images from a

TIMELESS WILDERNESS

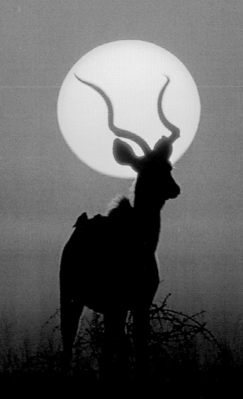

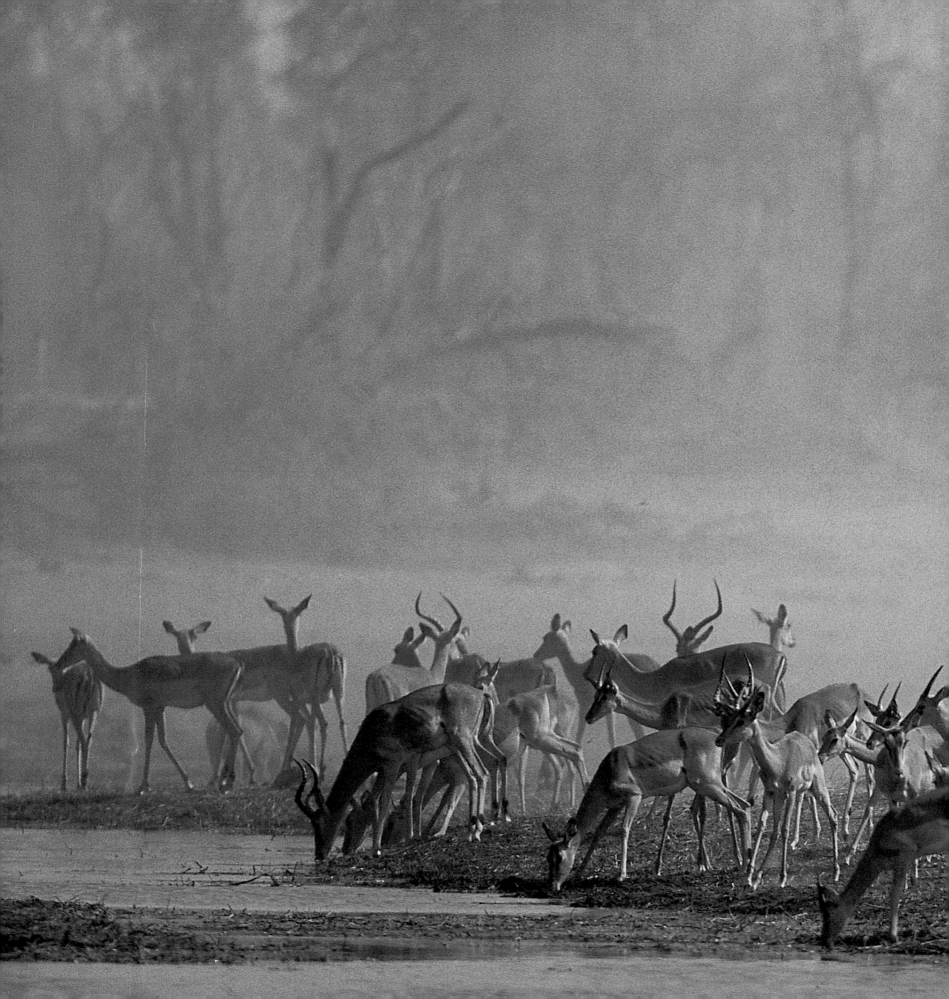

images from a
TIMELESS WILDERNESS

Photographs by Richard du Toit and Gerald Hinde

Text by Richard du Toit

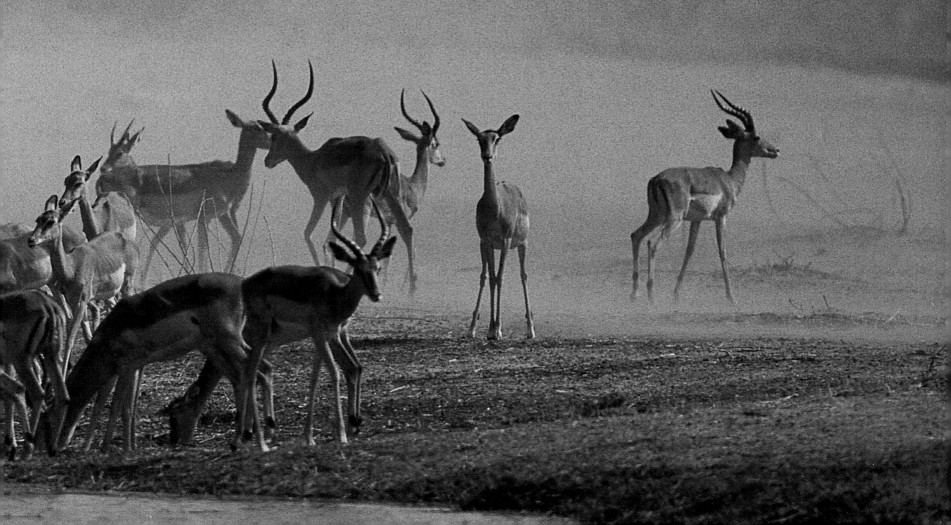

Struik Publishers (Pty) Ltd
(a member of the Struik New Holland
Publishing Group (Pty) Ltd)
Cornelis Struik House
80 McKenzie Street
Cape Town 8001

First published in 2000

10 9 8 7 6 5 4 3 2

Publishing Manager: Pippa Parker
Editor: Simon Pooley
Designer: Janice Evans
Proofreader: Helen de Villiers

ISBN 1 86872 502 2

Reproduction by Hirt & Carter Cape (Pty) Ltd
Printed and bound by Craft Print (Pte) Ltd,
Singapore

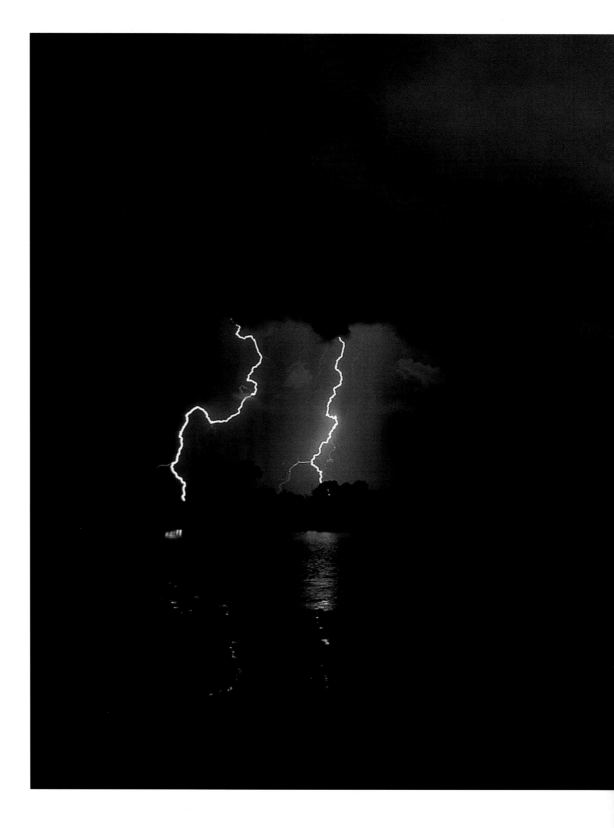

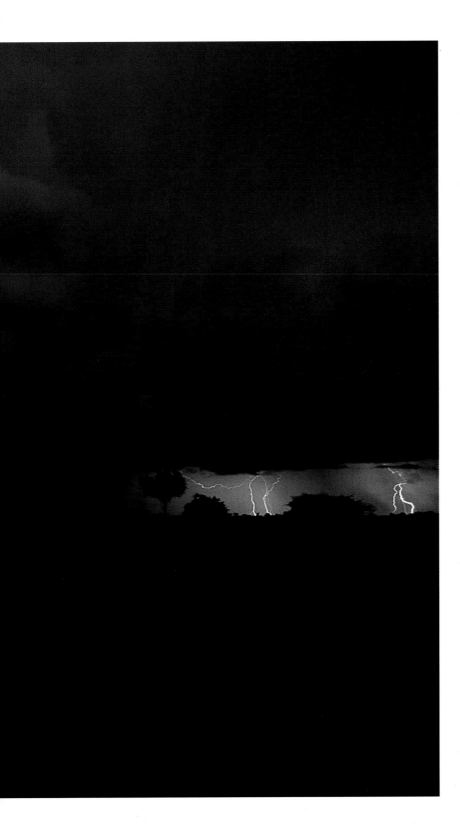

DEDICATIONS

Over the years I have had support and encouragement from my entire
family. My mother and father Pat and May Hinde, my wife Pam, our children
Wayne, Craig, Kevin, Sharon, Gavin, and Richard and my brother Ron Hinde and
his family. Thank you all for your love and that nudge when I needed to keep going.

The world and all that is in it belong to the Lord;
The earth and all who live on it are His.

Psalm 24:1

GERALD HINDE

For Mom, Dad, Judith, Elizabeth, Justin, Elizabeth and Alan.
And also for five young friends: Geoffrey Forbes, Jemma & Amber Rethman,
and Megan & Matthew Bolttler.

RICHARD DU TOIT

PICTURE NOTES

None of the photographs in this book were manipulated or altered with the use of
computers. These images are an accurate record of the behaviour of wild animals in a
natural environment.

For this project we used several zoom lenses, mainly the 17–35mm f2.8 and the
70–200mm f2.8. We made use of two long lenses – the 500mm f4.5 and the
600mm f4.

PICTURE CREDITS

RICHARD DU TOIT Cover, 4-5, 6, 7, 8, 13, 14 (top), 15 (bottom), 16-17, 19, 21,
23, 25, 26, 27, 28, 29, 30 (top), 31, 32, 33, 36, 37, 40, 41, 42-3, 44, 45, 48-9, 50, 51, 52,
53, 54-5, 56, 57, 58, 59, 60, 61, 68, 69, 71, 72, 74, 75, 76, 80 (bottom), 81, 82-3, 86, 87,
88-9, 92, 95, 97 (bottom), 98, 100, 101, 104, 105, 107, 108, 109, 110, 112, 114, 115, 120,
121 (top left, bottom), 122-3, 124, 128, 129, 133, 134, 135, 136-7, 138, 139, 143, 144-
5, 146, 147, 150, 154, 155, 156, 158, 159, 160, Back cover (lower 3 strips).

GERALD HINDE 1, 2-3, 11, 12, 14 (bottom), 15 (top), 18, 20, 22, 24, 30 (bottom), 34,
35, 38, 39, 46, 47, 62, 63, 64, 65, 66-7, 70, 73, 77, 78, 79, 80 (top), 84-5, 90, 91, 93, 94, 96,
97 (top, middle), 99, 102, 103, 106, 111, 113, 116, 117, 118, 119, 121 (top, right), 125,
126-7, 130, 131, 132, 140, 141, 142, 148, 149, 151, 152, 153, 157, Back cover (top strip).

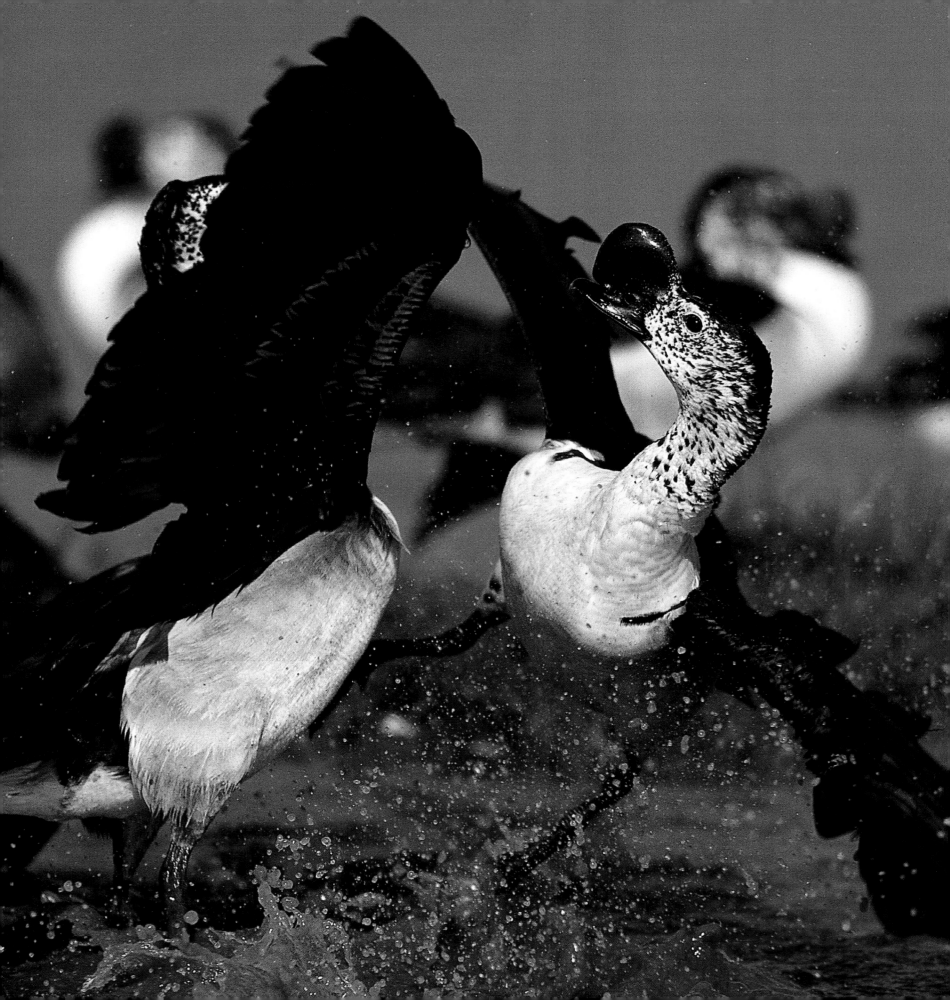

Preface

THIS BOOK IS NEITHER ABOUT THE Okavango Delta nor the Kalahari Desert but rather about the wildlife of a remarkable river system that links them. We chose to concentrate on the wildlife of the Khwai River, a narrow link between these two separate ecosystems, the permanent wetlands and the semi-desert. We travelled to this wild area to experience and photograph the cycle of the seasons: the summer rains; the arrival of the floodwaters in late summer; the gathering of the wildlife along the river in winter; and finally the dry months before the rains return. This is not a book about a particular group of animals – it is about Nature in all its extraordinary complexity and beauty.

As photographers we are fascinated with the interactions between different species, and the relationship those animals have with their environment. We wanted to capture the moods of this wilderness, and to portray the freedom and movement of the creatures that live here. The images we have chosen to include here are of the beautiful, the unusual and the extra-ordinary – images which we believe may convey to you something of the essence of this dynamic land. We chose the title to reflect the unchanging Nature of this ancient land.

We have visited the Khwai River region many times now, and its hold over us grows ever more intense. Its wildness and remoteness free the visitor from the cares of the urban jungle and reconnect one with Nature. We hope that many of you who read this book will one day have an opportunity to visit this part of Botswana.

We have not manipulated or enhanced any of our images in this book using computers. Each of these photographs is a faithful and accurate record of an instant in time as captured by the camera. All the photos were taken of animals that are wild and free. We believe that in this age of artificiality, this work has the integrity of a true document of events. We hope you will pick up this book, open it anywhere, and enjoy with us a journey into a Timeless Wilderness.

The Rains

revive the parched land

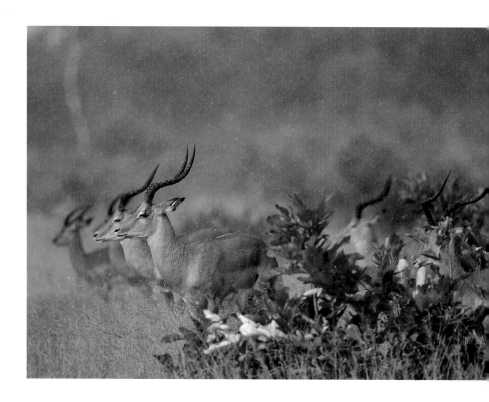

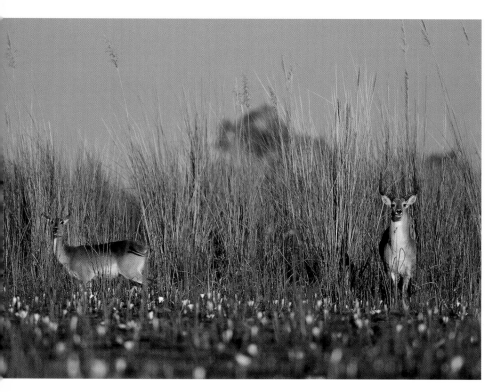

The Floods

arrive from the distant north

wet season

The Gathering

around the dwindling waters

82

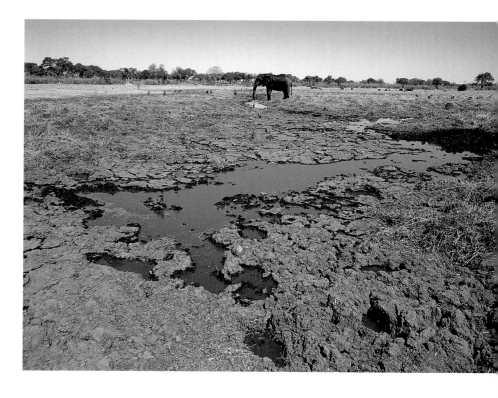

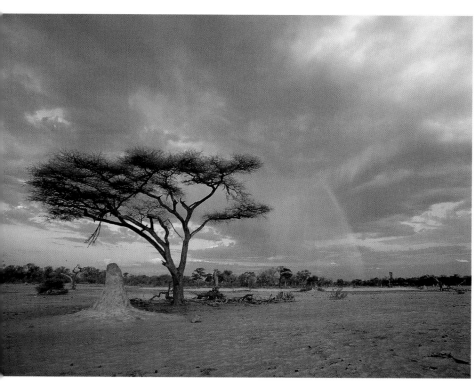

The Waiting

for the first stirrings of summer

136

Acknowledgements

TO PRODUCE AND PUBLISH A BOOK such as this requires the efforts and assistance of many people and organisations. Over the years we had the support and generosity of many people and friends to whom we owe our sincere gratitude. To Nick Seewer – a very special thanks for your ongoing help and support. To Peter Nelson, Malcolm Robinson, Margi Barnardt, Sandy Fowler, Alice Motlogelwa, Sello Motlotle and Ian Clarke, thanks for your friendship and assistance – it is much appreciated. To Julie Rose and Angela Clark in Cape Town thanks for your friendly help. The guides were always helpful in many ways – thanks to Buxton Masasa, Joe Bayeyi, Mothupi Moruthwa and Delux Moitshoki.

We extend our thanks to the Office of the President for providing us with permits and to the Department of Wildlife in Botswana for the running and protection of some of the finest national parks on the continent of Africa.

Thanks to Will Taylor, Linda Slaughter and Craig Kissick of Panthera Productions. To Bobby Haas of Dallas – thanks for your special contribution to cheetah and wildlife conservation in Africa. Thanks to Lance Smith, Pat O'Brien and Claire Millar from Avis Rental for their assistance whenever vehicles were needed. Thanks to Stuart and Lara Mackay of Mack Air in Maun for helping with air flights to and from the camps. Thanks also to Royston Knowles, Louis and Belinda Strauss, Shawn and Mandy Marshall and Tim and Cathy Reid. And finally to the talented and enthusiastic people at Struik Publishers – especially Pippa Parker, Janice Evans, Simon Pooley and Chris Gibbons – who put a great deal of work into this book; it was a pleasure working with you.

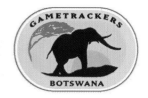

We owe a great deal to Gametrackers in Botswana. For over a year we made use of Khwai River Lodge as our base as well as Eagle Island Camp and Savute Elephant Camp. We took all the photographs for this book while we were based at Gametrackers camps. To all at Gametrackers we thank you for all the years of friendship and hospitality and for helping us in so many ways.

RICHARD DU TOIT AND GERALD HINDE

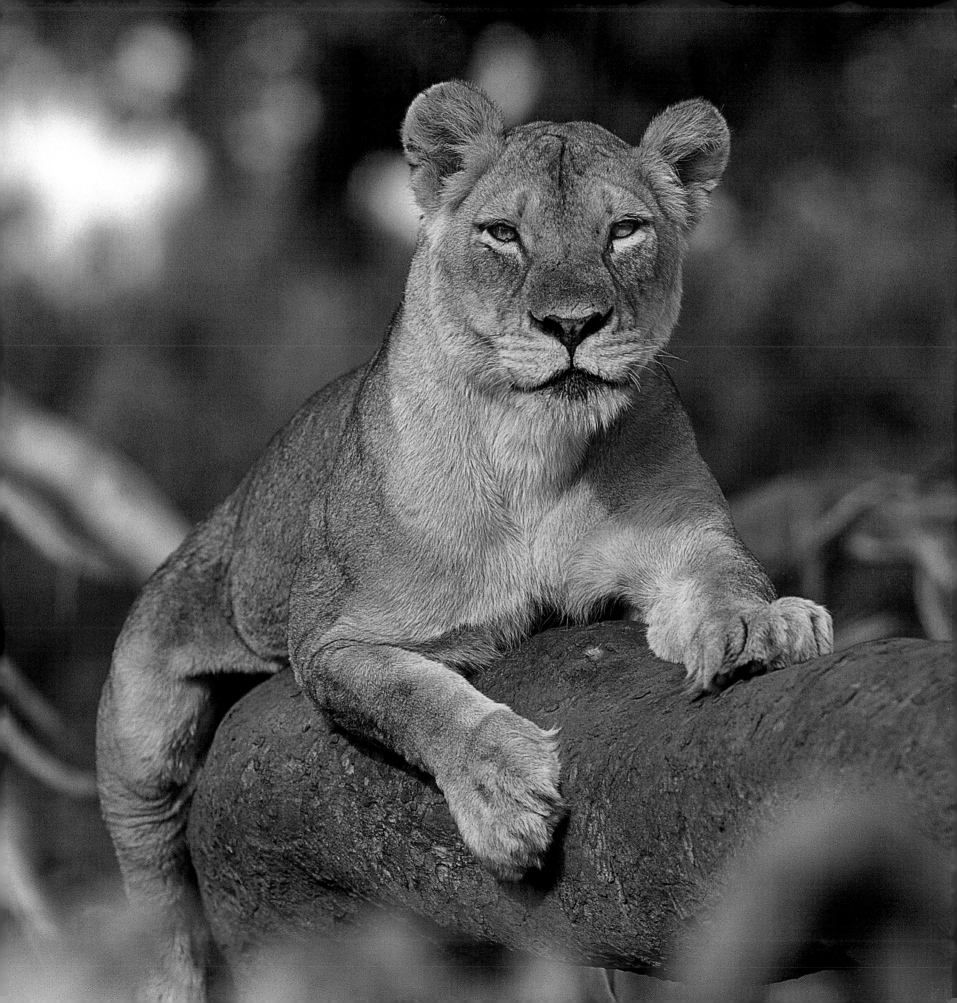

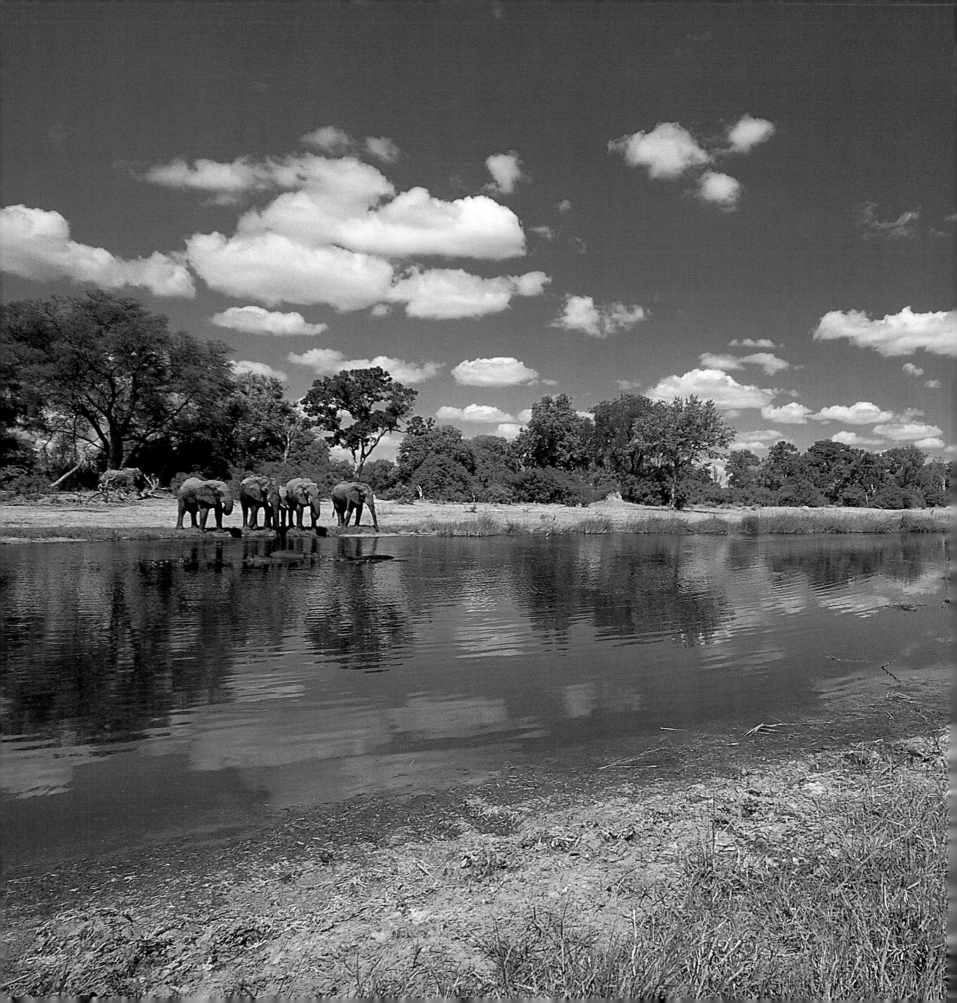

Introduction

A REMARKABLE RIVER SYSTEM LINKS THE OKAVANGO DELTA to the sands of the Kalahari. The vast Kalahari basin – the largest continuous formation of sand in the world – lies in the western half of southern Africa, stretching from South Africa northwards through Namibia to Angola, and extending into Botswana. Miraculously, in the heart of this great arid region there lies a paradisaical wetland wilderness – the Okavango Delta, the world's largest inland delta.

The Khwai River forms a thin thread linking the permanent Okavango swamplands with the mopane forests and acacia woodlands of the semidesert Kalahari. Gerald and I spent an exhilarating year in this timeless wilderness, documenting one great cycle of the progress of the seasons and the waters along the course of the Khwai River. The images in these pages represent the highlights of that year.

In this semi-arid region, where the annual rainfall averages around 500 millimetres, everything revolves around the ebb and flow of the waters. The water arrives in two separate and different inundations each year, and these are the major seasonal events which govern the movements and life cycles of the region's wildlife. The first of these is the summer rainy season (which peaks in December and January), a growing period for vegetation as the land turns a vibrant green. With water and food abundant, the animals, and in particular elephants, disperse widely into the mopane forests and grass-lands up to hundreds of kilometres away from permanent water.

Towards the end of summer the rain-filled pools begin to dry out, although food is still abundant. There is a slow transition towards winter as the grass starts to turn brown. Migrating birds leave and head north, and those mammals dependent on water slowly head back to the rivers and swamps. It is now that something extraordinary occurs: by May the year's second inundation arrives in the Okavango. These waters eventually reach the Khwai River in July (midwinter) – when one would least expect them! Slowly, the flood waters flow in, refilling the drying river pools and pushing back towards the parched sands of the desert. It is a remarkable thing to witness, this annual miracle that supports a host of wildlife in the middle of the dry winter.

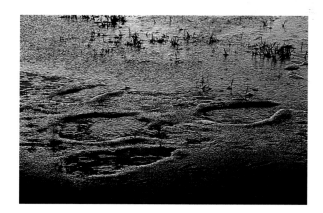

Above Elephant footprints fill with water as summer rain drums down on a pan's edge. As the water dries up wading birds will search for small crustaceans trapped in them.

Opposite Elephants drink from the River Khwai in summer.

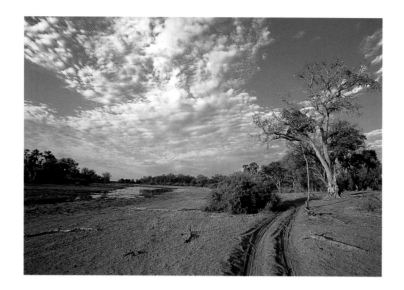

By late winter the passage of hungry herbivores has denuded the river edges of all grasses, and many trees will stand devoid of leaves.

The flood waters that fill this swampland originate in the distant highlands of the Benguela Plateau in Angola. Every year, a deluge of summer rains fall over this mountainous region. The waters travel quickly at first, but as they descend onto the flat lowlands their momentum gradually slows. Broadening to form the Cubango River, they flow into Namibia's Caprivi Strip in the southeast, where they are known as the Okavango River. In northeastern Botswana the river is constricted within faultlines in the earth, the most southern fractures of Africa's Great Rift Valley, to form the stretch of river known as the 'Panhandle'. At the southern extent of the Panhandle, the Okavango divides into several smaller rivers, and in times of flood the waters fan out to form the delta. Ultimately, the waters will travel for nearly a thousand kilometres and for almost a year. The Khwai River, which links the swamps of the delta to the desert, is one of the final destinations for flood waters that will never reach the ocean.

In some years the Khwai River will flow through to the Mababe Depression, which is an ancient lake bed, now dry for more than a century. In late summer the zebra migration arrives in the Mababe from Savute in the North. This part of the world is home to some of the largest concentrations of wildlife on the continent. In particular, it is a sanctuary to the largest population of elephants in Africa, and the elephants certainly dominate the region. It is most impressive to witness the gathering of these giants, and other wildlife, that occurs when the flood waters gradually seep into the desert sands, or are lost to evaporation beneath the relentless African sun. After the great dispersals of the wet season, life concentrates once more around the rivers and pools, and this is an exciting time to observe interactions between many diverse species which have no other choice but to coexist in an ever decreasing habitable region. Then comes the long wait for the rains to return...

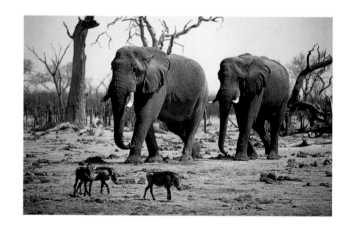

Winter is a hard time for the larger animals that cannot hibernate and must continue to search for food and water.

Most travellers get their first glimpses of the Okavango from the air as they fly to their safari destination, and flying along in a small bush plane is certainly the best introduction to this part of the world. It is far easier to understand this unique and mysterious desert wetland from the air. Flying in, we saw scruffy woodlands carpeted with short green grass and a few single-track roads snaking their way across the flat, featureless bush below us. The woodlands ended suddenly as we encountered the permanent swamp, a mixture of blue lagoons and winding waterways fringed with thick green reed beds. From the air these form a fascinating tapestry of palm islands and deep, meandering channels in a sea of lush green papyrus swamps.

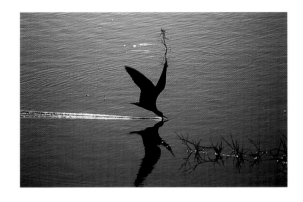

The African skimmer's lower mandible is elongated to scythe the water for small fish and invertebrates.

Our destination in sight, we could make out the smallest of gravel runways in among the patterns of woodlands and flood plains ahead of us. Then suddenly we were bumping along on the ground, francolin and hornbill scattering ahead of the plane. In the dappled shade of a nearby rain tree a bull giraffe stood daydreaming. It was already a month into the wet season, and the bushveld was verdant. The grass was knee-deep and the trees resplendently green. A visitor journeying a month previously would not have recognized the transformed landscape. The elephants that had congregated in their hundreds were long gone, and the thick grass was already beginning to hide the presence of the narrow river.

We set out through this timeless wilderness in mid-summer. The floods were still months away, but when they arrived we moved with them, along the course of the Khwai towards the Kalahari. We saw the waters swell with the summer rains, contract with the onset of winter, then miraculously flood the Delta as the Okavango River delivered rainwater from far-off Angola. Then the waters ebbed, gathering the animals in around the river's shrinking margins as they waited for the cycle to come full circle, and the rainy season to return.

We invite you to share the most memorable moments of our journey along the Khwai River.

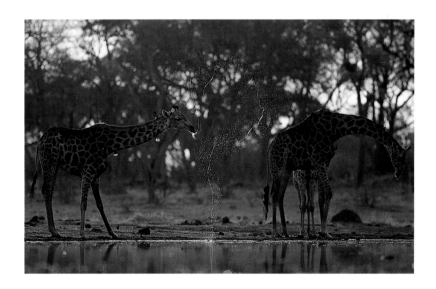

A giraffe head-flicks as she drinks from a glass-still pool at dusk, leaving a delicate tracery of precious water hanging in the air for a moment.

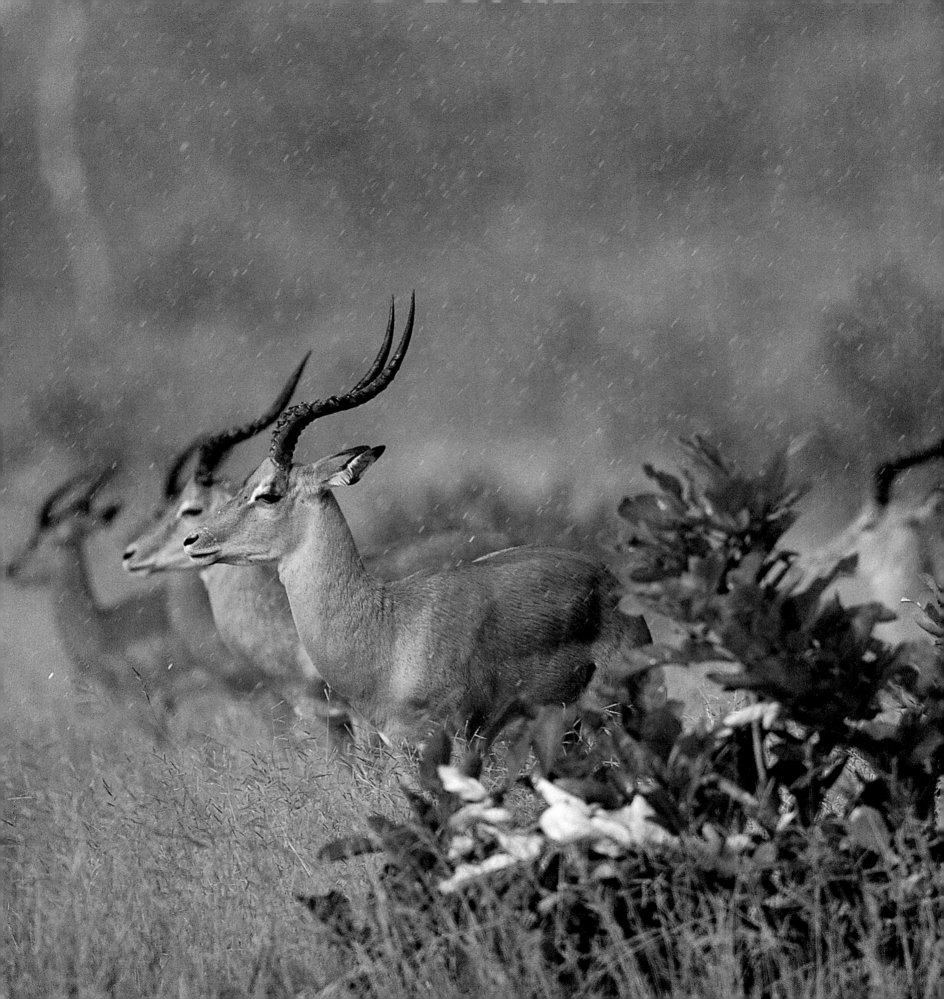

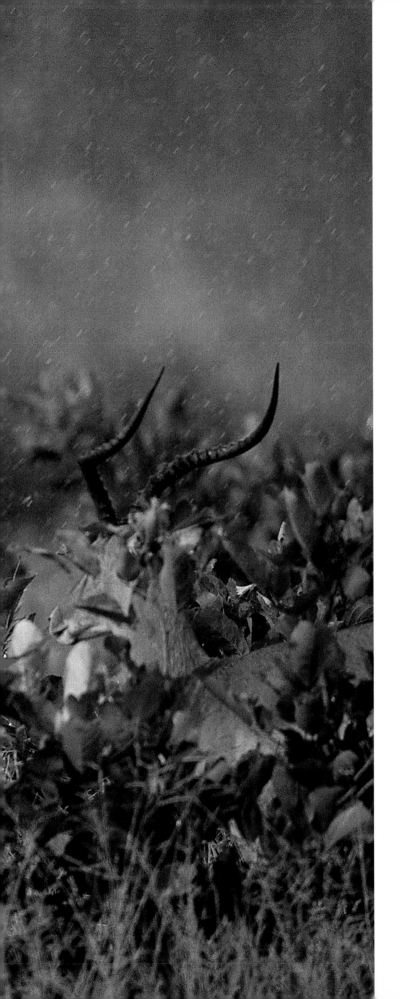

The Rains

revive the parched land

THE PRELUDE TO SUMMER IS A period of exciting and rapid change in the Khwai River region. The catalyst for this change is the arrival of the summer rains, and these usher in the next great cycle of the seasons.

At noon on a typical baking hot November day, giant storm clouds quickly mushroom out of nowhere and in the distance the rumble of thunder spills through the bushveld. A sudden squall of wind races through the trees, tumbling dry leaves in its path; the birds fall silent and flee to shelter. Carried in on the gusts of cooler air is a new and unfamiliar smell. It is, finally, the sweet scent of imminent rain, after the weeks of empty promise.

The arrival of the thunderstorm is sudden and spectacular. Cold, heavy raindrops burst on the ground, exploding in fine puffs of dust. Rapidly and relentlessly the drumbeat of the downpour increases. A fierce noisy squall thrashes the trees, as the storm closes in all around.

The storm lasts an hour, passing quickly by and rolling away into the distance to reveal blue skies. The earth is sodden and puddles lie everywhere before the thirsty sand swallows the surface water. A fresh earthy smell rises from the ground, the air is clear and still and the trees and grass are washed clean of their layers of winter dust. Life returns to normal and a busy traffic of birds resumes as the storm's sudden violence is survived and forgotten. Metallic glossy starlings flutter and jaunty hornbills bounce out into the open, gobbling up emerging harvester termites.

Rain showers fall daily on the entire region throughout November. With these first major rains a new seasonal cycle has rolled into place, and within hours of the first rains the dry bushveld will change in extraordinary fashion. A great awakening will occur, insects, tortoises and frogs that have been cocooned for months in dry mud will emerge from hiding, plants will suck the moisture from the soil and seeds will swell with life.

Summer is a time of plenty for all plants and creatures.

Previous pages Despite the discomfort of this sudden summer downpour these impala rams remain vigilant, for storms can be dangerous for them. Apart from crashes of thunder, the showers are noisy occasions as the rain smacks down through the vegetation. The swirling air hides the smell of danger and every bush shakes in the wind. The impala are nervous, as it is almost impossible for them to detect the approach of danger. Furthermore the ground quickly becomes soft and slippery. It is a perfect situation for predators to attack them, and both leopards and lions are masters at exploiting such opportunities.

Right Weaverbirds are common residents, but only in the summer breeding season do the males sport their colourful plumes. Here a male weaver displays frenetically to attract the attention of the seemingly nonchalant females.

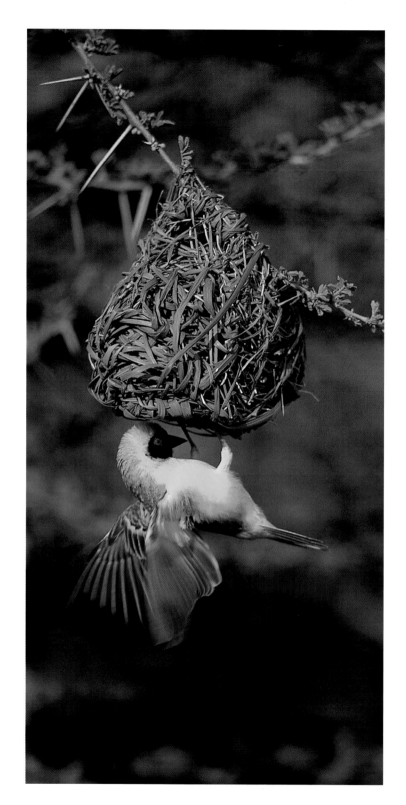

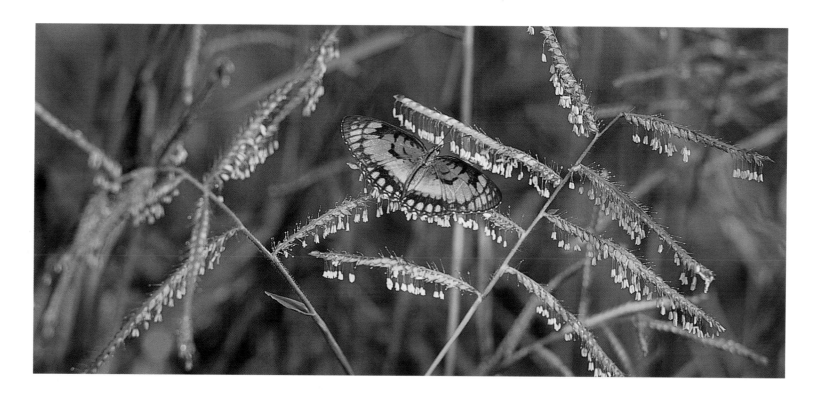

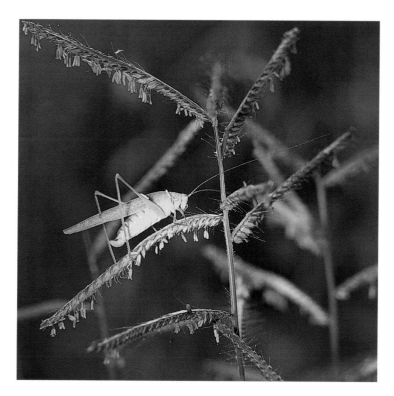

Above Insects have evolved many elaborate behaviours for hiding, and camouflage patterns to avoid detection. Another way to remain uneaten is to be unpalatable or even poisonous, and then to conspicuously advertise this fact. This is a common strategy in the insect kingdom, and is seen in many butterfly species.

Left Discovery will probably mean death for this long-horned katydid, a close relative of the grasshopper. In order to escape sharp-eyed birds it is best for these insects to remain unseen. Most birds are diurnal, and to avoid these predators many insects are active at night. The long antennae of katydids are covered with sensory receptors that enable them to navigate in the dark.

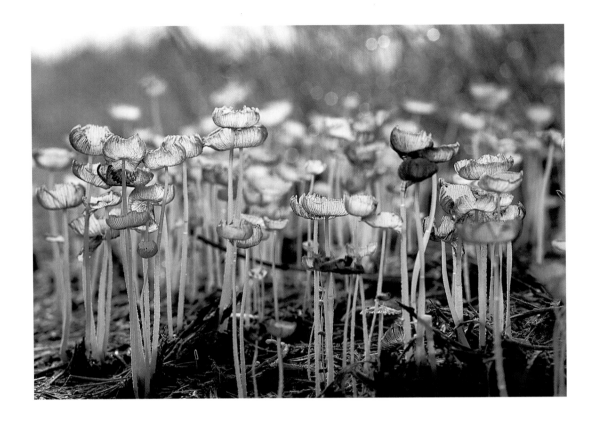

Above   During the summer, dung beetles and other insects, along with fungi and bacteria, play a role in the decomposition of animal droppings. Carpets of grey mushrooms sprout up overnight on piles of elephant dung, only to wither after a day of summer sunshine.

Opposite   Adult elephants can consume up to 300 kilograms of vegetation per day, and being such abundant animals this translates annually into thousands of tons of dung. The coarse elephant dung has accumulated during the dry season, forming brown carpets where the elephants have congregated. It is the humble termite that undertakes the vital role of breaking down and eating this huge resource, a process which takes place mainly in the warm and wet summer months. If you turn over a ball of dung you will discover busy workers with well-armed soldiers in attendance. To protect themselves from the sun and birds, they construct a thin protective layer of mud over much of the surface of the dung, wherein they tunnel and feed. Termites are the most significant decomposers of dead vegetation in this wilderness ecosystem and themselves provide an important food source to a host of birds and other creatures.

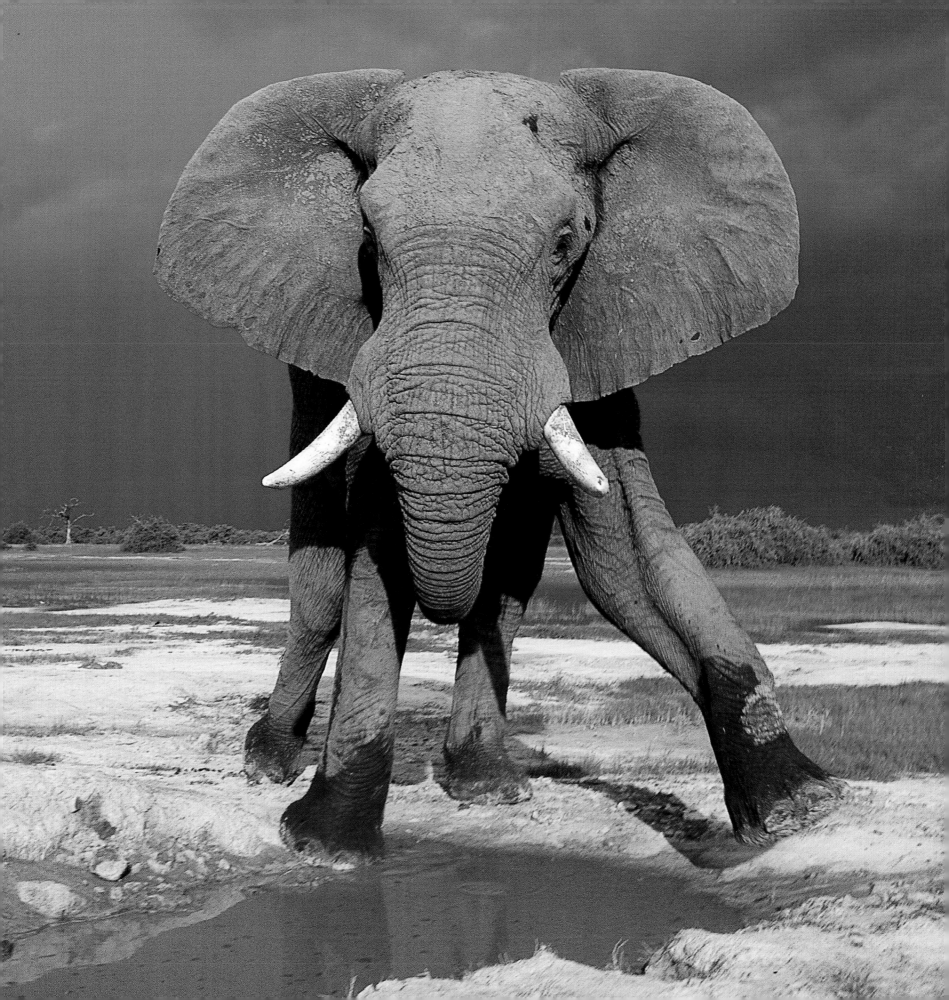

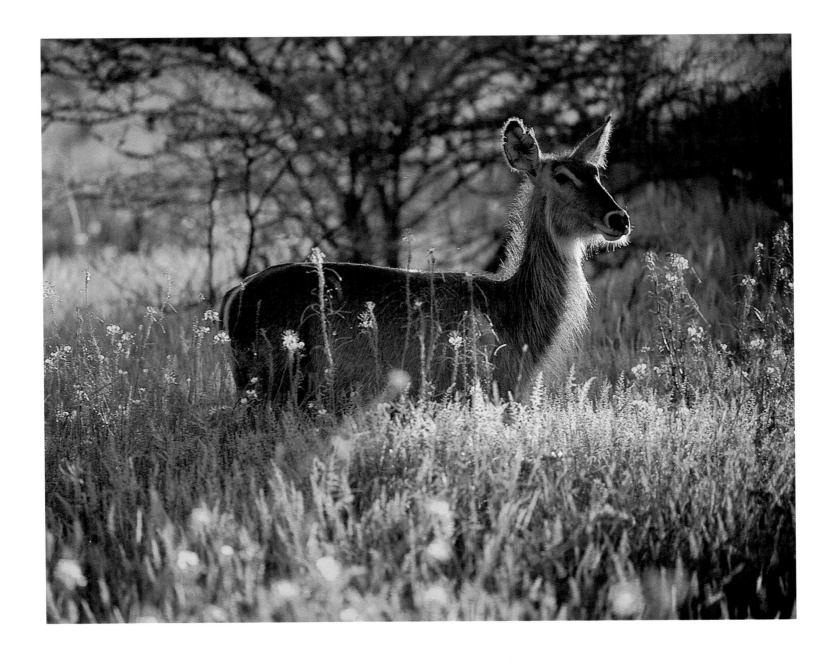

A shaggy-haired waterbuck ewe revolves parabola-like ears for signs of danger, for in the tall grass nearby lies her hidden calf. As they are too big to hide, large herbivores need to be totally in tune with their environment to survive, making use of every clue that will benefit them. The longhorned males may be seen singly or in bachelor groups, whereas the females maintain a loose herd structure with occasional males present. The waterbuck is famous for its musky smell and oily, unpalatable flesh, but despite the myths of predator invincibility, this does not dissuade lions from eating them.

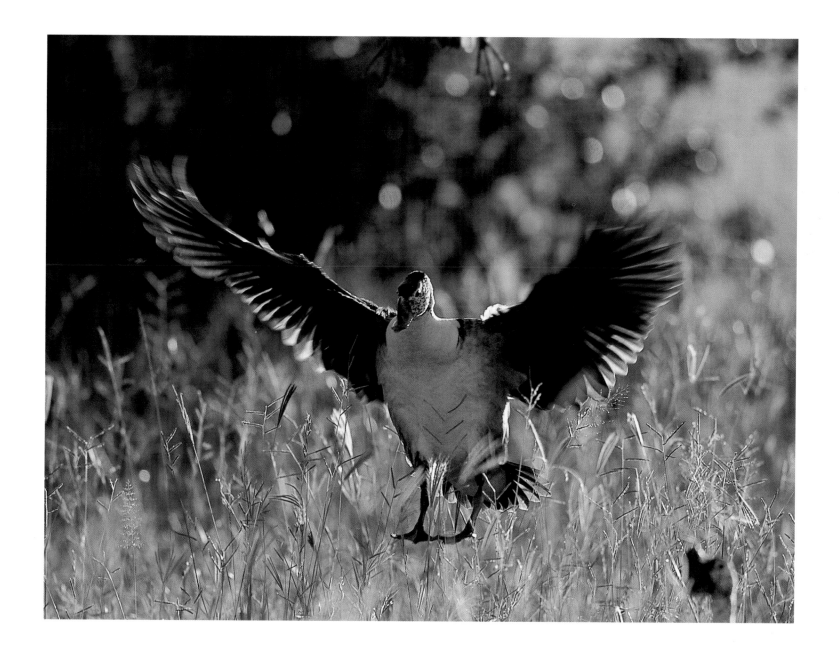

In summer the knob-billed ducks are highly gregarious in areas where their favourite grass seeds abound, congregating in temporary flocks of hundreds of birds. Using their fleshy serrated bills they strip the grass heads of seed. Baboons and warthog are also very partial to this food source and feed in a similar way. Many of the spilled seeds will lie dormant through to winter, sustaining huge flocks of quelea and doves, long after the ducks have left.

Below On some summer mornings mist lies over the grassland and heavy dew settles during the night. As it heats up it burns off quickly. Insects and spiders take refuge from the heat and sharp-eyed birds by retreating inside thickets and to the bottom of the six-foot-high grass. There is an extraordinary variety and number of invertebrates in the region which, although small, are ecologically very significant.

Opposite The pretty lady is common in summer; its bright colours and sweet nectar attract insect pollinators.

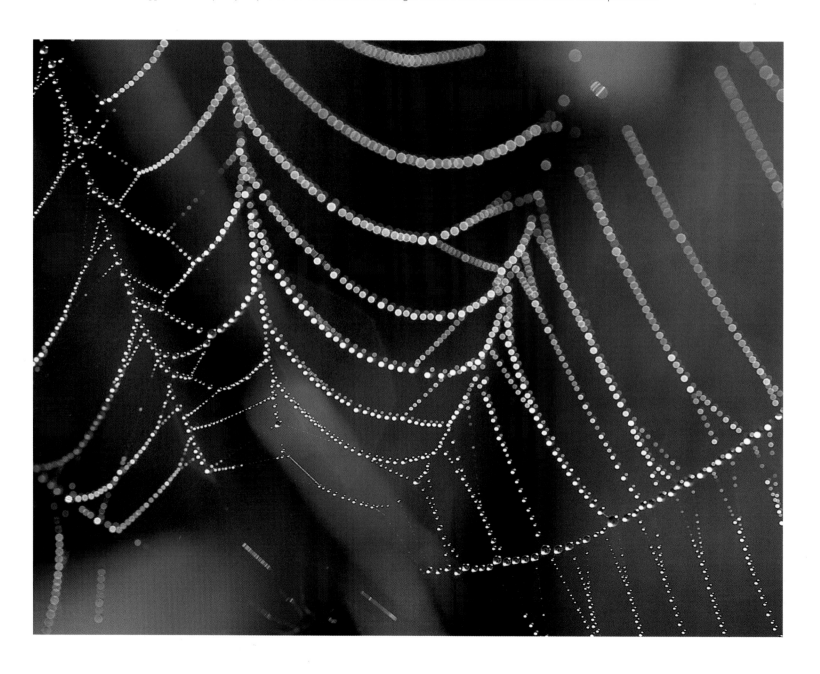

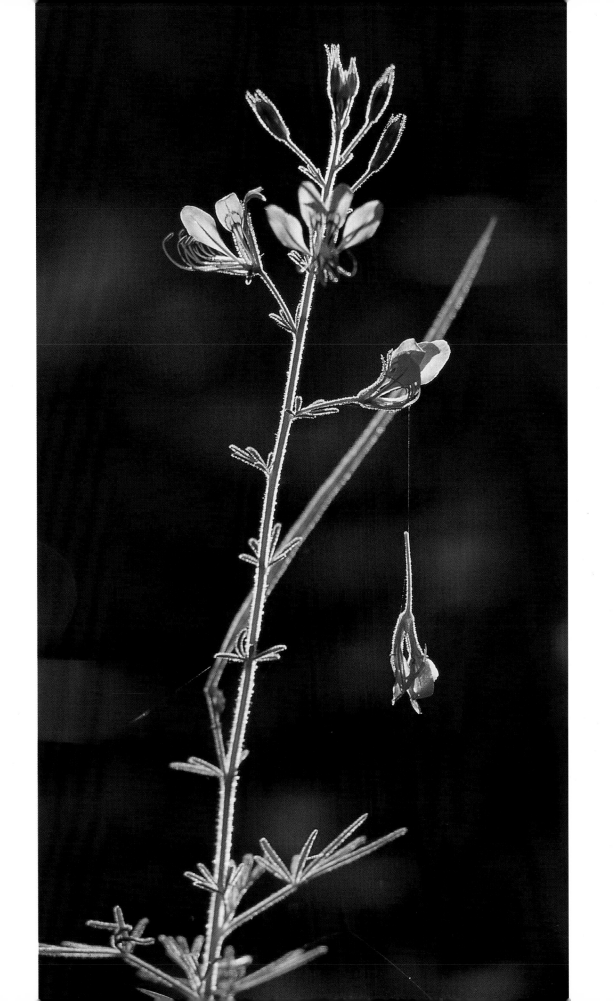

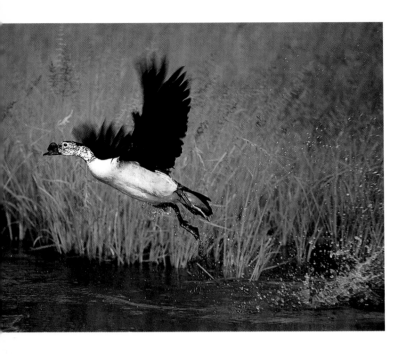

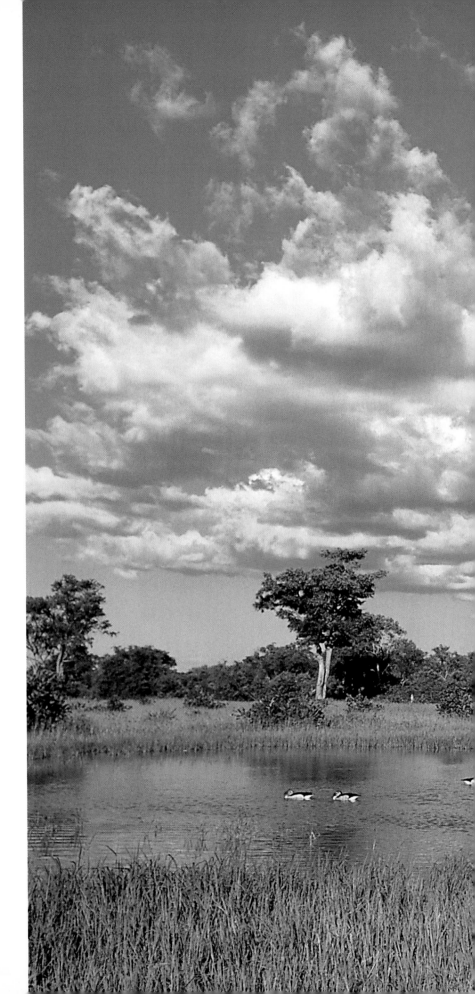

Above and Opposite True geese do not occur in southern Africa, and the spur-winged and pygmy geese are incorrectly named. In the case of the knob-billed duck, which is also sometimes erroneously called a goose, only the males sport the impressive fleshy knobs that are most prominent during the breeding season. In the rainy season, conditions provide extra time and the perfect requirements for nest building and raising of chicks. Like the migratory birds, many of the resident birds are opportunists, travelling regionally to any area where food is plentiful. True to the nature of winged freedom, entire flocks of birds can be here one day and gone the next.

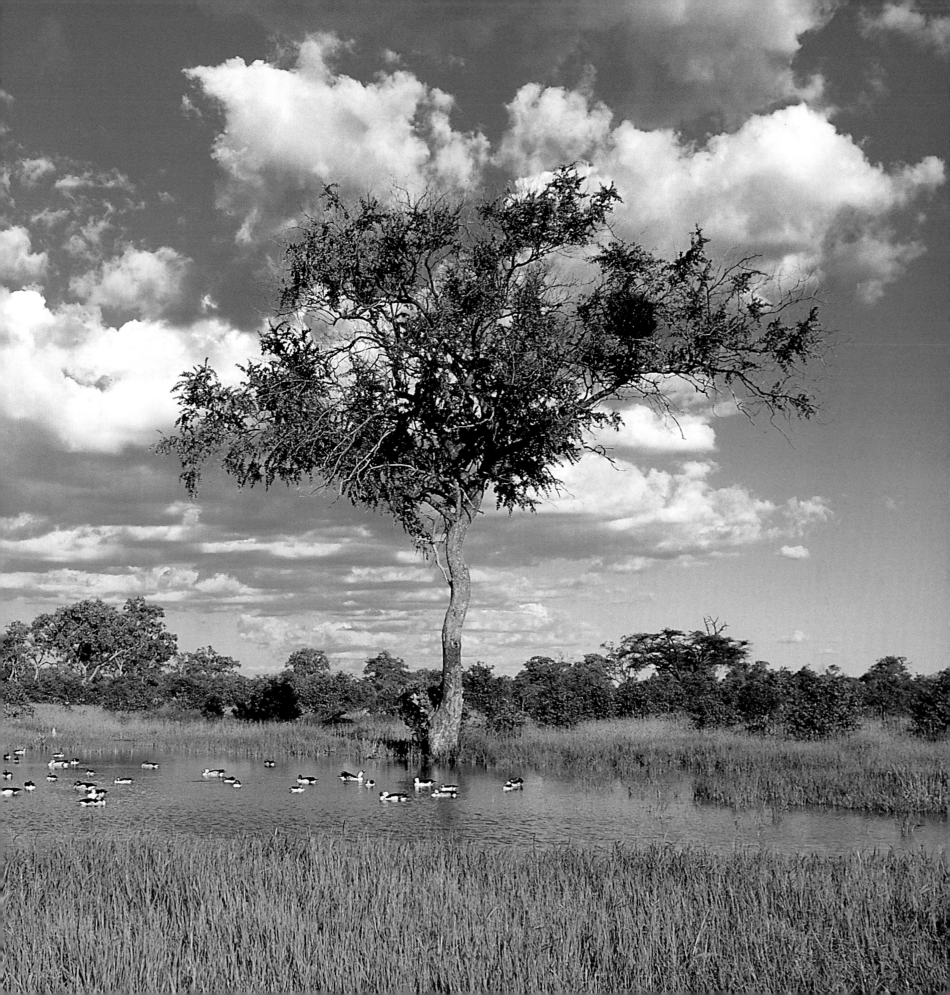

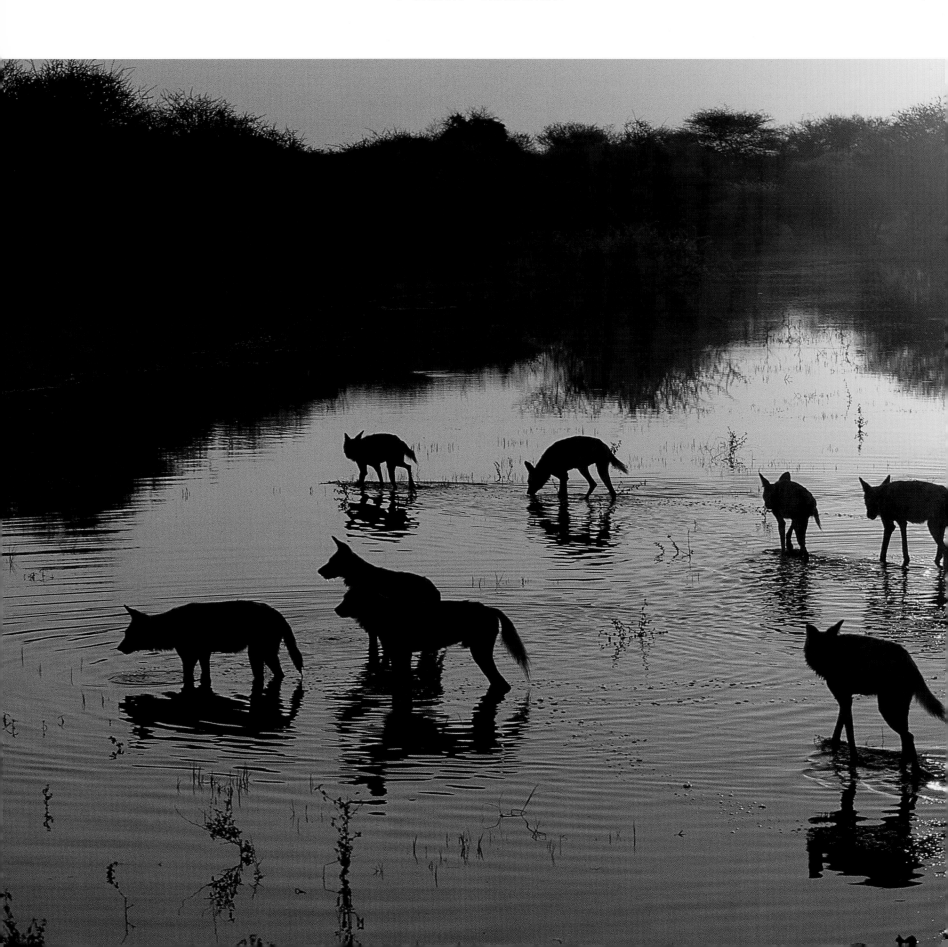

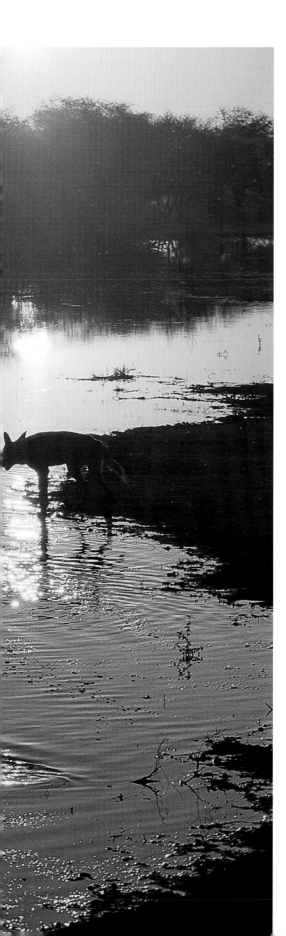

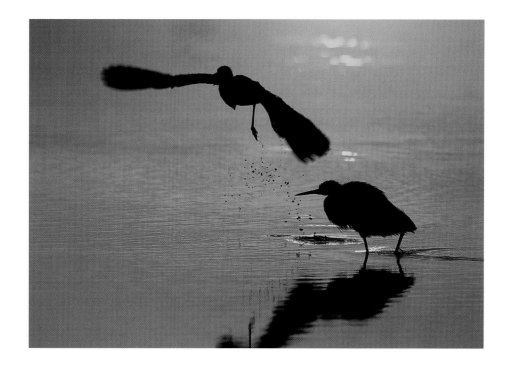

The dawn colours are at their resplendent best for a brief few minutes before sunrise, as the fleecy clouds are washed with burnished gold. But the colours fade quickly as the sun rises.

Opposite Wild dogs are considered diurnal hunters but they often make use of the moon to hunt during the night hours. After drinking, they splash playfully through the river.

Above Little egrets fish in the predawn stillness. The beautiful plumes that gave these white herons their name were in such huge demand for fashion purposes a century ago that several species were threatened with extinction.

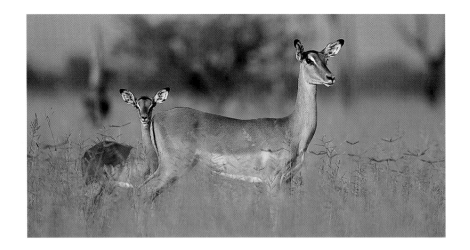

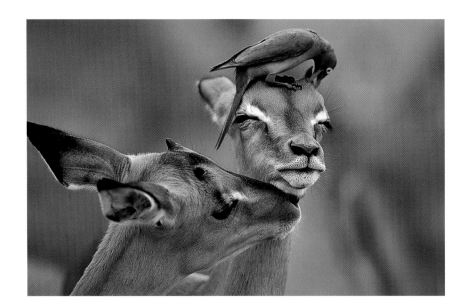

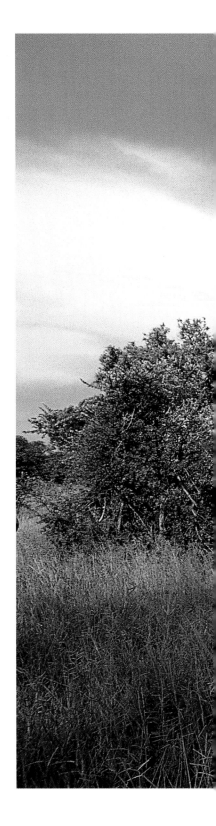

Impala are one of the African bushlands' most common and adaptable antelope. They are both grazers and browsers, and can go for long periods without drinking. In early summer the babies arrive in a synchronized birth, and within days they are strong enough (*top*) to run with the herd. Impala are the only antelope that engage in allo-grooming (*above*), although it is a common practice in other mammals. This involves the reciprocal grooming of body parts they cannot reach themselves. Impalas' loose-fitting lower incisors function to remove ticks and other ectoparasites. When an impala scrapes a herd mate, the latter replies with almost exactly the same number of scrapes.

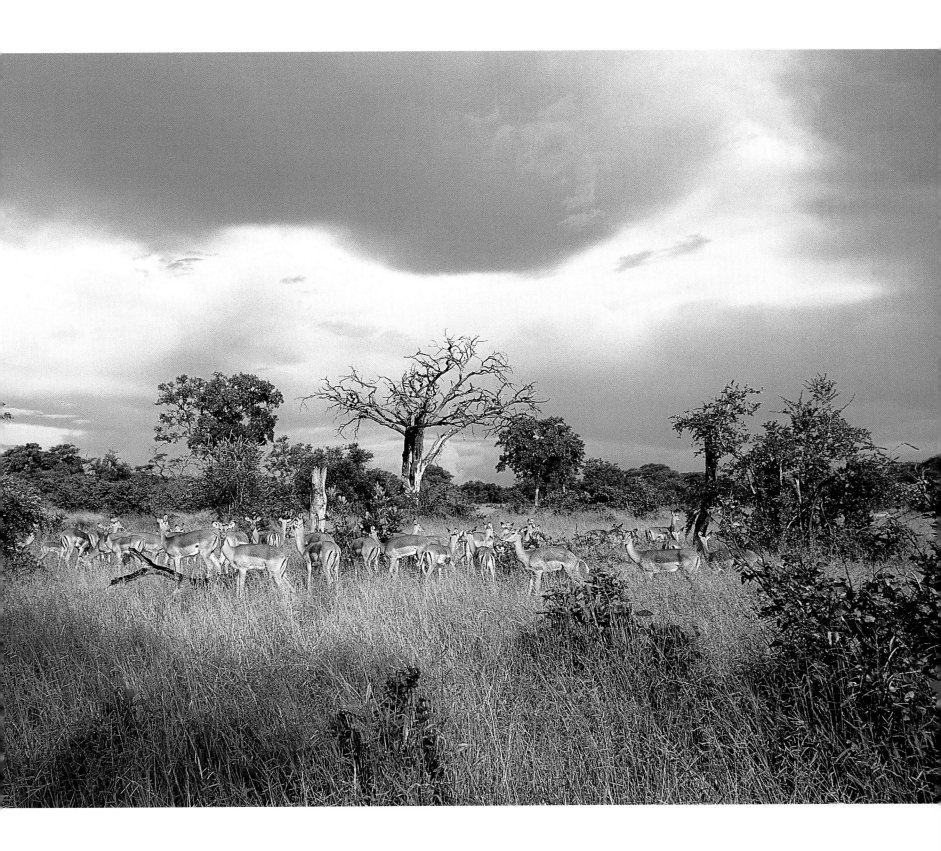

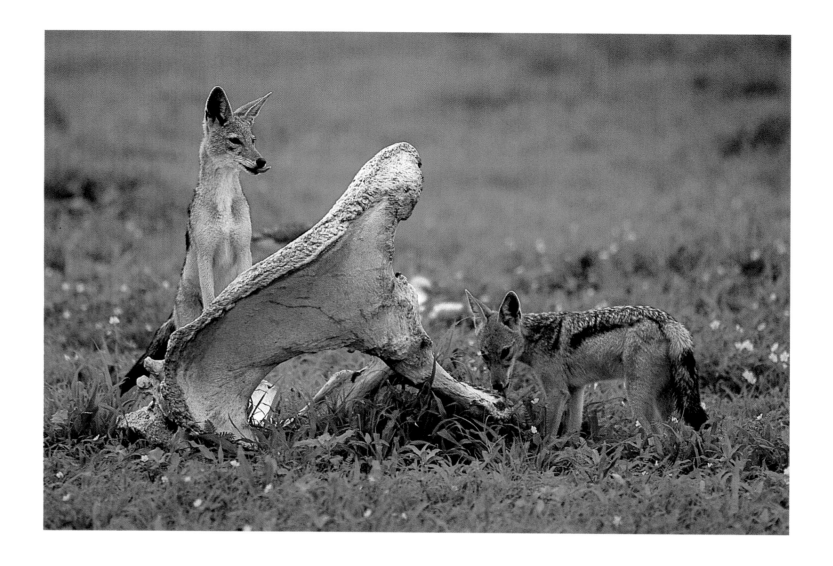

Black-backed jackals have a cosmopolitan diet, feeding primarily on small mammals, birds and insects that they catch themselves. They also eat fruits and the scraps from kills made by the larger predators. This family of jackals was foraging as they trotted through the grasslands. They spent a few minutes gnawing on the giant pelvis bones of an elephant bull that had died the previous winter.

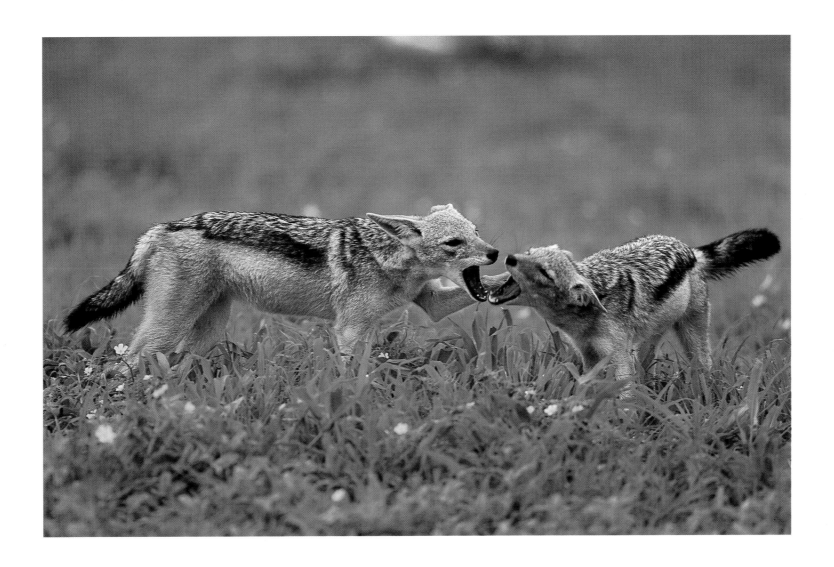

The distinctive trilling howl of jackals at sunset could well cause unease amongst the hoofed denizens of the open grasslands. Each evening the jackals herald the onset of night, a time when prides of lions and clans of spotted hyaenas reign supreme.

Lions are the dominant African predators. The key to this success lies largely in their social nature, which manifests itself in the pride structure. At the core of this social system are small groups of females (*opposite*), often closely related, that live together in prides and maintain close bonds for life. The larger males come and go, and in some areas their tenure will last only a few months before they are ousted by a stronger coalition of new males. This pair of lion cubs (*below*) made use of a termite mound as a playground; as adults they will use mounds as vantage sites from which to spot prey. These castles of clay are the protective homes of a primitive yet enormously successful insect – the humble termite. Often incorrectly known as white ants, these insects have the most ancient social organisation of any animal. Inmates work 24-hour days, which are spent mostly in total darkness. Many birds and animals prey upon these soft-bodied insects, and even people relish this protein-rich bounty. The mounds are largely dormant in winter, but once the first rains have softened the earth and made the air humid enough for the termites to venture out, the mounds grow anew. Some mounds reach five metres in height and accommodate hundreds of thousands of individuals.

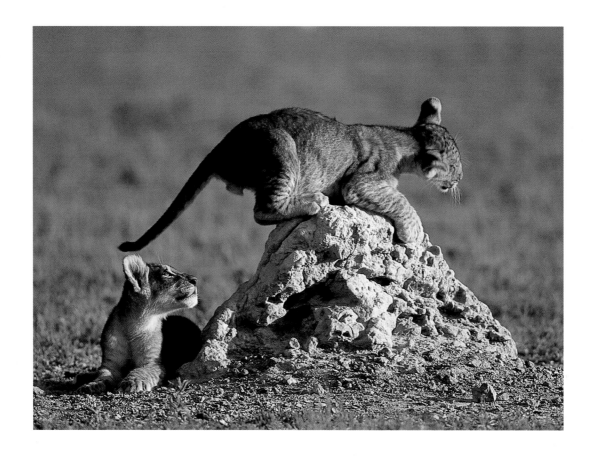

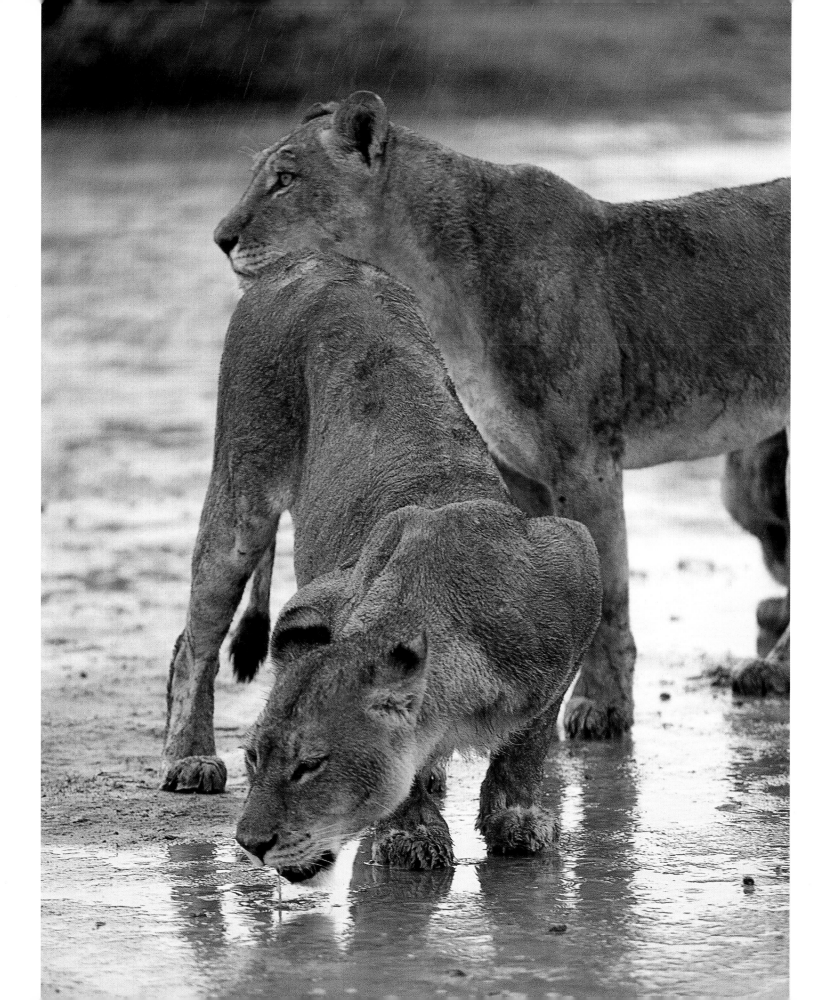

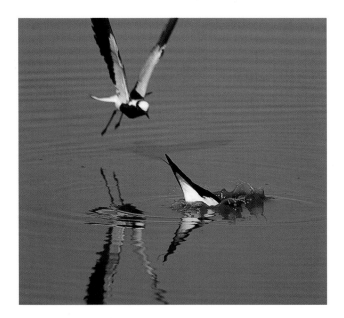

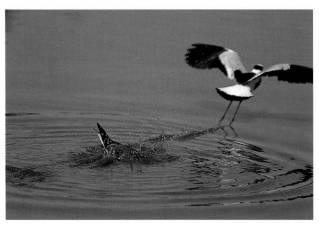

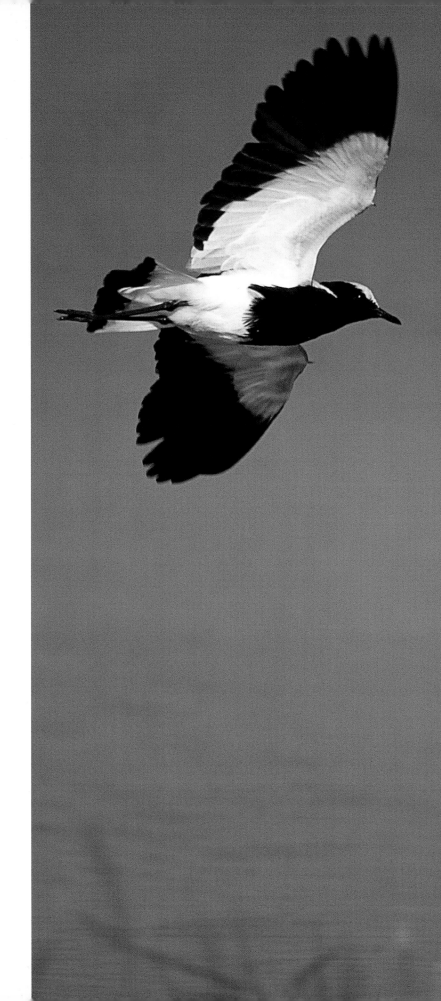

Although well known for their bold and aggressive nature, the blacksmith plovers surprised me with their intolerance of black-winged stilts. I'm not sure of the reason as they don't compete for the same food. This plover launched a repeated dive-bombing attack on a feeding stilt, backslapping him with trailing feet. Plunging momentarily before the plover could hit him, the stilt would then bob to the surface, cool and unfazed, and resume his insect eating. Then the chasing would resume; here (**right**) they bank at high speed on the edge of a pan.

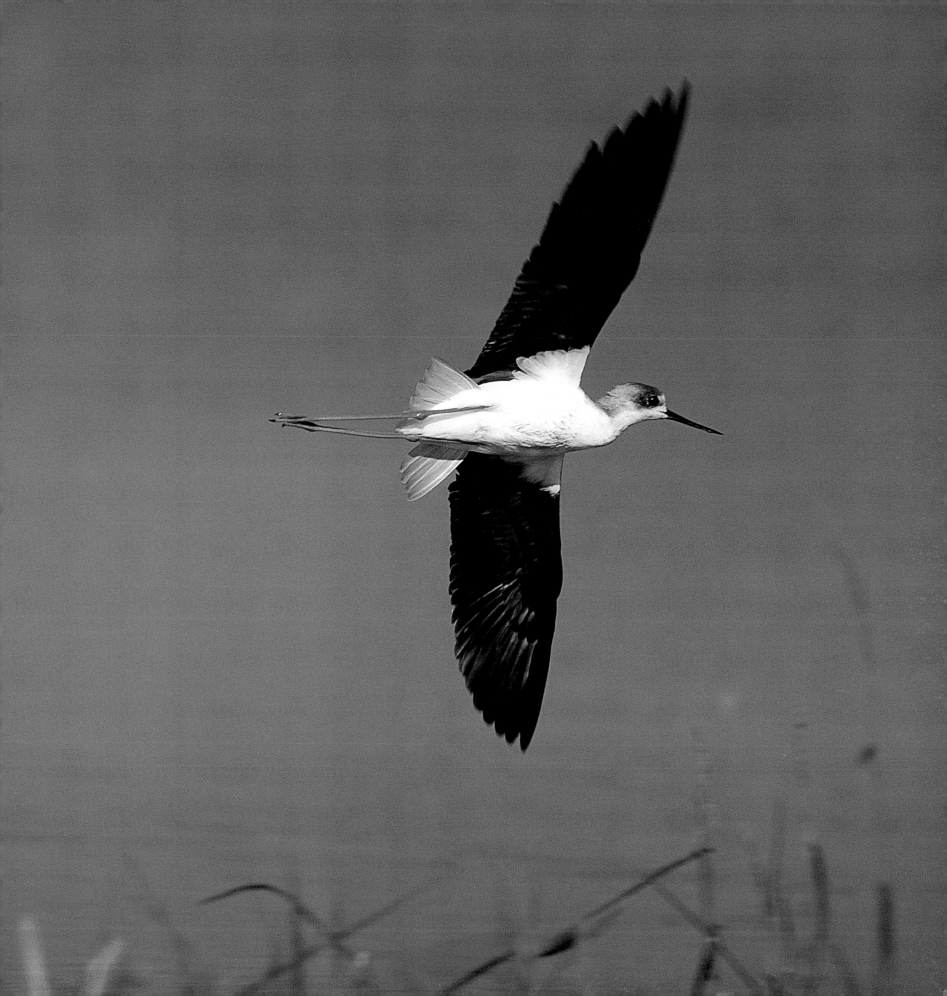

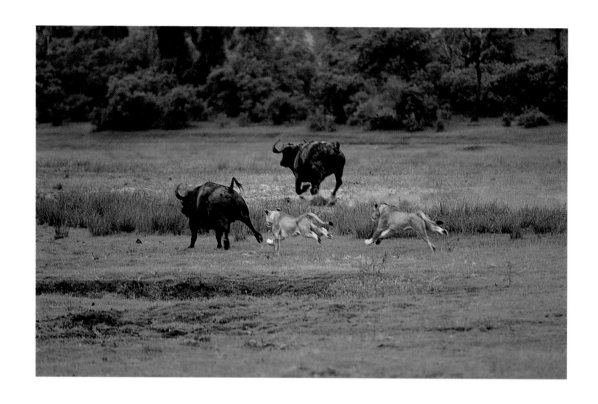

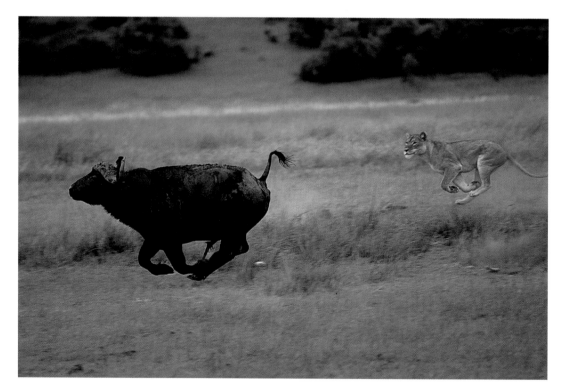

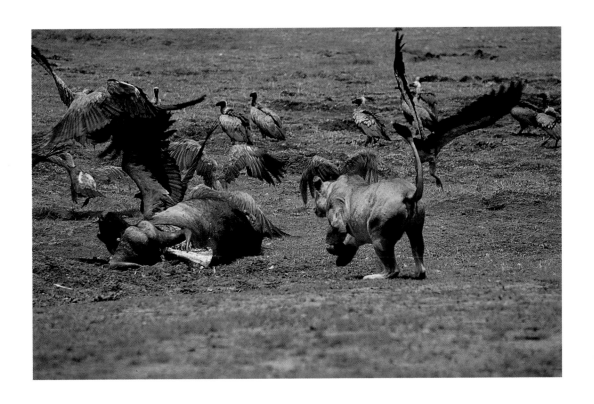

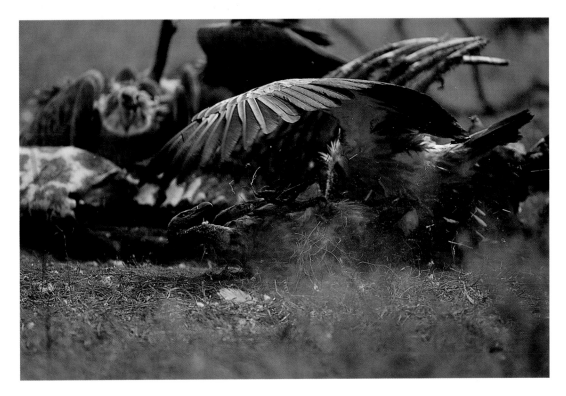

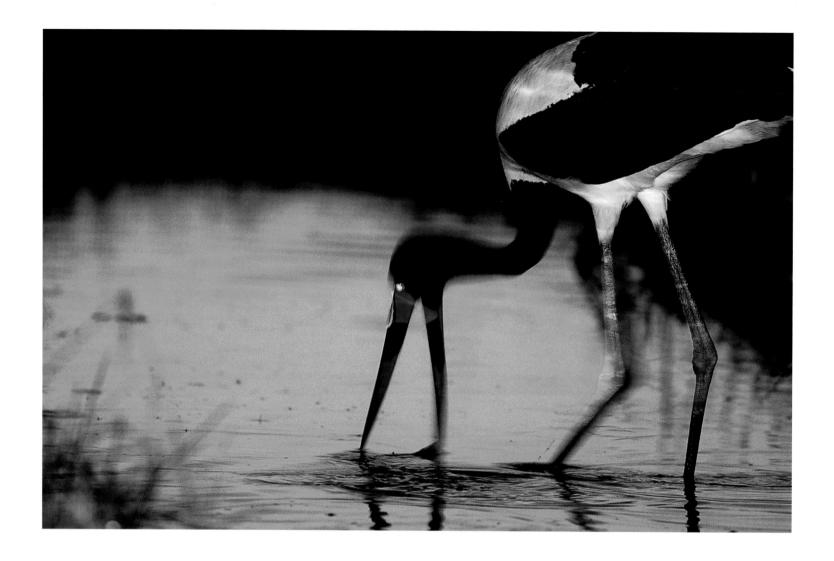

Previous pages   The lions of northern Botswana are famous for catching buffalo, and prides will often tag
along behind large buffalo herds for days, catching the occasional straggler at the back of the herd. The herds
are noisy and conspicuous, and this herd was soon noticed by the resident lion pride. After a protracted hunt
in the predawn hours, they caught a cow. When the growing summer heat had driven the feasting lions into
the shade of nearby trees, white-backed vultures descended in their droves. One of the lionesses ran out
repeatedly to chase them away, and on one charge managed to leap and catch a vulture in midair. She killed
the great bird with a single bite and left its broken body uneaten. Although generally disliked, vultures are
fascinating birds that play a significant ecological role. They occupy a diurnal scavenging niche, one which is
largely unexploited by the primarily nocturnal carnivores. Vultures do scavenge from predator kills, but they
obtain most of their food from the carcasses of animals which have died of natural causes.

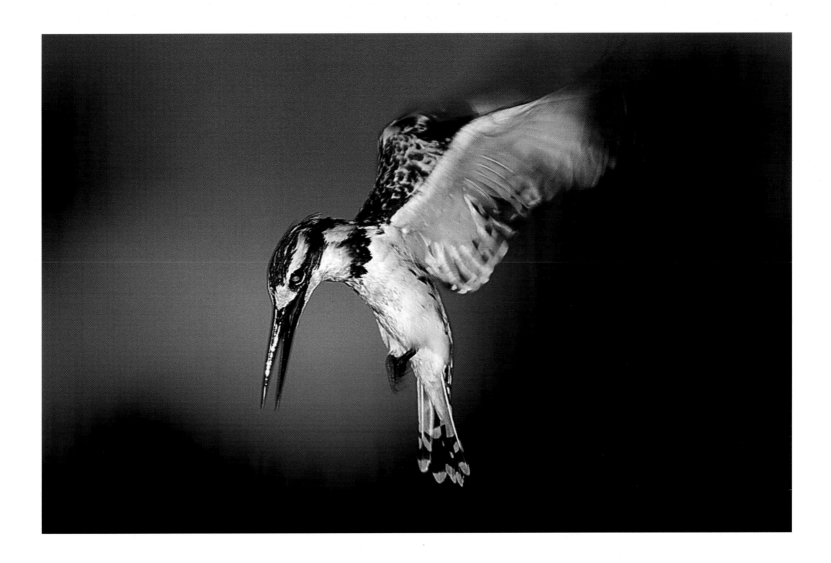

Opposite   In years when the summer rains are particularly heavy, the floodplains adjacent to the rivers become inundated. Large pools of water quickly fill up from the main course of the river and are soon colonized by a multitude of fish, frogs and invertebrates. By late summer these pools have become isolated and full of trapped fish, and are quickly invaded by a multitude of birds. Saddlebill storks feed by wading around and stabbing for frogs and fish that they secure with their huge serrated-edged bills.

Above   At first light the pied kingfishers would arrive at a small pool on the Moremi floodplain. They fished busily all morning, hovering, plunging, and emerging with small silver fingerlings. The other fishermen would also arrive early: saddlebills, hamerkops, sacred ibises and rufous-bellied herons all catching tiny fish using their own various fishing strategies.

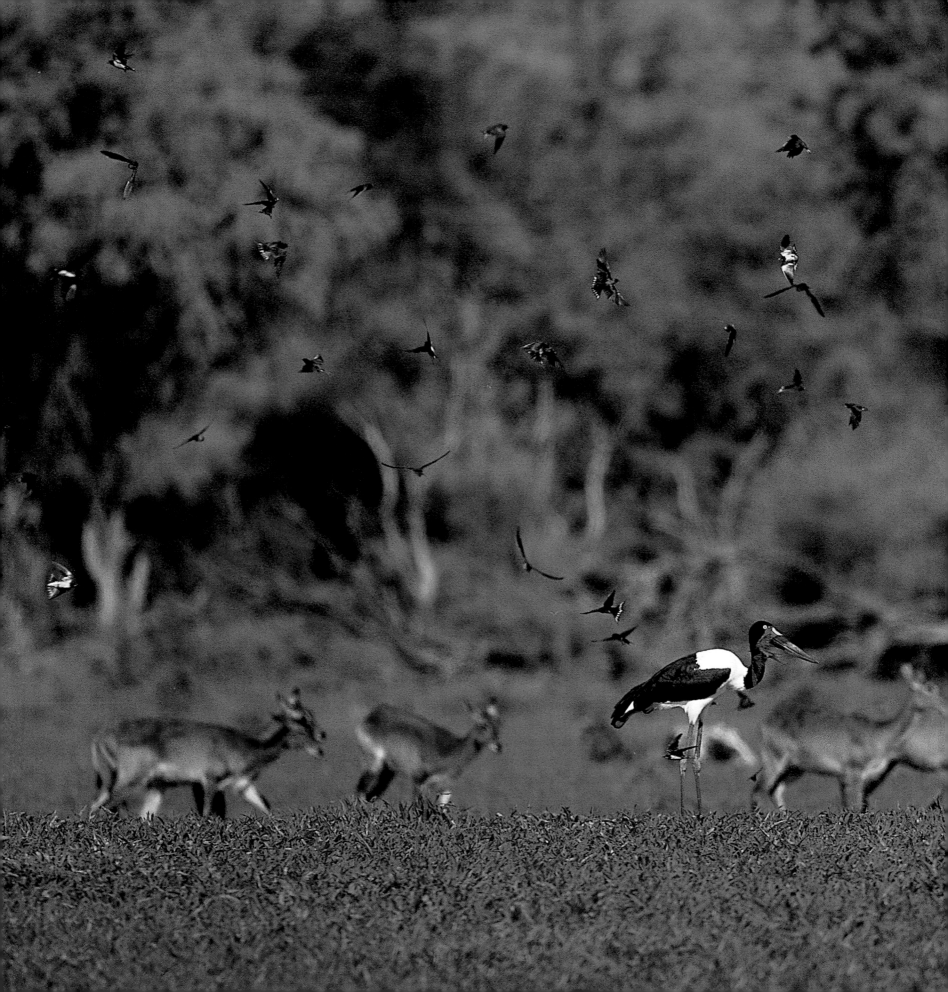

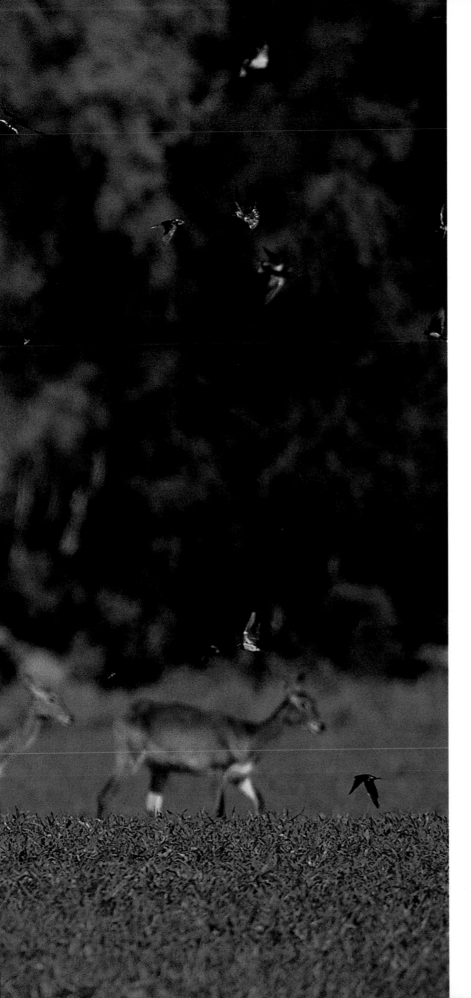

The Rains

The warm humid conditions following soaking rains
are ideal for termites to establish new colonies. Deep
underground in chambers of clay, thousands of these
winged reproductive termites will have waited months
for this moment. Throughout a given area, all the mounds
will release their flying termites simultaneously. How the
termites determine that conditions are perfect outside
or who gives the signal for this diaspora is a mystery.
A phalanx of soldier termites protect the emergence
holes, but frogs, lizards, spiders and mantids all feast
themselves silly on this unexpected winged bounty.

A termite emergence can be a very impressive
spectacle. Thousands of these silvery-winged insects
emerge and flutter out into the bright sunlight,
attracting huge numbers of birds within minutes. Here
European swallows and a saddlebill stork gather to feed.
The first waves of termites stand no chance, as hungry
bills snatch up every single one. But the apparently
suicidal mission is not entirely fruitless. So many termites
emerge that the birds feed to capacity, until with bloated
crops they can eat no more. If one pair in a million
termites escapes to establish a new colony, it has been
a successful endeavour.

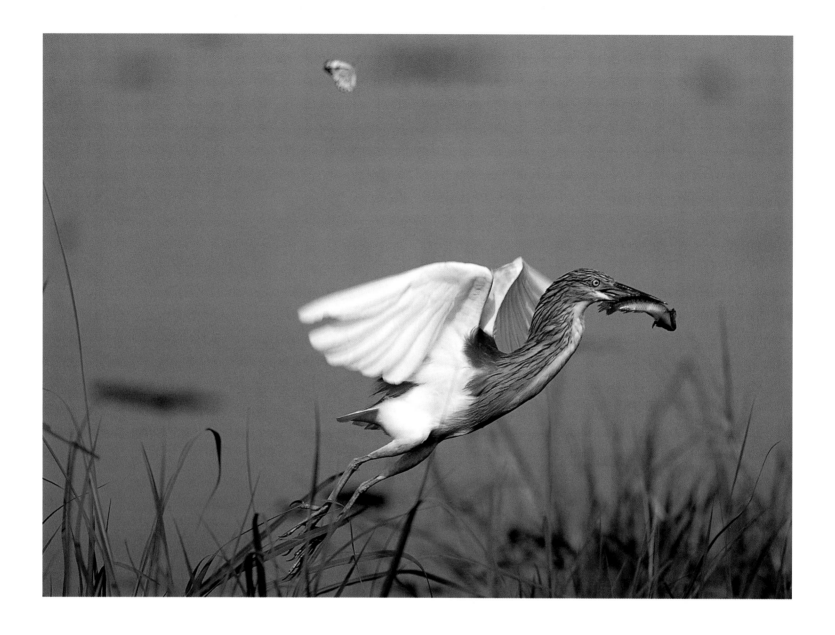

Squacco herons are easily overlooked as they skulk motionless on the fringes of the green-brown reedbeds. Like most of the other small herons they are stealthy hunters, waiting patiently for fish and other morsels to reveal themselves. They can swallow surprisingly large fish, and after a quick bill wash and drink, they resume fishing. In the low half-light of dusk the day's urgency slows and squacco herons fly off white-winged to their communal roosting trees.

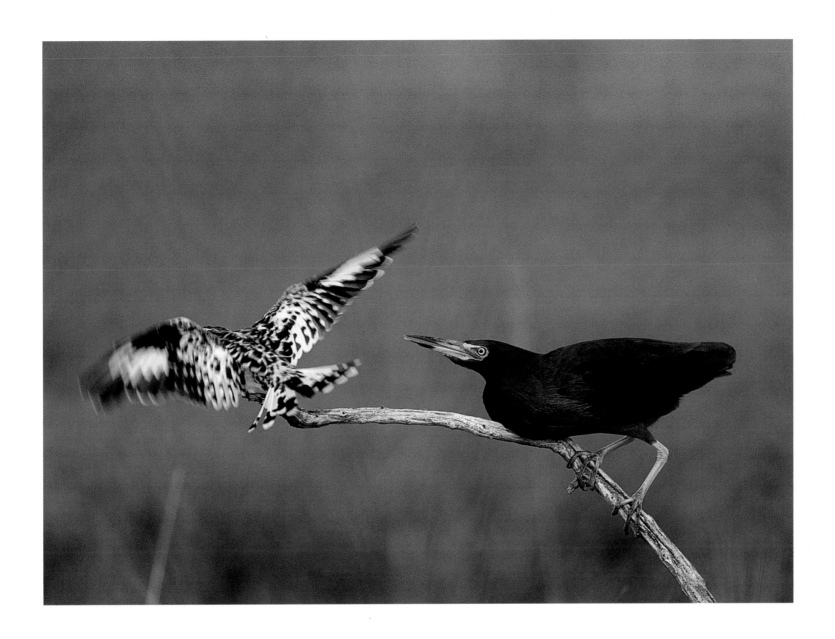

The reedbeds and temporary pans of summer can host the most unexpected waterbird visitors. Rufous-bellied herons are seldom seen out in the open and this pied kingfisher appeared surprised and annoyed to see one when he returned to his favourite waterside perch. These small herons, along with bitterns, snipe and moorhens usually lurk in the well-vegetated shallows. It is well worth taking some time to scan the watery areas with your binoculars, as these masters of camouflage are more common than one realizes.

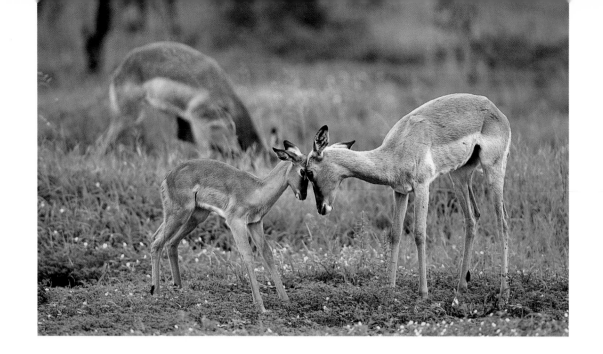

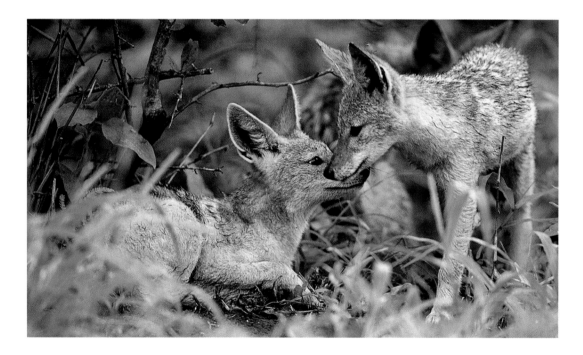

Impala (*top*) are seasonal breeders, giving birth in the optimum conditions of midsummer. Not only is food abundant and conditions mild, but the synchronized birth of the vulnerable youngsters ensures that at least some will escape the rapacious jaws of a host of predators. Young jackals (*above*) are born in underground burrows in the early spring, and the youngsters remain close to the dens for safety, for even as predators, a host of threats exist. Young vervet monkeys (*opposite*) have much to master; they must learn to identify the many alarm calls that the adult monkeys utter, each in response to a particular threat.

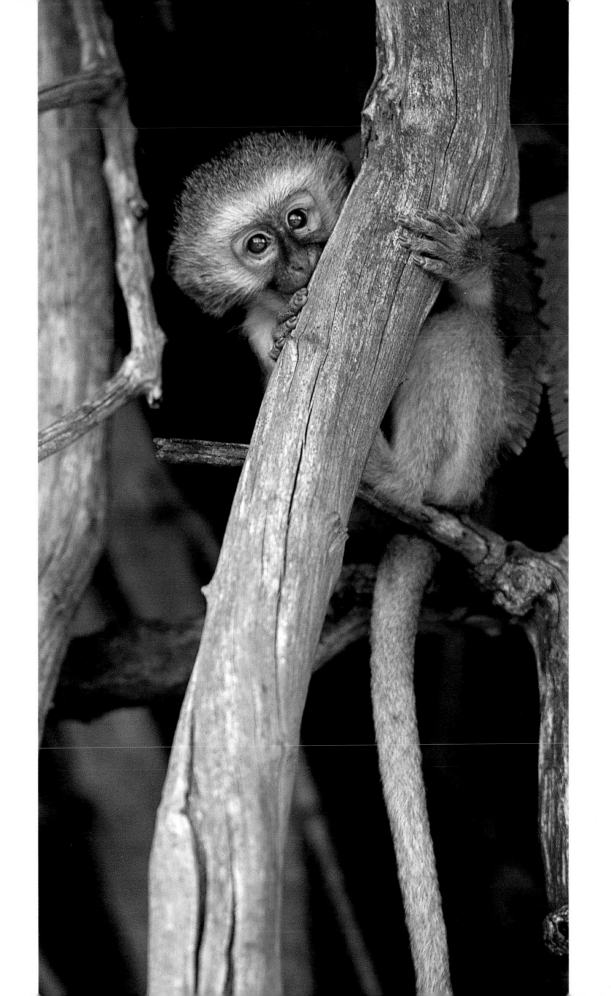

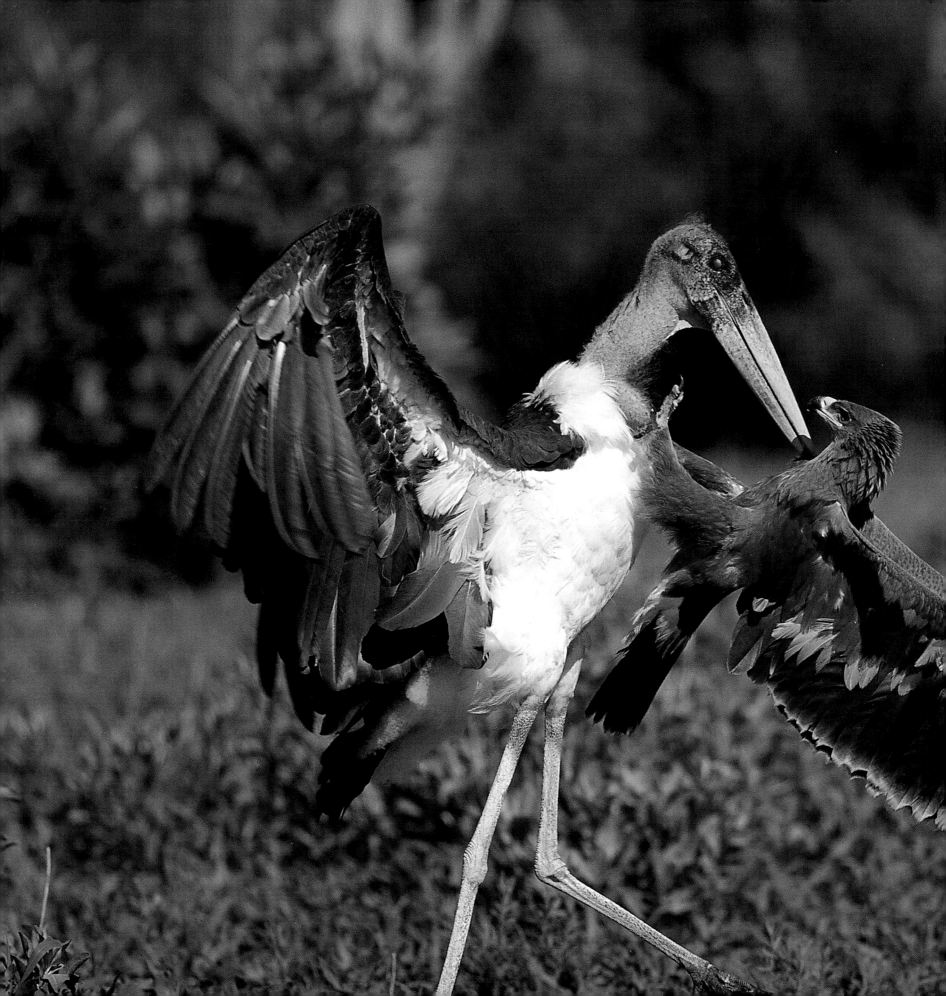

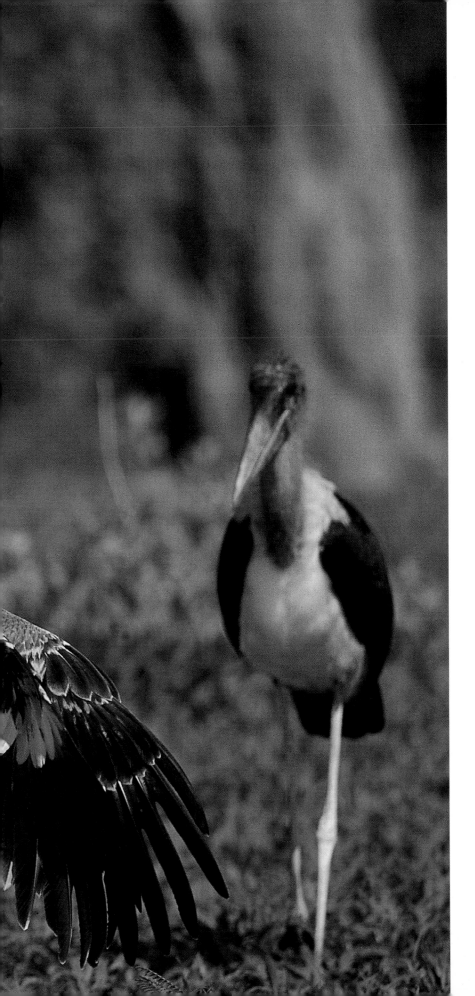

Attracted by swallows chasing winged termites, several eagles and heavy-billed marabou storks wing their way in. With the angry clap of a bill and a sudden explosion of feathers, these two birds risk injury in a contest over a tiny insect. The steppe eagle is a common summer visitor, flying all the way from its distant breeding grounds in Eastern Europe and Kazakhstan. Around 20 per cent of southern Africa's bird species are migratory, and they fall into two similar-sized groups, namely the intra-Africa and the Palearctic migrants. In spite of the great distances involved, migration is clearly a successful strategy and many of the most abundant summer birds are migrants. One of the major reasons why so many birds migrate is the seasonal abundance of food in two separate regions.

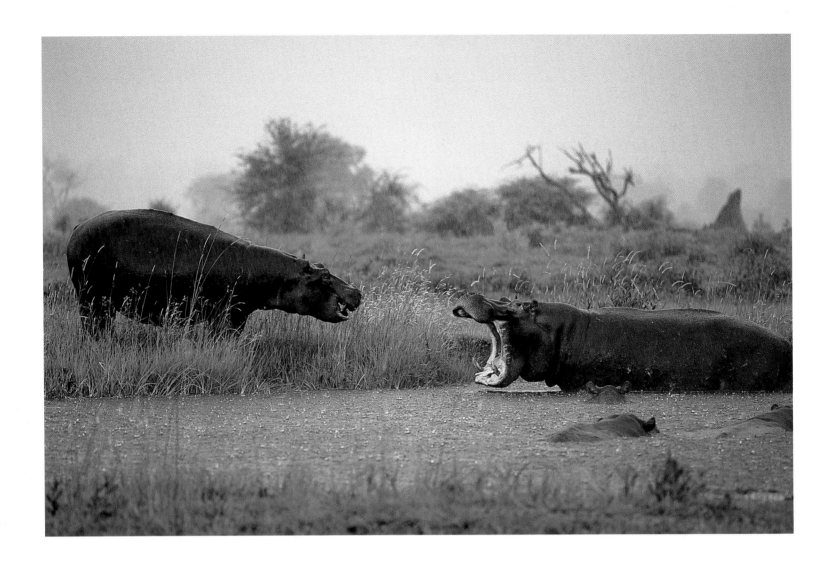

Above High summer temperatures can cause overheating and dehydration problems for large animals, of which the hippo is particularly vulnerable. The hippo solves this by being amphibious; during the heat of the day it wallows in pools and rivers, and ventures out to graze during the cooler nights. There are always exceptions to the rule, and on occasion the hippos will be out grazing or sunning themselves during the hottest days, albeit briefly. This passing midday rainstorm caused some excitement for this pod of hippos.

Opposite Threat yawning is used by hippos to expose and display their massive canines. These huge teeth are kept sharp by grinding against each other, and can reach 50 centimetres in length in adult males.

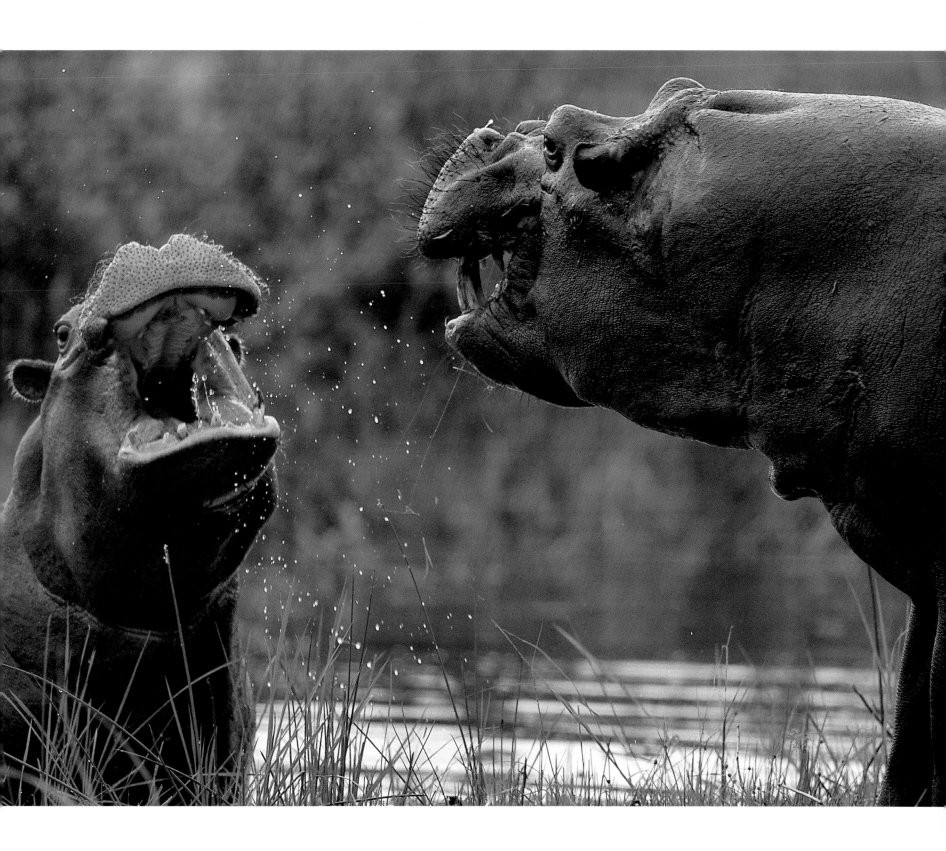

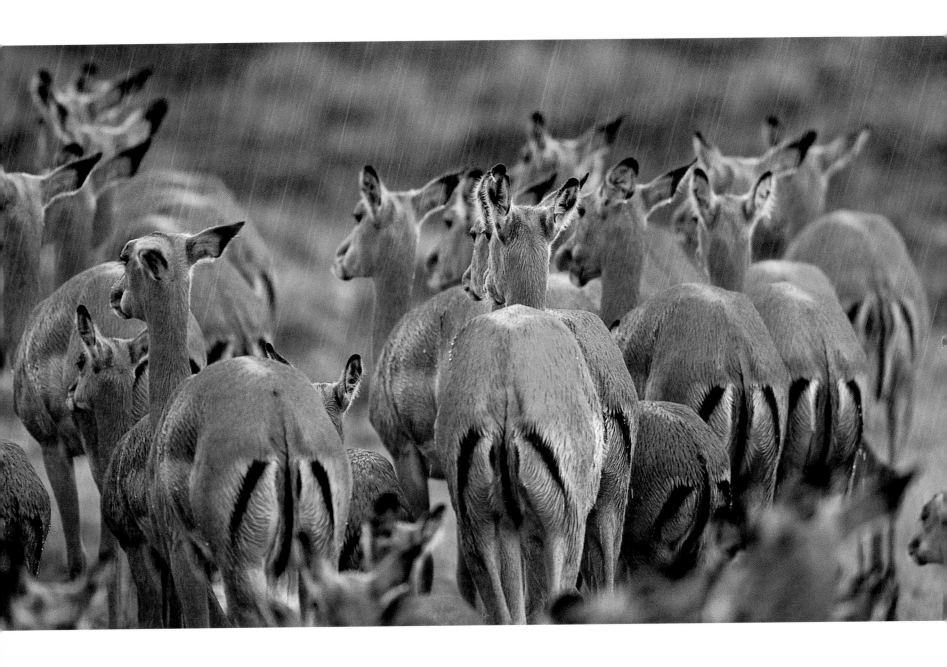

Throughout the hot summer months clouds build up daily out of clear blue skies, with several storms sweeping over each day. From midday on thunder can be heard in the distance and the big clouds roll in quickly, low and dark, bringing with them a deluge. Such sudden rain showers are a phenomenon well known to the animals here. As this squall of rain suddenly began to fall these impala ran from the treeline and bunched together in the open. With their backs hunched towards the chilling downpour, the ewes waited stoically for the intense shower to pass.

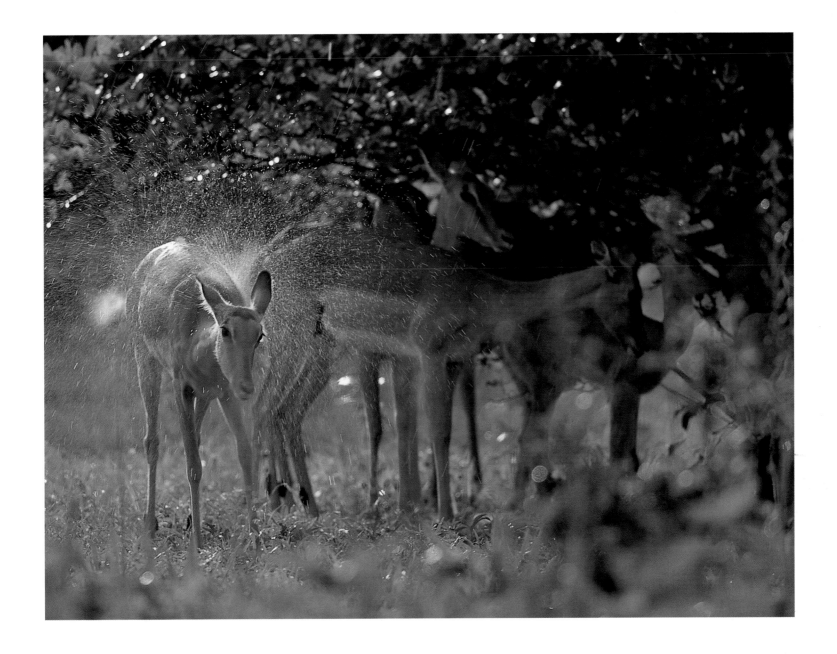

The storm is over quickly and the ewes shake themselves dry. This is one of the last showers of summer. The porous earth has sucked up the months of rain and thousands of pans lie full of muddy water. It is a season of plenty and the impala make the most of it. The rams need to gather strength for the imminent rutting season, and in the near future the ewes will fall pregnant and carry their calves though the driest part of the year. It is vital now to build up fat reserves and strength for the difficult times to come.

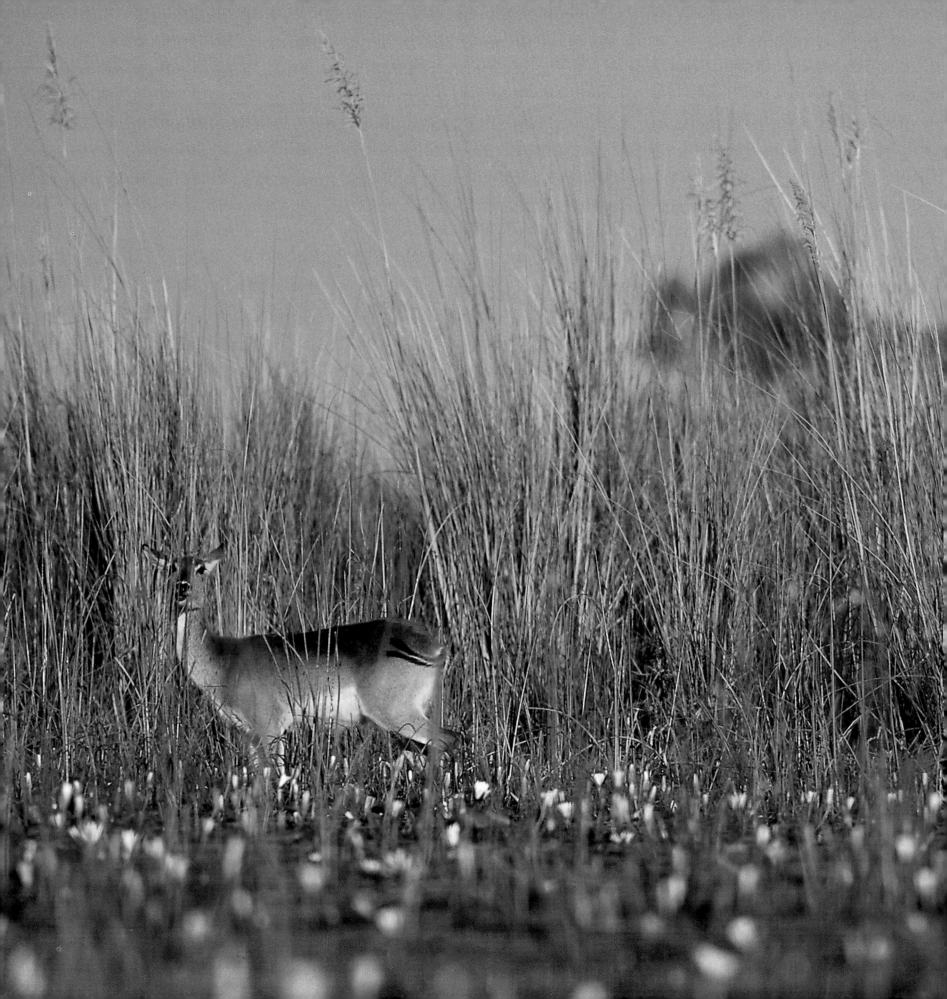

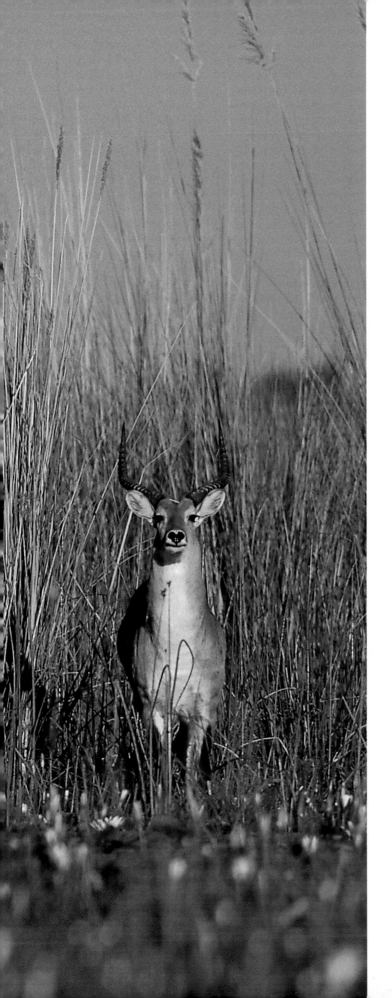

The Floods

arrive from the distant north

THE FLOODS NORMALLY ARRIVE in the delta in April, after the cool clear waters have travelled down the narrow panhandle of the Okavango River. This rather inappropriately named 'flood' is actually a slow and gentle process, the flood waters appearing silently and often unnoticed. One day the waters suddenly start to rise and dry stream beds begin to flow with water again. The water enters thousands of nameless rivers and channels that meander and oxbow before spreading out into the great swampland itself. As the floodplains become inundated, the frontline of the flood pushes down towards the Khwai River.

The open floodplains adjacent to the Khwai are home to lechwe, impala, giraffe and baboons, but an examination of the tracks at the river's edge will reveal little traffic. Out in the mopane forests there are still pans filled with water and there is no need yet for the animals to make the journey to the river to quench their thirst. Most noticeable by their absence are the herds of elephant — neither massed tracks nor fresh dung indicate their often destructive presence. For the vegetation this is the recovery season — a chance to grow again before the hungry giants return en masse.

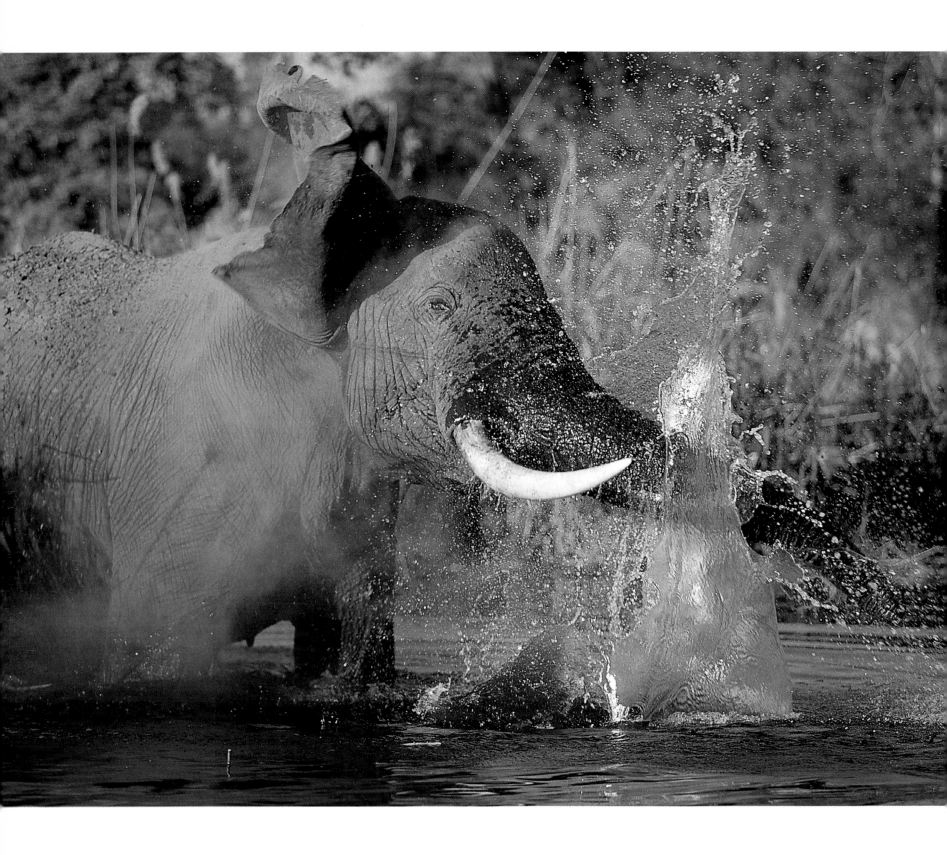

On the broader stretches of the upper river the chatter of numerous birds and the hum of insects carries clearly across the water. There is an abundance of squacco herons, although they are almost invisible in the reeds until they flutter off. The carpets of waterlilies that cover patches of river are home to shy pygmy geese, their whites, browns and greens rendering these seemingly conspicuous birds almost invisible. The russet and white African jacanas that trot over the surface are far bolder.

Floating down a narrow delta channel in a *mokoro* (dugout canoe), we glided silently along, so low that we could dip our fingers into the water (something we were reluctant to do as we tried to forget campfire stories of giant crocodiles!). The slightly tea-coloured waters were surprisingly clear, silt-free from being filtered through a giant sieve of papyrus. The only sound that interrupted Nature's chorus was the soothing splash of the boatman's pole.

Mazes of channels offered themselves as we entered a small lagoon, and wet fronds brushed against our faces going through a tunnel in the papyrus. Gliding back into an open stretch of water, we were soothed by the pure tranquillity of this waterland. Malachite kingfishers darted along the lily-covered surface, startling tiny fish below. A loud exhalation of air from the channel announced the presence of a bull hippo. Hippos always look huge and, at eye level, we felt very vulnerable. He gave us a beady stare and submerged – a bow wave betraying his position as he submarined away – to our considerable relief.

We hugged the shallows and glided silently by, next spotting a group of buffalo bulls feeding knee-deep. They ignored us even though we poled close by. The clean dark water was restful as it proceeded on its slow journey to the distant Kalahari.

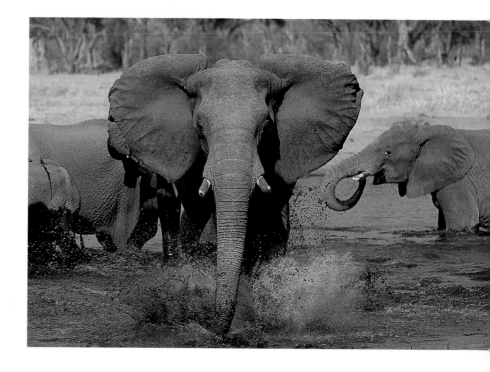

Previous pages   Lechwe are at home in the shallows where they feed among the waterlilies and papyrus. The neck of the male is much thicker than the hornless female. Aided by powerful neck muscles the males use their horns to good effect in fierce territorial battles with rival males.

Opposite   Some of the elephant herds in this region are nervous, and on catching human scent will startle and hurry away. However, we have also been on the receiving end of some furious charges! These elephants probably come from remote regions where people and vehicles are seldom encountered.

Above   Headshake, earflap, trunkslap – an explosive display of displeasure from an old bull elephant.

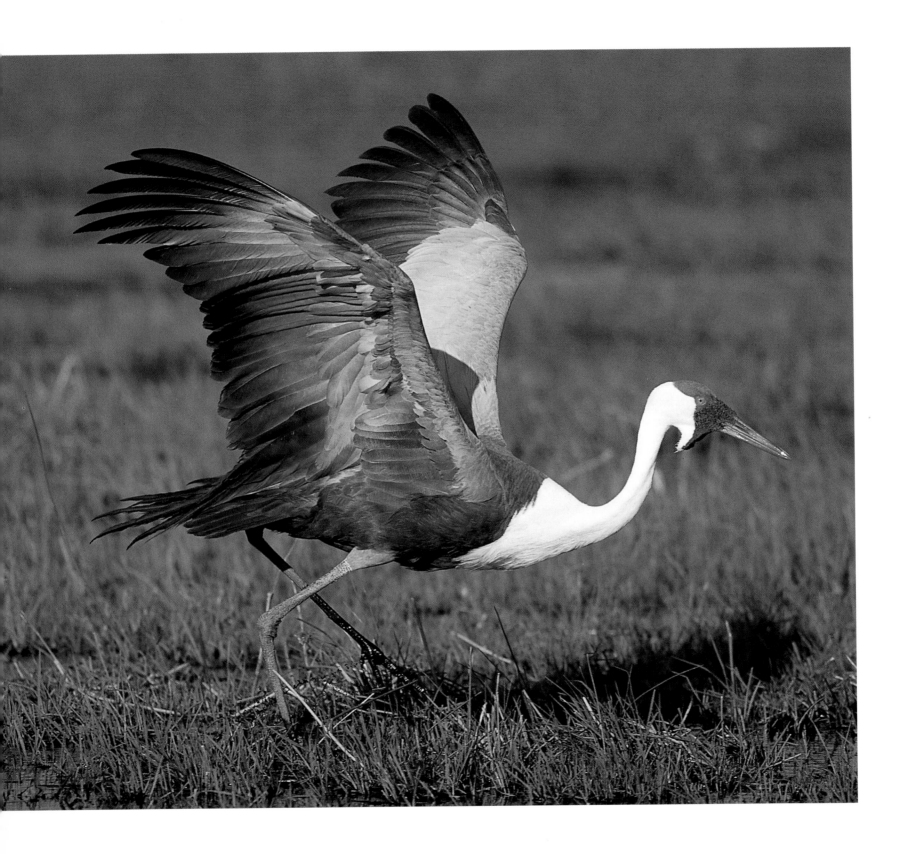

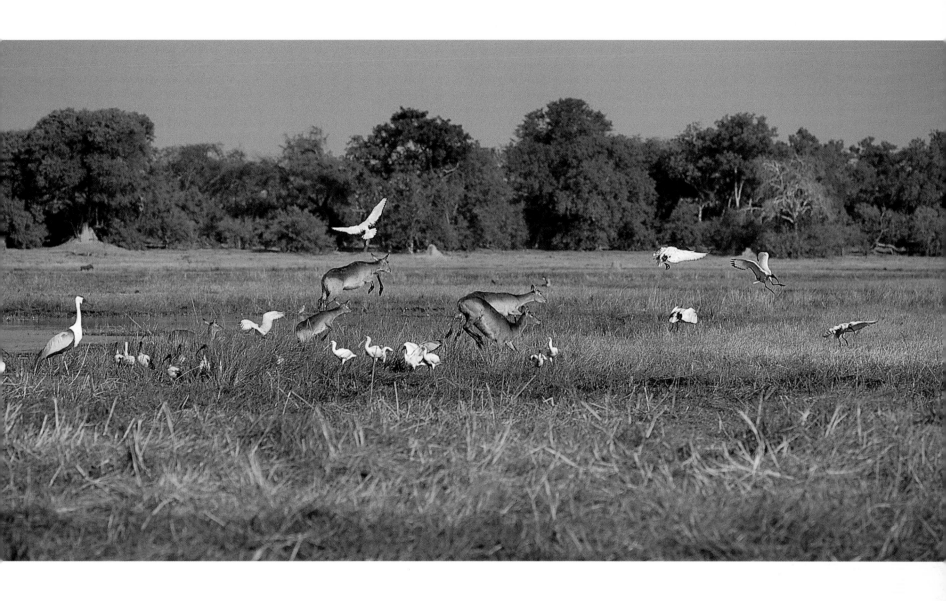

Sacred ibises scatter in fright (***above***) as red lechwe bound across the river. Here on the floodplain the river loses its narrow form, and splays out into a shallow marsh that provides a rich hunting ground for a wide variety of waterbirds. Many of these – the egrets, herons, ibises, spoonbills and storks – nest in colonies many kilometres from where they feed. However, the stately and endangered wattled crane (***opposite***) breeds right here in the marsh. These striking birds' courtship involves an impressive display of open-winged dancing to show off their long wing plumes and unusual facial adornments. Out here in the open a pair of cranes build a low platform nest of reeds, grass and mud, where the female will lay one or two eggs. Both birds take turns to incubate but only one chick is raised. Many large bird species with slow reproductive rates are very long lived, and the wattled crane may reach fifty years.

Marabou storks would feed at this river pool for about an hour in the early morning, plunging their beaks into the murky water to grab fish and frogs. These large storks are efficient hunters of fish, catching and swallowing impossibly large catfish that probably keep them replete for days. After catching one of these, they would wander off and stand in the shade for the rest of the day. Marabous also scavenge from the carcasses of dead animals; their bald heads and necks are featherless to reduce contamination by blood and flesh.

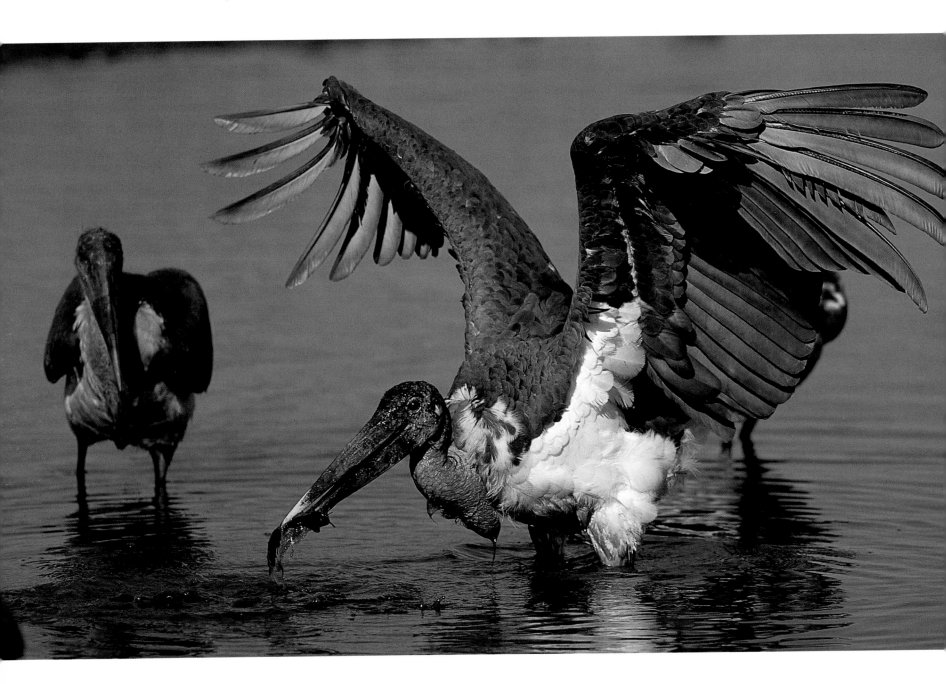

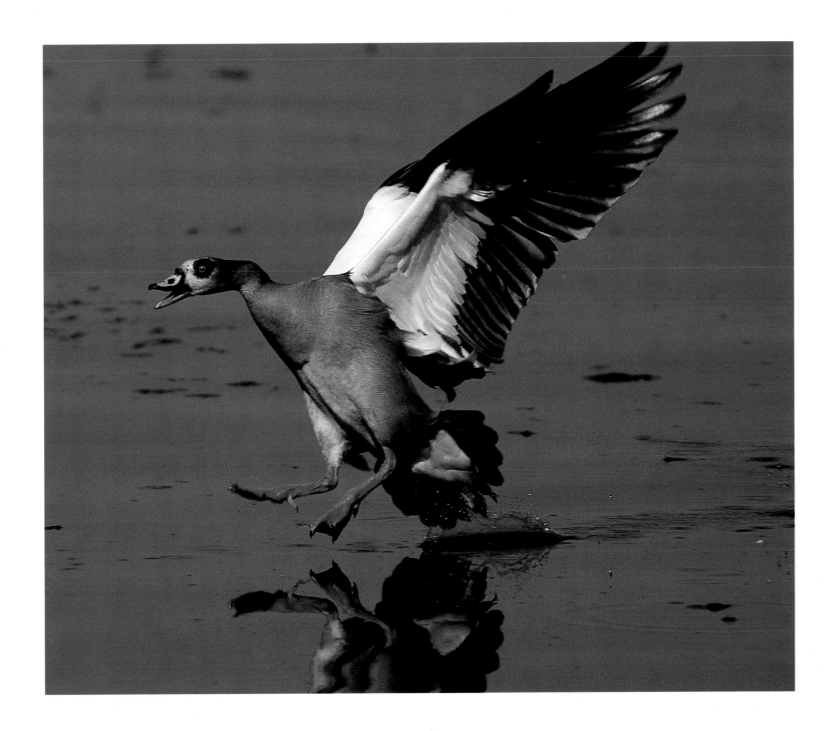

An Egyptian goose lands stiff-legged. The large, webbed feet function as waterskis to facilitate a smooth water landing for this heavy bird. Along with the sacred ibis, the Egyptian goose was revered by the ancient Egyptians. Both of these birds have a wide African distribution.

The red lechwe, a water-loving antelope that exploits the seasonally flooded river edges, is always close to permanent water. These antelope have distinctly elongated and widely splayed hooves that help them negotiate the soft marshy ground of this habitat. They feed on grasses and sedges, sometimes grazing belly-deep for hours. Rivers provide both food and protection for the lechwe.

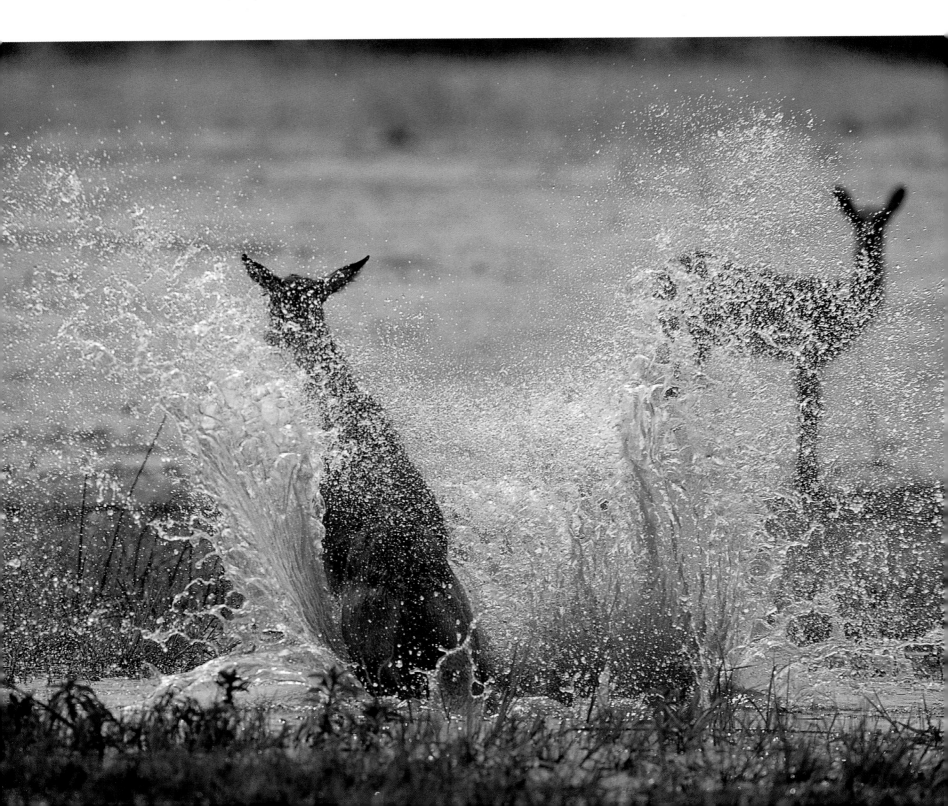

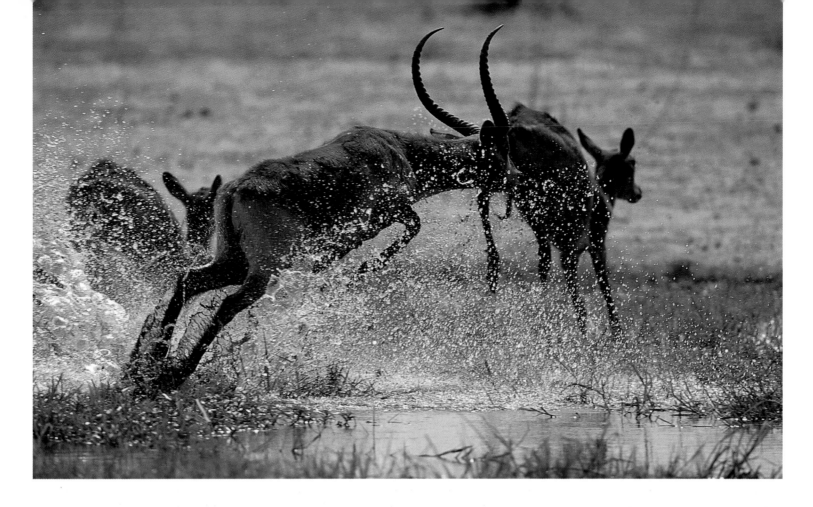

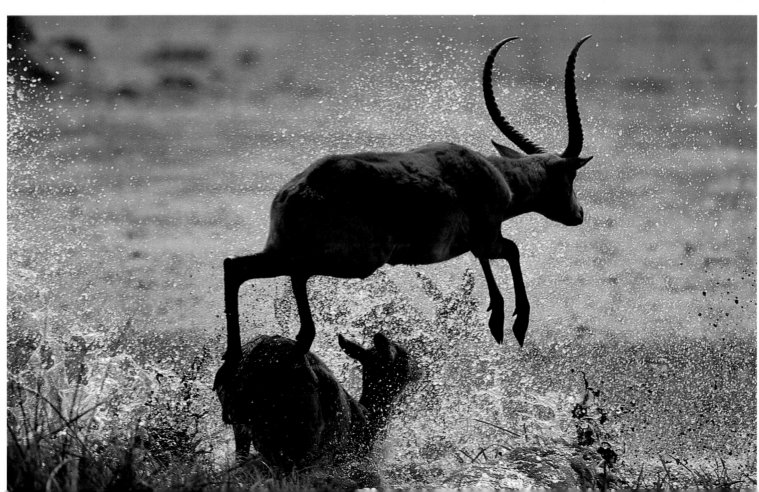

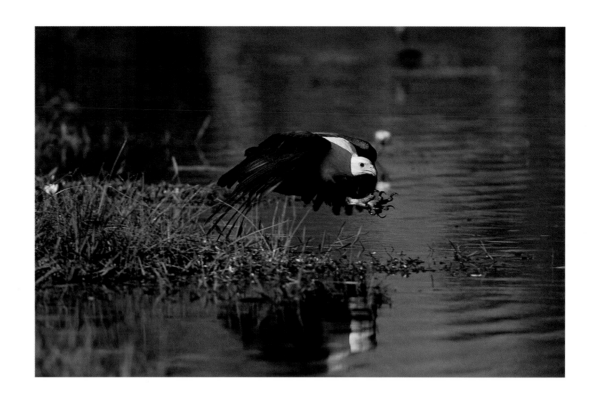

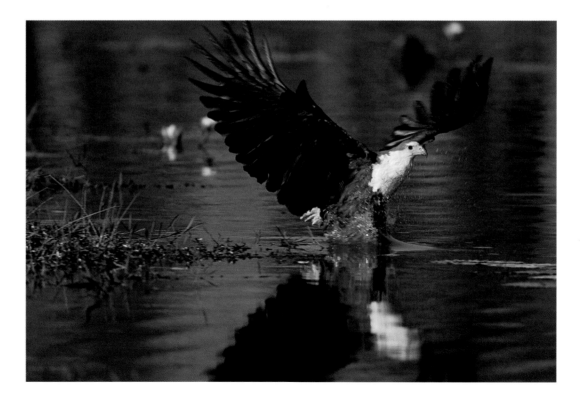

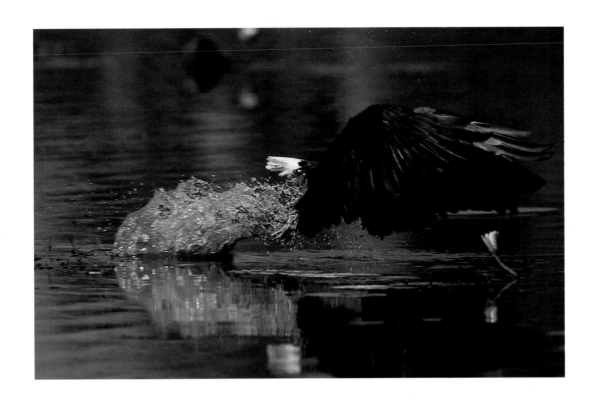

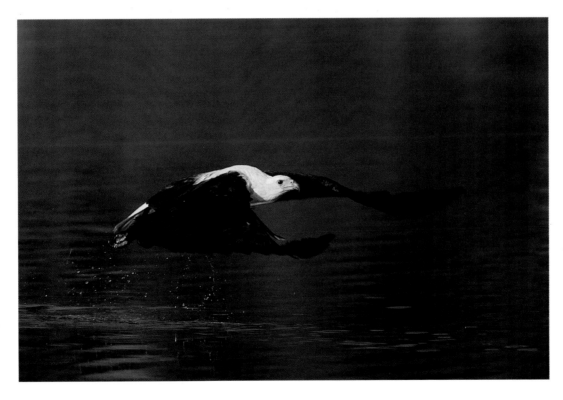

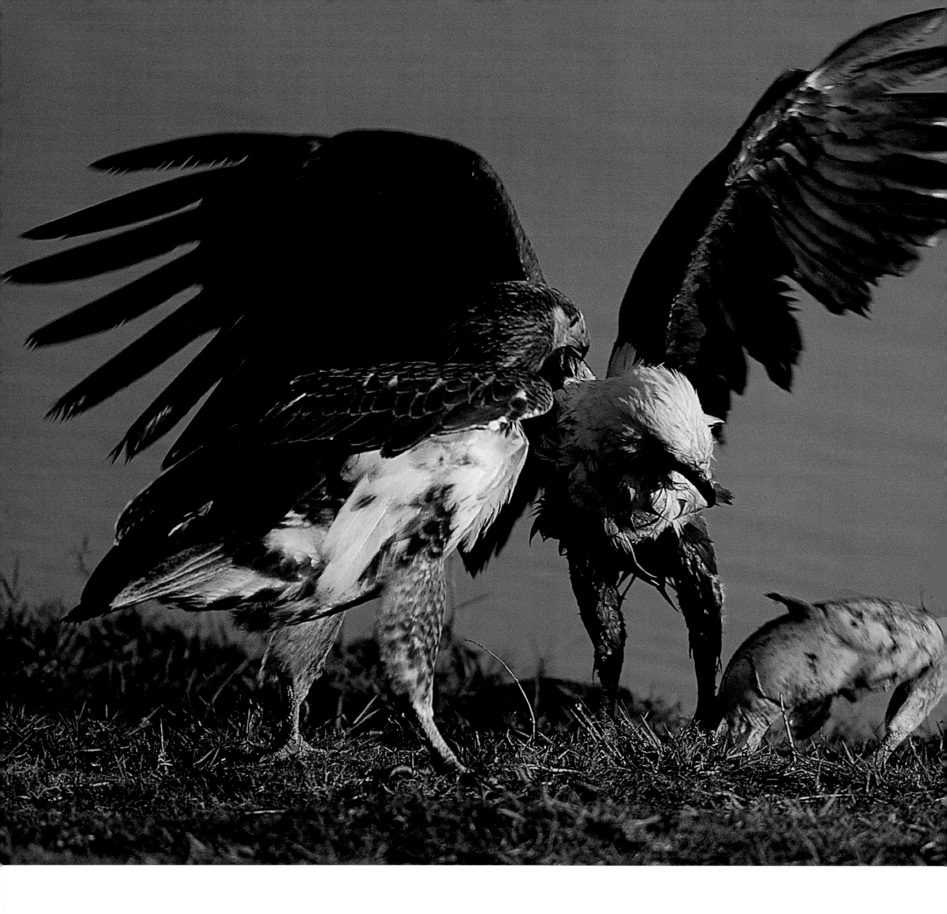

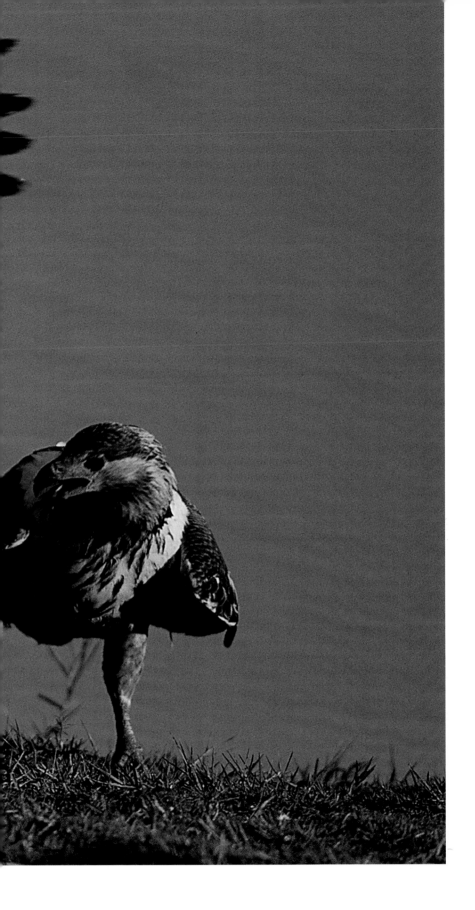

Previous pages   The common and conspicuous African fish eagle is a magnificent bird, its clarion call a symbol of the waterways of Africa. Eagles hunting in the wild are a rare sight but the African fish eagle provides birdwatchers with some of the finest demonstrations of aerial skills. They carefully survey the water for signs of fish – either from a high perch or while on the wing – swooping down and snatching their victims from the surface in a spectacular splash of spray. They will plunge into the water after larger fish, some as heavy as themselves, which they need to drag ashore to eat. In the lower reaches of the Khwai River they eat mostly catfish, but their diets include birds such as turtledoves and red-billed quelea that they hawk in mid-air with surprising dexterity.

Left   Fish eagles belong to the genus *Haliaeetus* which includes the American bald eagle, a similar-looking bird that also has a distinctive white head and tail. Fish eagles are generally territorial, but occasionally concentrate in gatherings of dozens of birds. The immature eagles are scruffy-looking birds, with a mottled plumage of white, brown and rufous, which they maintain until about four years of age. Here they squabble over a catfish.

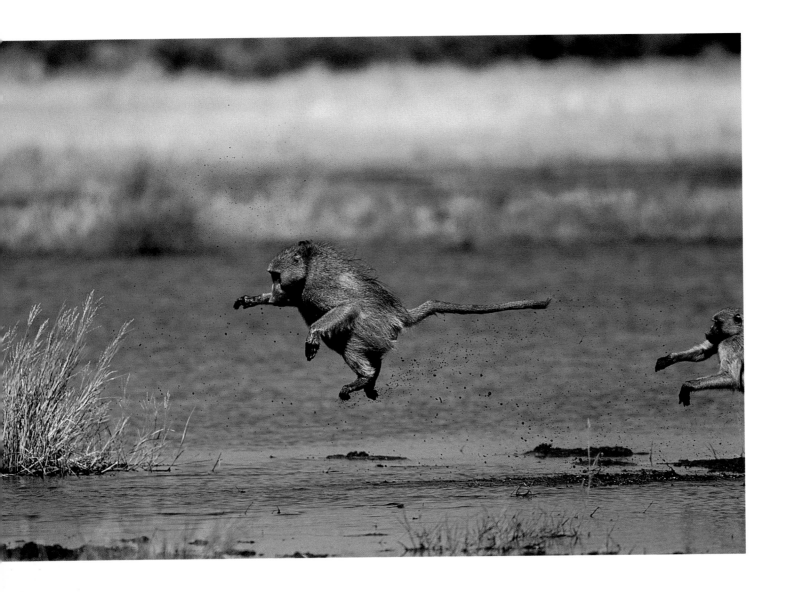

Above   The baboon troops roost in the large jackal-berry trees on the edge of the floodplain. The daily wanderings of the troops are longer during the dry season when foraging is less productive. They are terrified of crocodiles and most leapt fearfully over these narrows.

Opposite   Wild dogs are long-legged hunters designed for high-speed chases and remarkable endurance. These pack hunters specialize in catching antelope such as lechwe and impala. The dogs cornered these lechwe on a bend in the river, but the water-loving antelope had been in such situations many times before. In an impressive splash they plunged into the deep waters and through onto the other side, the river a safety-line to counter enemies. The dogs showed no interest in following, their dread of crocodiles keeping them dry.

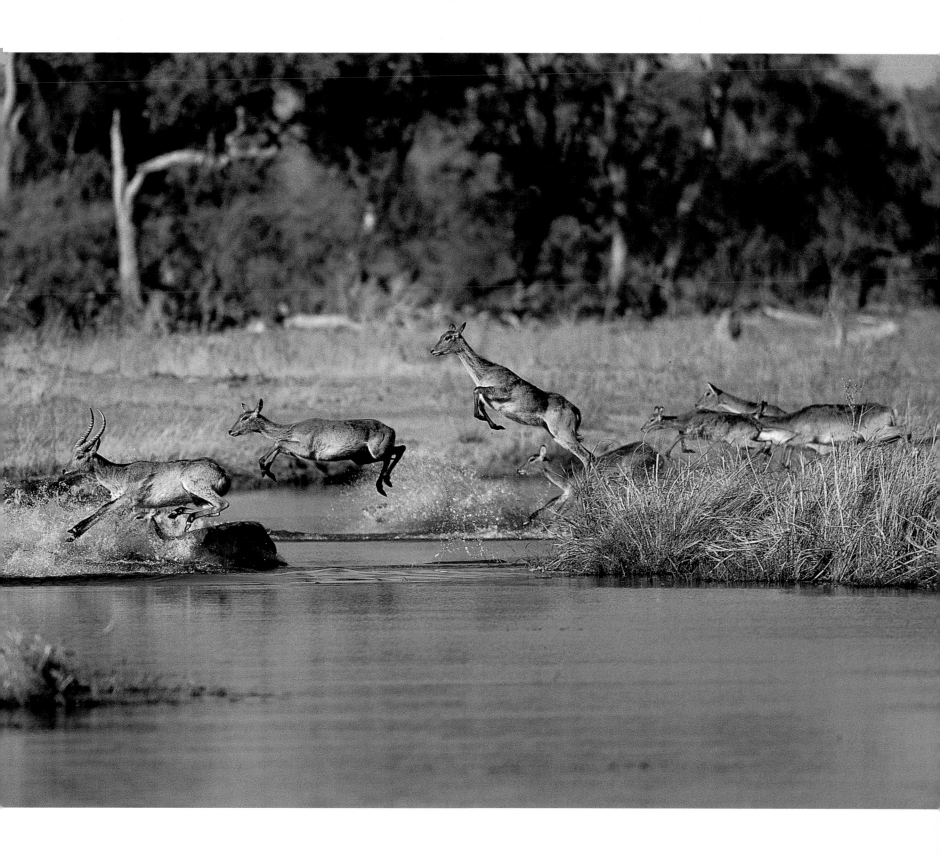

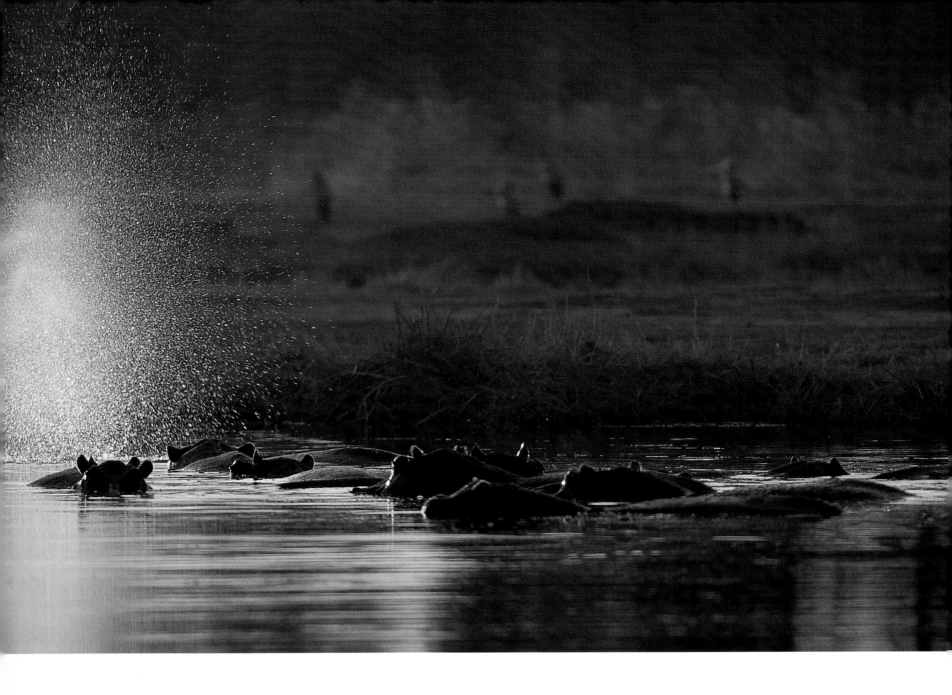

Hippos are well adapted to their aquatic life with eyes, ears and nose being situated on the top of the head (**above**). They close their nostrils and fold back their ears when they submerge, for up to five minutes at a time. After surfacing from a dive, hippo release great blasts of air, like the blows of surfacing whales. They are very vocal, their familiar roaring grunts functioning to advertise their occupation of a stretch of river. I had been sitting on a riverbank watching a bull hippo roll (**opposite bottom**) and snort, when he suddenly demonstrated his threat charge (**opposite top**). Posturing and snorting, he got his message across. Mock charges and demonstrations of size and strength are generally adequate to chase away unwanted visitors, but if unsuccessful, violence can follow. Hippos are one of Africa's most dangerous large mammals.

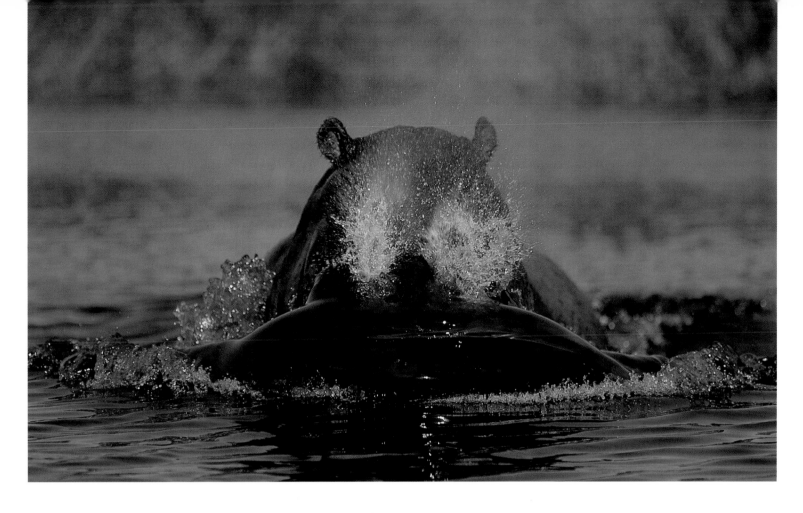
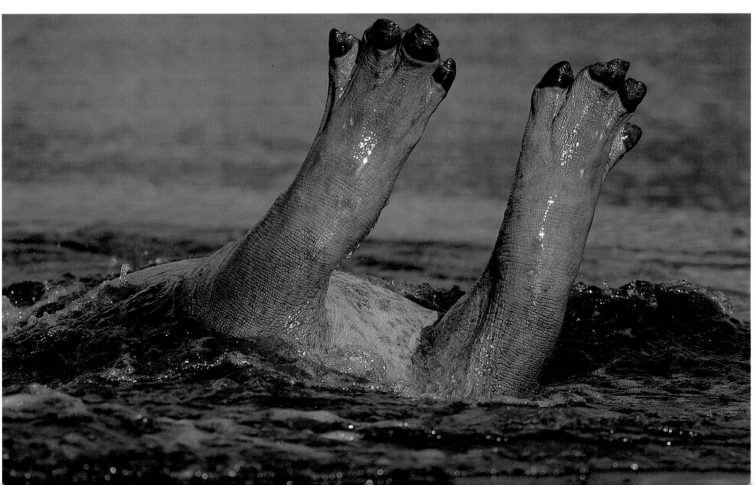

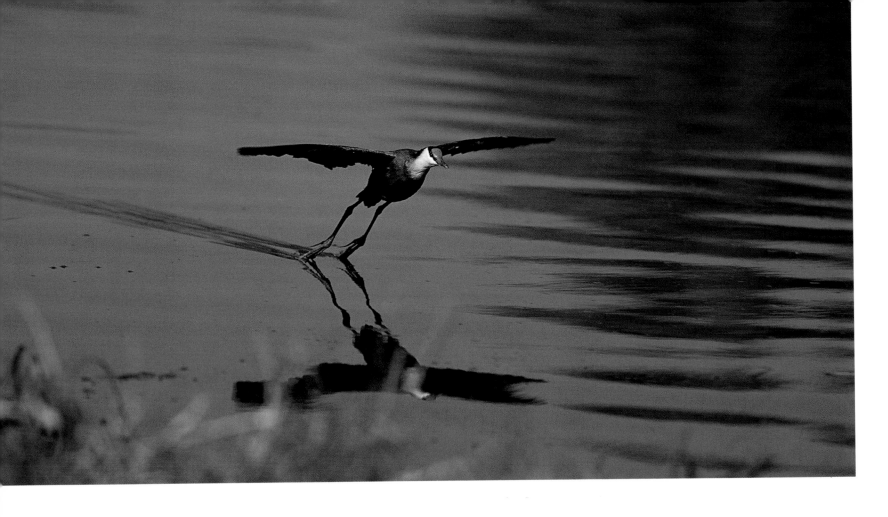
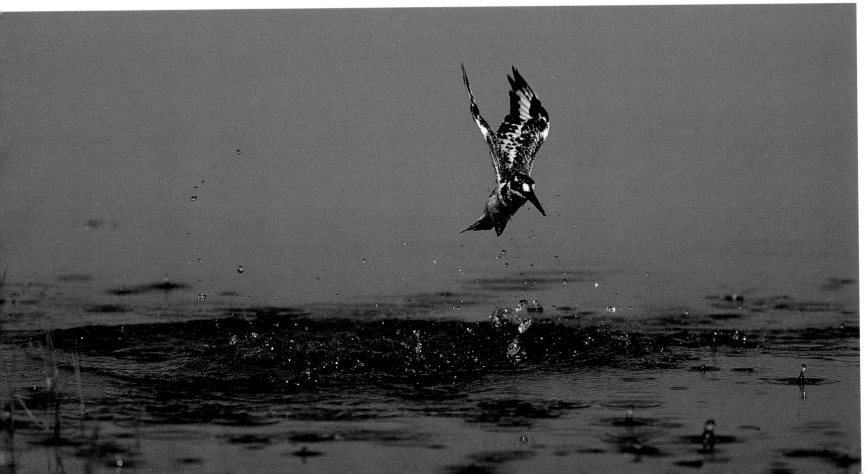

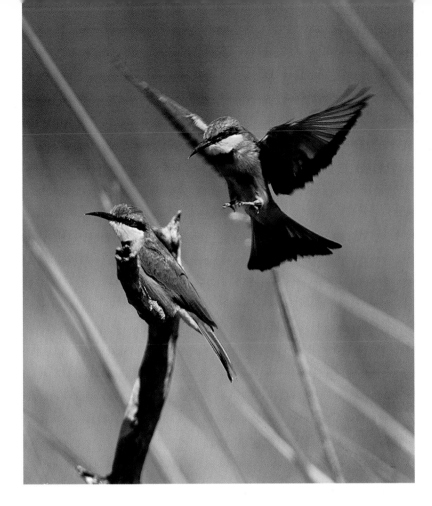

Just as birds come in a bewildering variety of sizes and shapes, so too have they evolved an extraordinary range of behavioural adaptations for obtaining their food from watery environments.

Opposite top   An African jacana drags its long toes before landing. The jacana is a common bird, spending much of the day wandering over the lilies, inspecting them for insects and seeds. In common with the painted snipe, the jacana has an interesting but uncommon breeding strategy. Jacanas are polyandrous; a female courts several males in succession, for each of whom she lays a clutch of eggs on a mat of floating vegetation. The male then incubates the eggs, which are covered with an ornate pattern of dark scrolls and streaks on a background of dark yellow-green.

Opposite bottom   A pied kingfisher explodes from the water after an unsuccessful dive. These birds are masters at hovering, which precedes a dive and a torpedo-like plunge under the water to catch fish. Some of their victims are surprisingly large, and are bashed to death on a perch before being swallowed headfirst.

Top   Little bee-eaters are attracted to the water's edge by an abundance of flying insects, for which they wait on a convenient perch. Darting out like jewels to catch their food, they are capable of remarkable aerial manoeuvres.

Left   The common hamerkop is normally a wader, stalking frogs and fish in the shadows. On occasion it will fly over the water with feet trailing and snatch up the water creatures it disturbs.

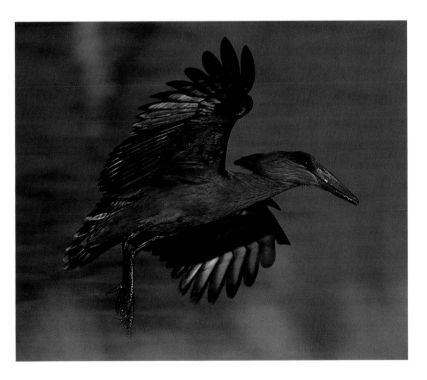

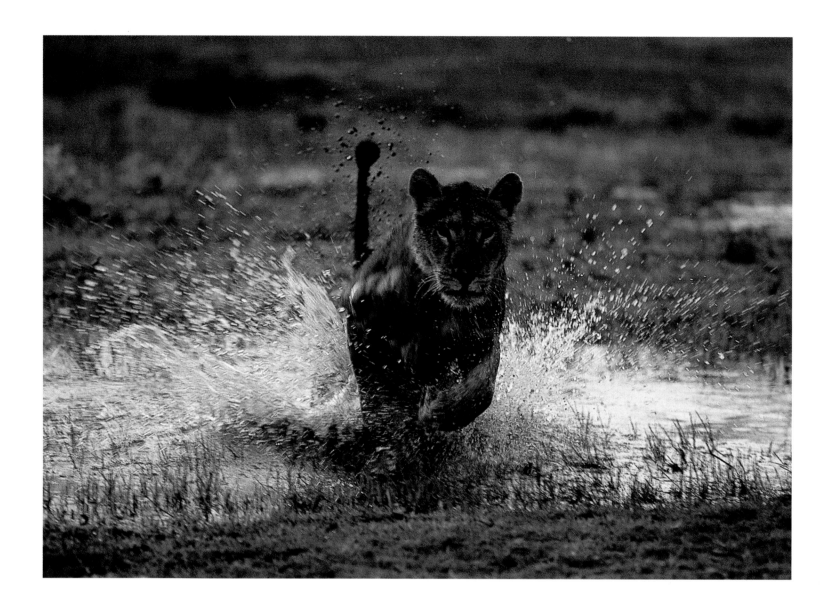

At dawn one morning I came across a lion pride by the river. Although cats have a reputation for disliking water, the lions that live close to rivers and swamps are generally unfazed by getting wet, often wading and even swimming. The large cubs of this pride actually seemed to revel in their watery adventures, indulging in wild play-fighting as they chased each other back and forth across the shallows of the river.

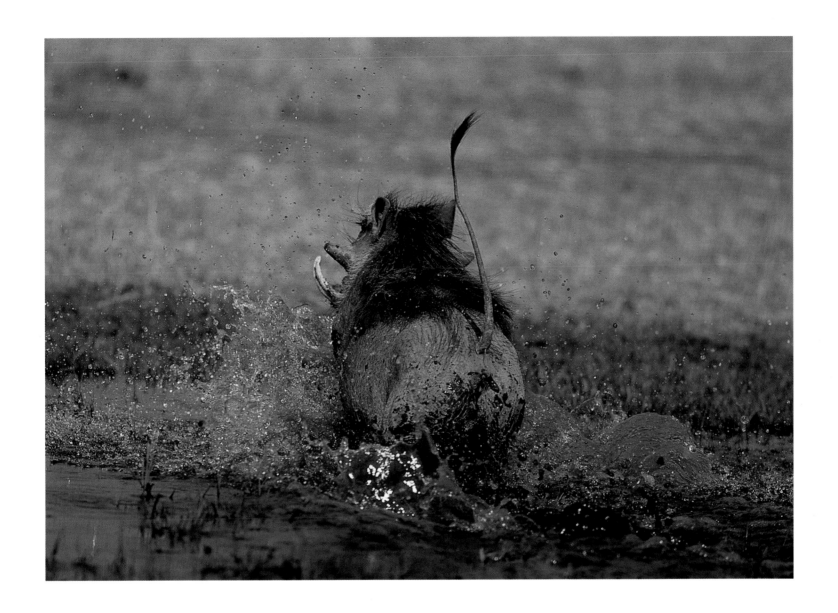

Warthogs may be short and squat but they are sprinters of note. Here a crusty old male spins around and dashes off through the shallows. I have always liked these tough creatures; they are one of my favourite bushveld characters. Warthogs are underdogs, their days spent avoiding the constant threat of lions and other predators. Their nights are spent in dusty burrows where they are tormented by fleas and biting flies, and to make matters worse, the lions will even attempt to dig them out!

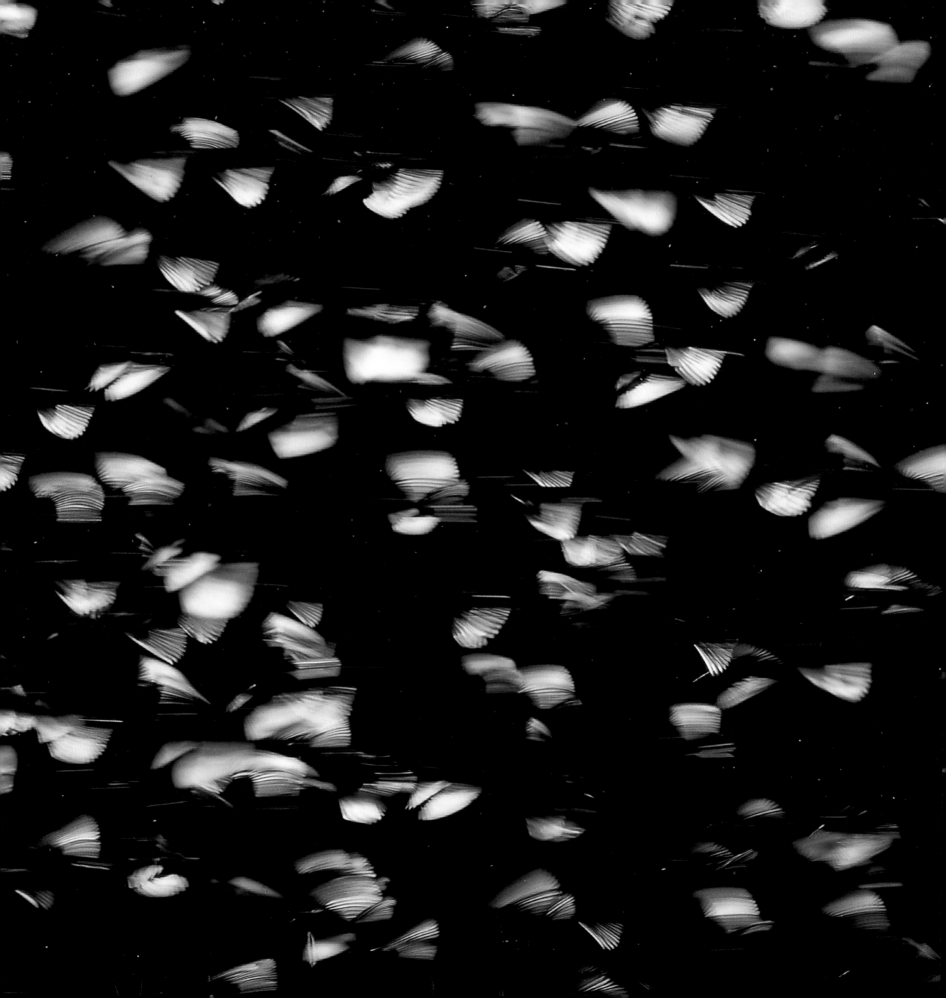

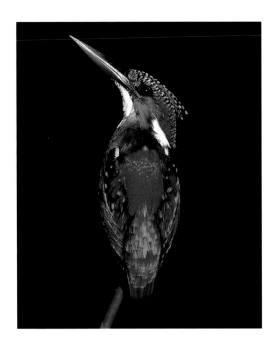

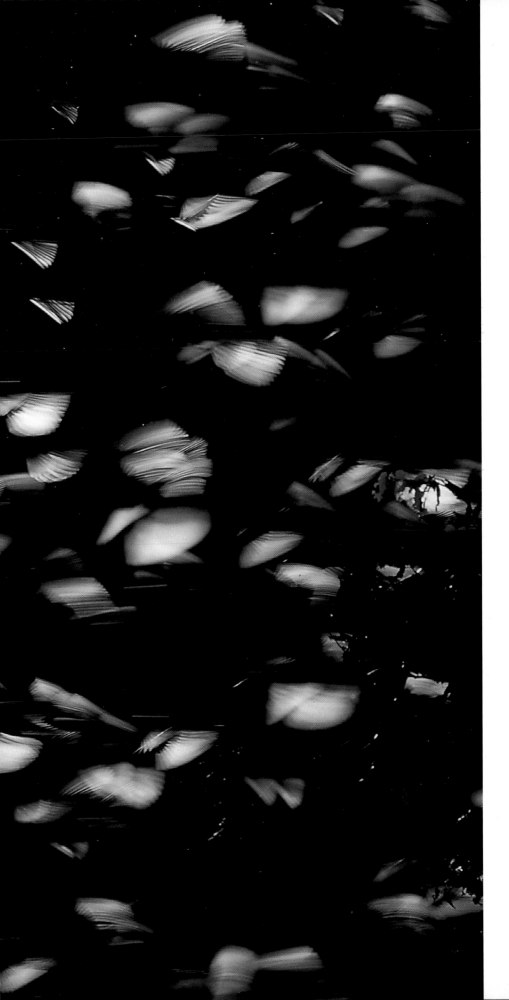

Above The malachite kingfisher is one of Africa's most colourful birds, but despite its striking plumage this little bird is often overlooked. It is a perch hunter and uses reed stems, from where it plunges into the water after tiny fish and tadpoles. Kingfishers – along with other colourful birds such as the rollers and bee-eaters – are hole nesters. Here in the darkness camouflage is not necessary for the birds or their eggs (the latter are pure white). Quite why these birds are so colourful remains a mystery.

Left The red-billed quelea is probably the most abundant bird species in the world. Flocks of tens of thousands swarm and roll like silver smoke across the grasslands as they feed, their sheer numbers puffing up clouds of dust and seed. This is one of Nature's most impressive spectacles; the sight and sound of these flocks is staggering.

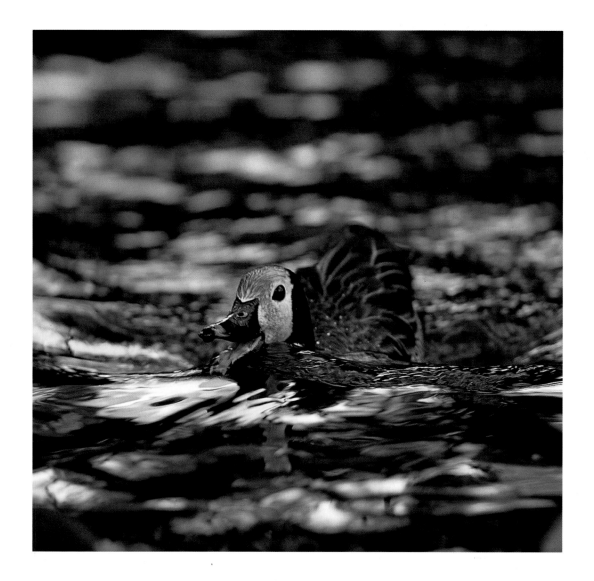

Above and Opposite top The white-faced duck is common in southern Africa and may occur seasonally in flocks of several thousand. These ducks have a very distinctive whistling call, which can often be heard at night as they fly to new feeding grounds.

Opposite bottom The spur-winged goose is a huge bird and Africa's largest indigenous duck, males weighing in at up to ten kilograms. It is appropriately named; large spurs on the 'wrists' make it a formidable customer.

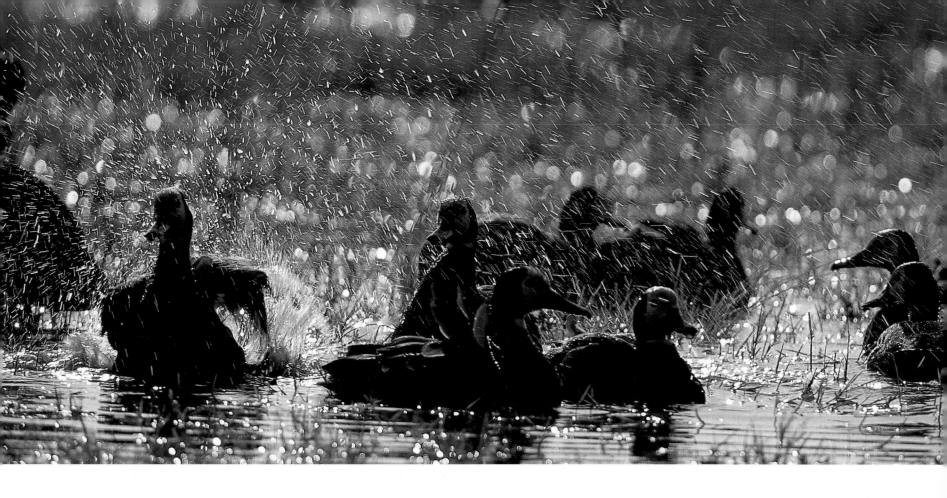
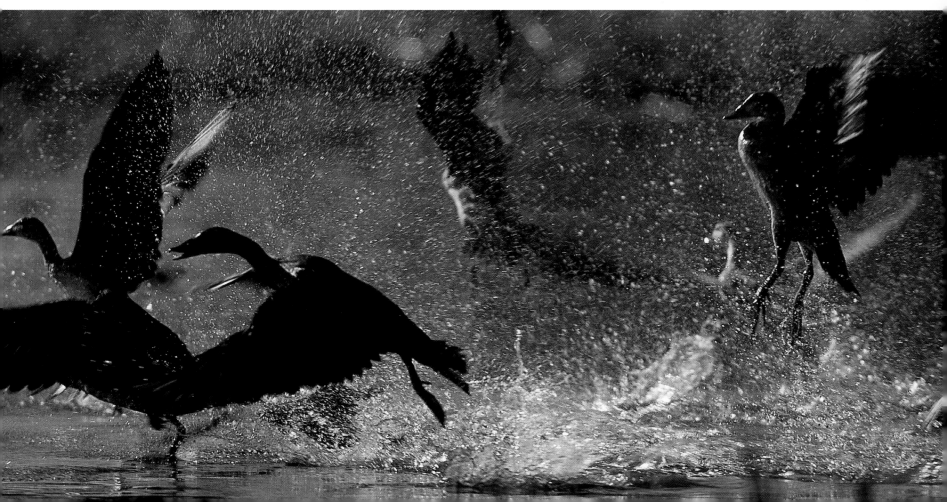

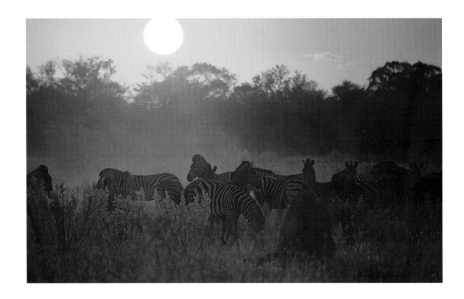

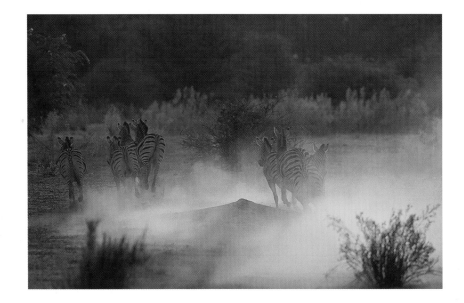

The annual migration of thousands of Burchell's zebra, from the Linyanti in the north down to the Mababe Depression, is Africa's second-largest migration after the vast Serengeti herds. Although the zebra gather in herds of hundreds, within these congregations there exist distinct family groups, each consisting of a dominant stallion, his mares and offspring. This annual migration does not pass through the floodplains of the Khwai, but several family units of zebra are resident here all year round.

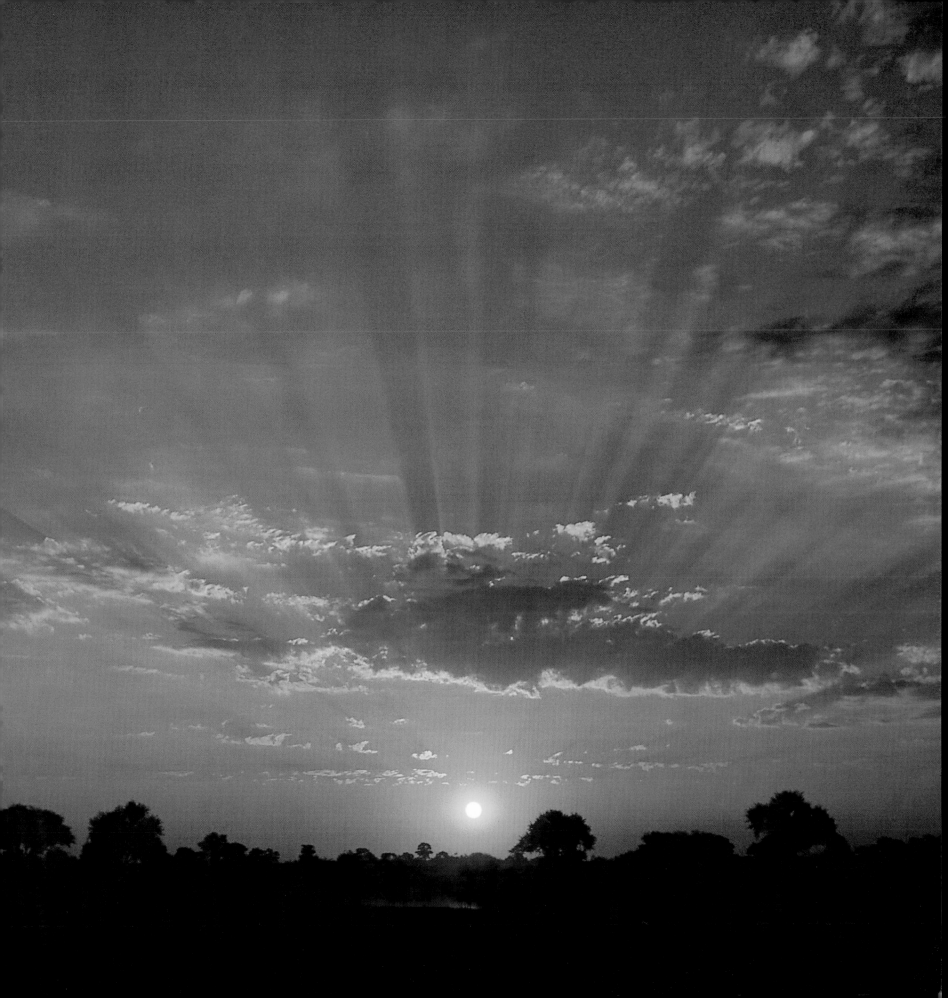

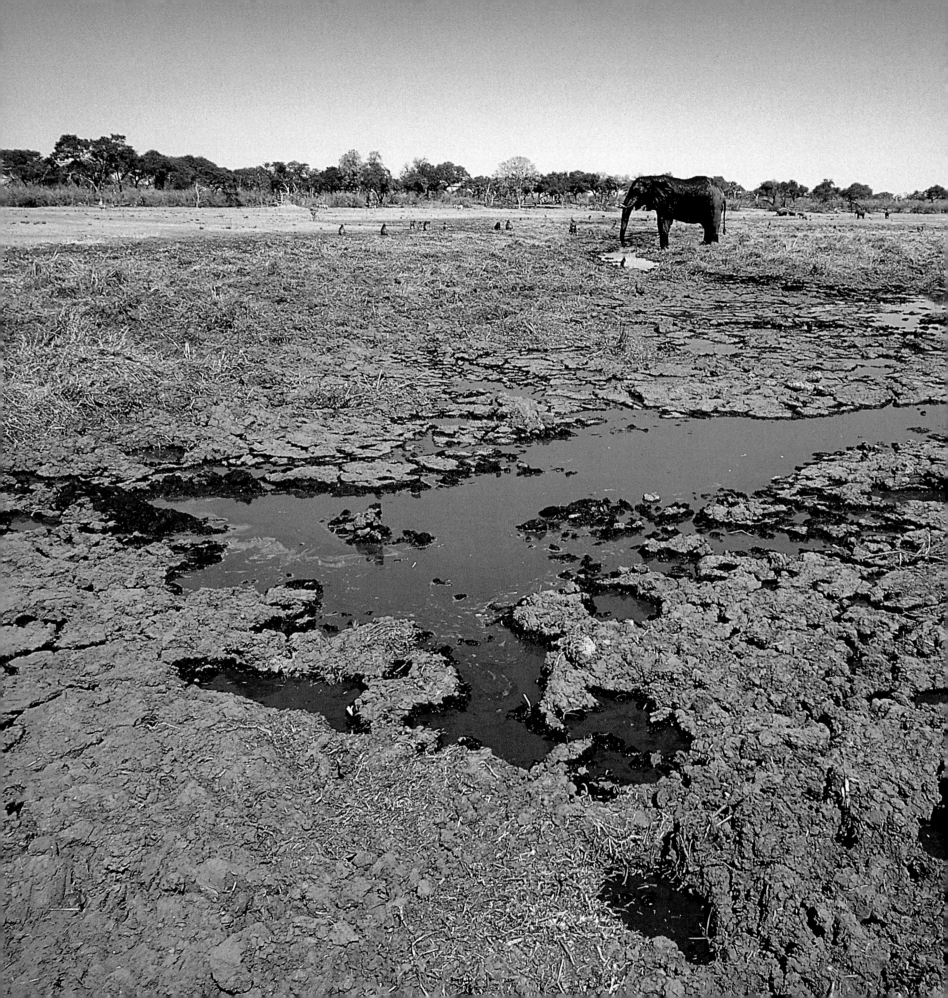

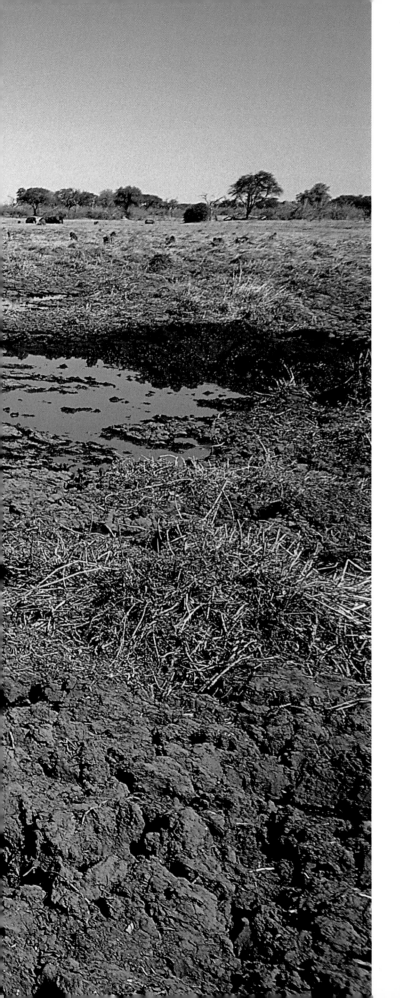

The Gathering

around the dwindling waters

ONE FREEZING WINTER MORNING we departed the small northern Botswanan town of Maun before dawn, travelling the first stretch of our journey on a newly tarred road. For wilderness lovers who have travelled here in years gone by the tar roads are an incongruous and slightly disturbing new development. The tentacles of civilization are reaching slowly but insidiously towards the heart of one of the world's most unspoiled wildernesses.

Within an hour the tar turns to gravel and these feelings of unease slip away quickly. We pass a string of small villages, which radiate a feeling of peaceful simplicity as some friendly children wave a welcome. Skinny dogs trot alongside our vehicles for a few moments, with groups of lethargic cows and multicoloured goats decorating the roadside. Shortly after passing through the last village we arrive at the buffalo fence, one of the long barriers set up to separate wildlife from domestic stock. Our destination, the Moremi Wildlife Reserve, has no fences at all. With a wave to the gatekeeper we leave civilization behind us completely; now time and dates are of no consequence. The road becomes a twin-rutted track as we pass through mopane forests, woodlands and open meadows.

Where pools lay in the road last summer there are now only dark rutted depressions. Our vehicle's tyres spew up a thick choking dust that hangs in the air long after we pass, and the roadside trees are caked in layers of it, a testimony to months without rain. Seed-gathering turtledoves explode from the road ahead, and spoor imprinted in the dust provide clues to what lives in the area.

At midday we arrive at the dry Khwai River bed and proceed to drive upstream, searching for the headwaters. The distinctive silhouettes of a few hamerkops reveal a small pool being fed by a trickle of brown water. It is a curious sight, water seeping slowly along the surface of the parched earth. The river is still (just) flowing, fed by the summer rains that fell some nine months ago in the distant highlands of Angola. How far the river reaches varies each year, and this makes for much lively discussion, for all have an opinion. Last century this river flowed right through to the Mababe Depression to the east, forming a huge, shallow swamp. Now there is no water to the east of this.

The mud pans in the woodlands have long since dried up and thirsty beasts must now make the journey to the river. In the winter incredible concentrations of animals occur along the river's course; it is a time of hunger and stress for herbivores, and a time of plenty for carnivores. The winter gathering is the occasion for the most dramatic and complex interplays of the wildlife of this region.

Previous pages   An elephant drinks from the dwindling river.

Right   As the dry season draws on, food becomes scarce, especially close to the river. Here, foraging baboons and buffalo ignore each other in the failing light of a hazy sunset. In winter a shroud of dust hangs over the land, stirred up by the prevailing easterly winds.

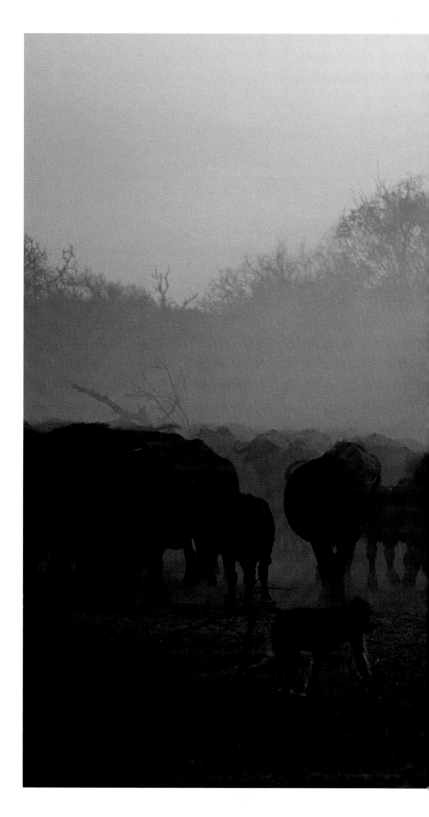

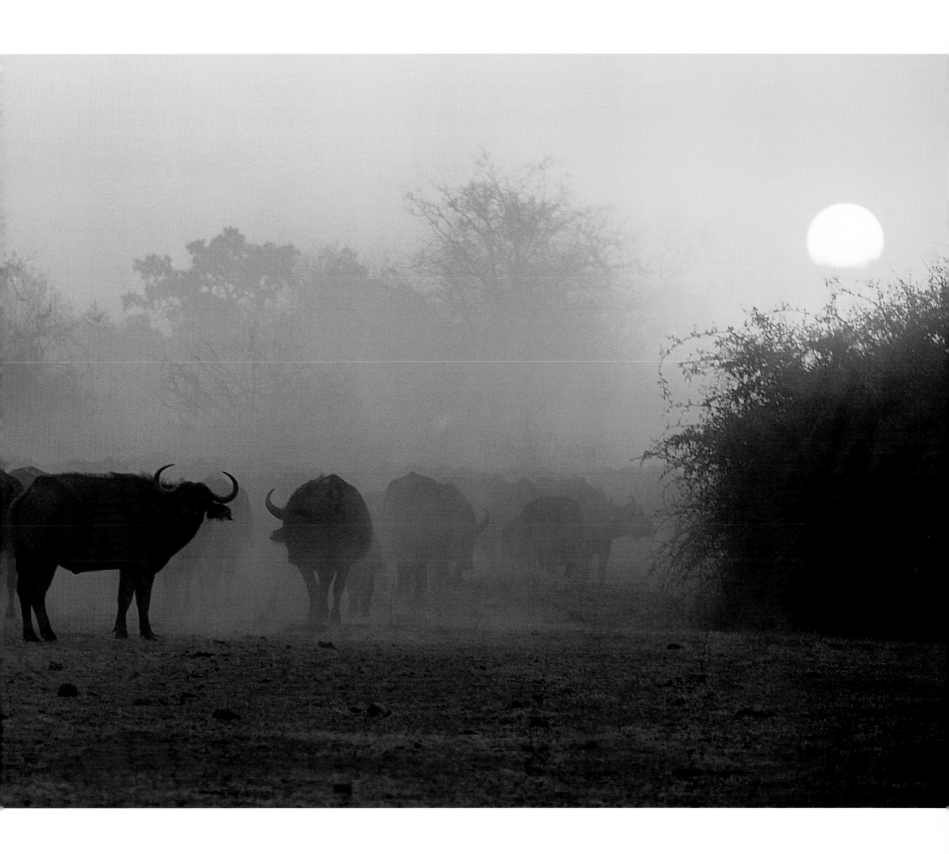

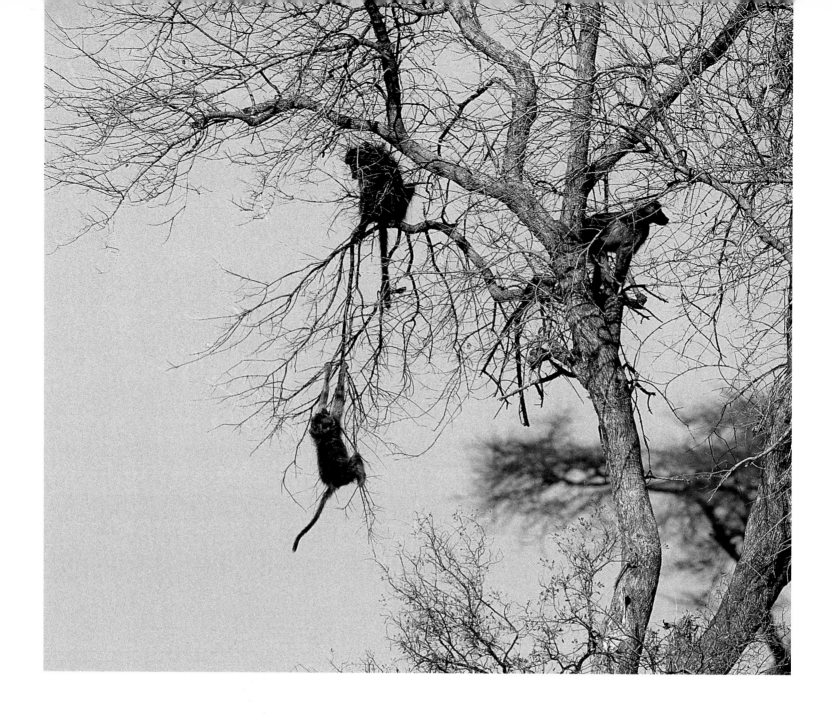

Baboons are socially one of the most complicated of African mammals. Status is all-important for these gregarious apes, and the achievement and maintenance of dominance is an ongoing and important aspect of their daily behaviour. Here (*above*), a dominant male terrifies a lower-ranking individual out onto the thin outer branches of a tree. The smaller male's display of subordination, along with much screaming and posturing, was to no avail – and he took a long fall down to earth (*opposite*). Adult male baboons are formidable beasts, sporting fangs longer and sharper than those of a lion. Their co-operative spirit of defence against predators means that, in daylight, they can roam in the open without having to fear leopards or cheetahs.

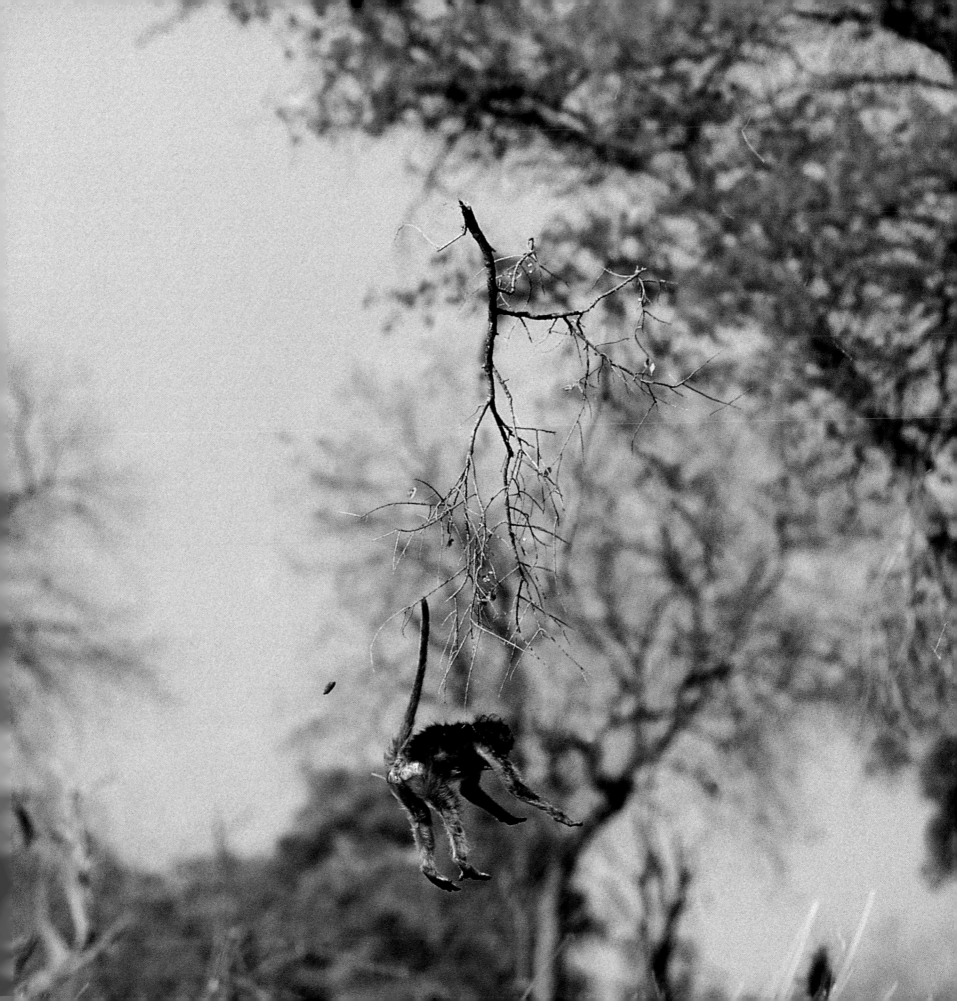

The largest herds of African elephants occur in
Botswana, and all together tens of thousands of
elephants roam the woodlands and swamps.
Ecologically, they are the most significant animals
in this region and the evidence of their massive
impact is everywhere. This is especially manifest
in the devastated forests where countless trees
are left broken-limbed, debarked or simply pushed
over. A small group of bull elephants (**right**)
wanders along the river on their way back into
the mopane forests where they will feed.
Throughout the night the elephant herds have
visited; drinking, splashing and cavorting. Water-
loving and water-dependent, these giants must visit
the river regularly, no matter how far the walk.
In the morning the river is once more quiet, with
just footprints carpeting the waters' edges, a
testimony to the hundreds of elephants that have
passed by in the preceding hours of darkness.

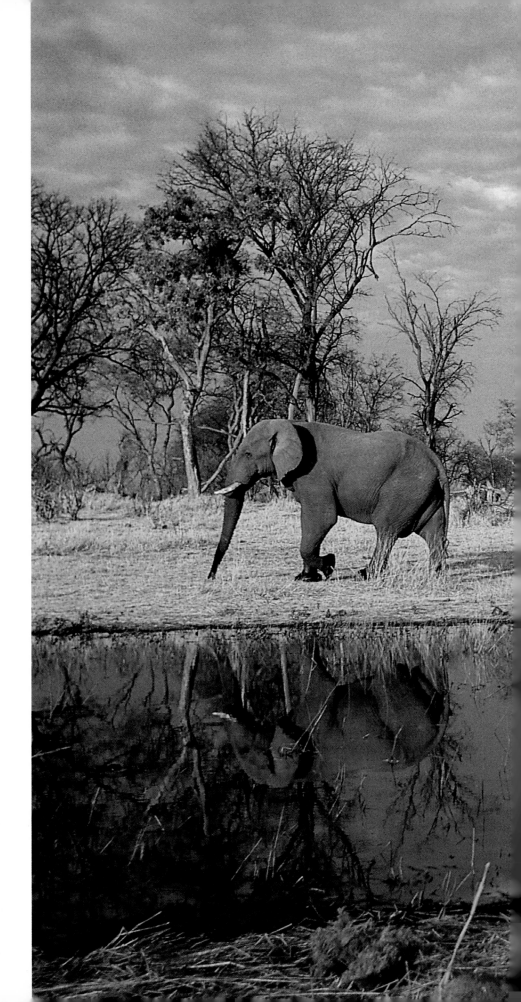

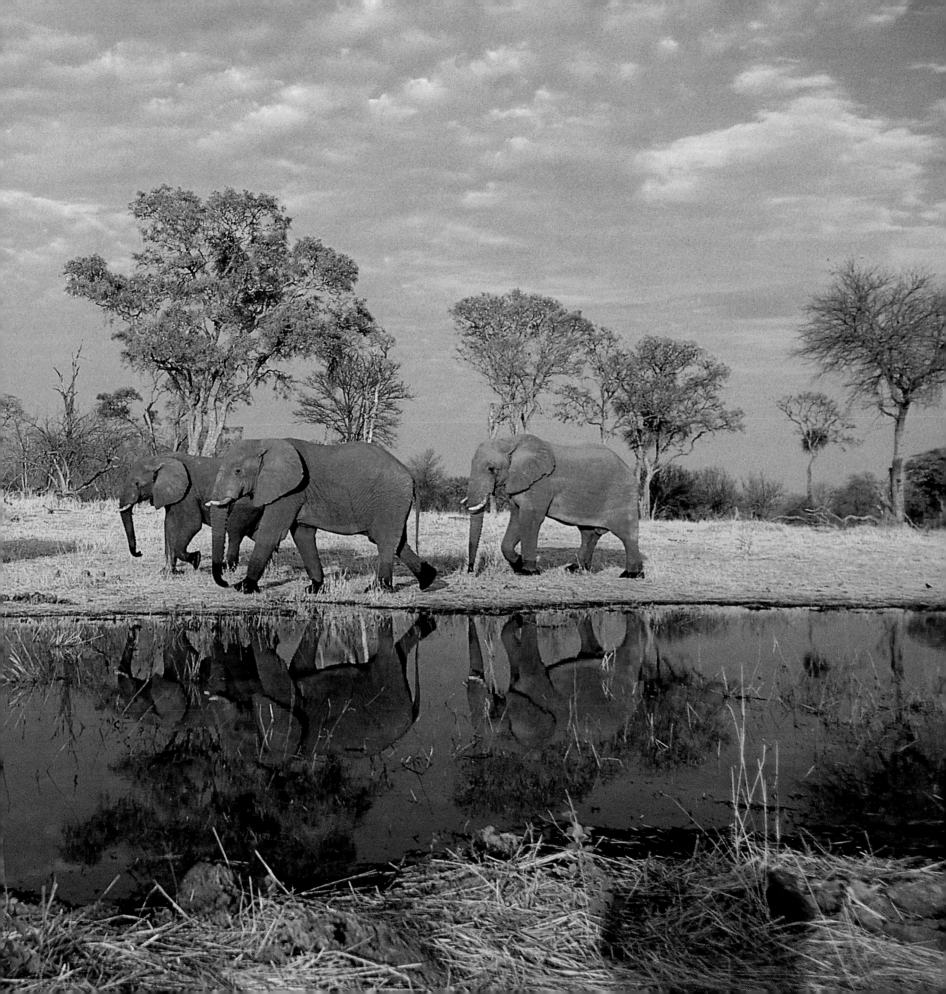

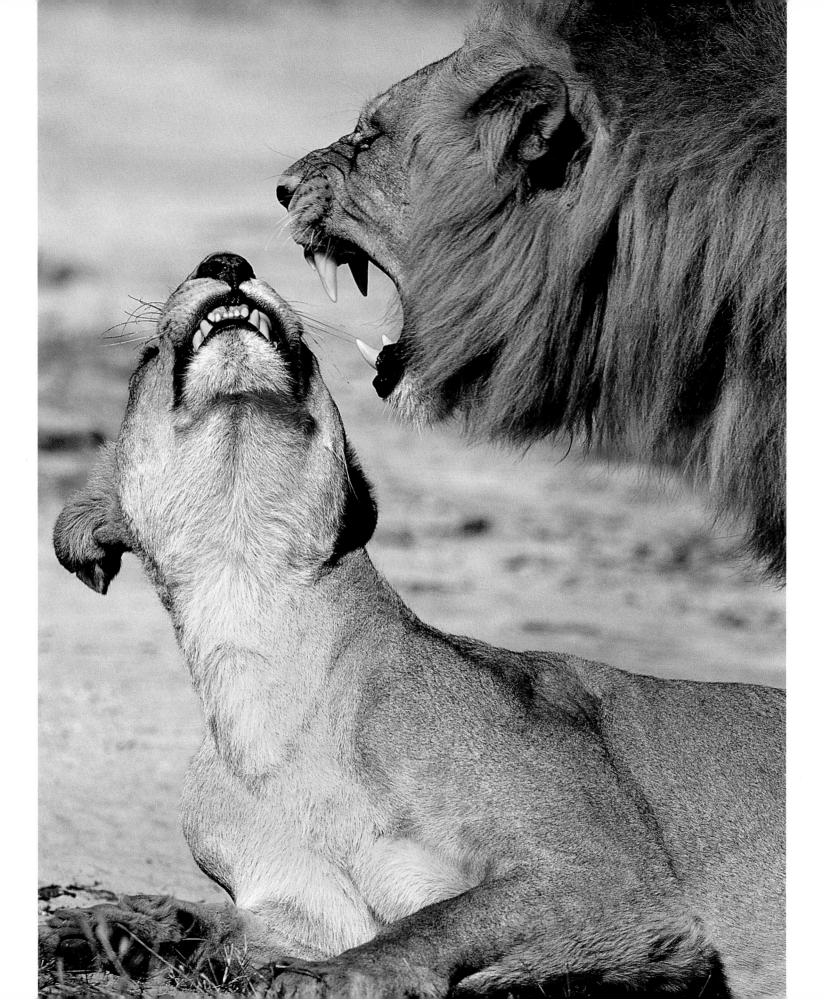

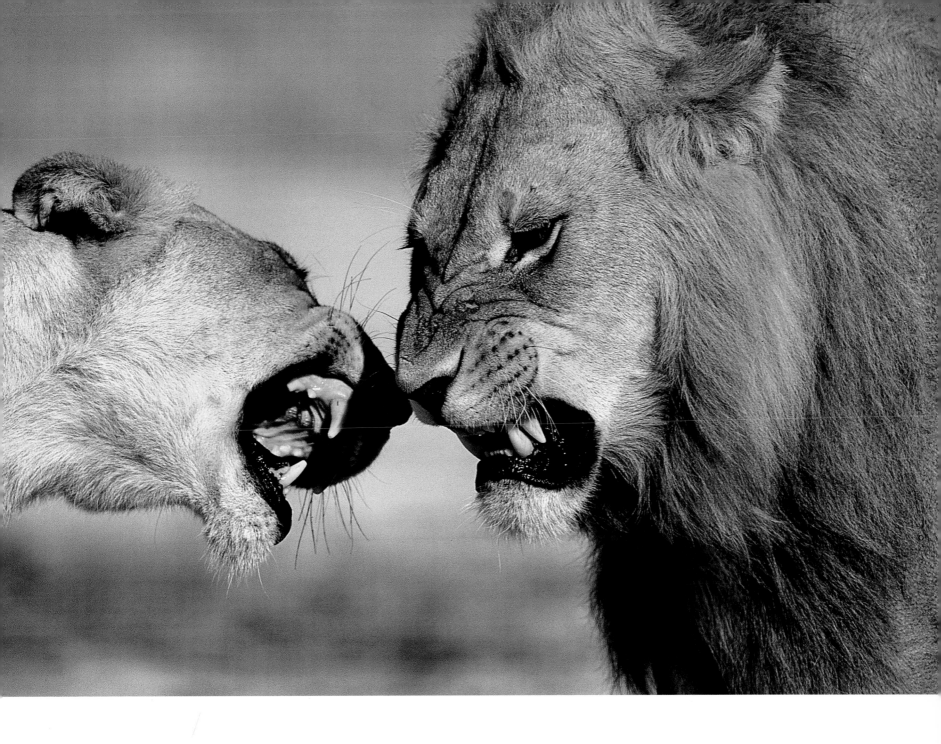

The mating prowess of lions is legendary. As creatures at the top of the food chain, lions are similar to humans in that under normal circumstances only they can control their population numbers. During her lifetime a lioness can produce dozens of cubs, but normally fewer than one in five make it to adulthood. There is simply no space in Nature to accommodate a rapidly increasing population; infanticide and gang warfare take their toll. Lions are under threat in Africa as wilderness ranges diminish, but fortunately this is not the case in Botswana where some 17 per cent of the land is protected in national parks.

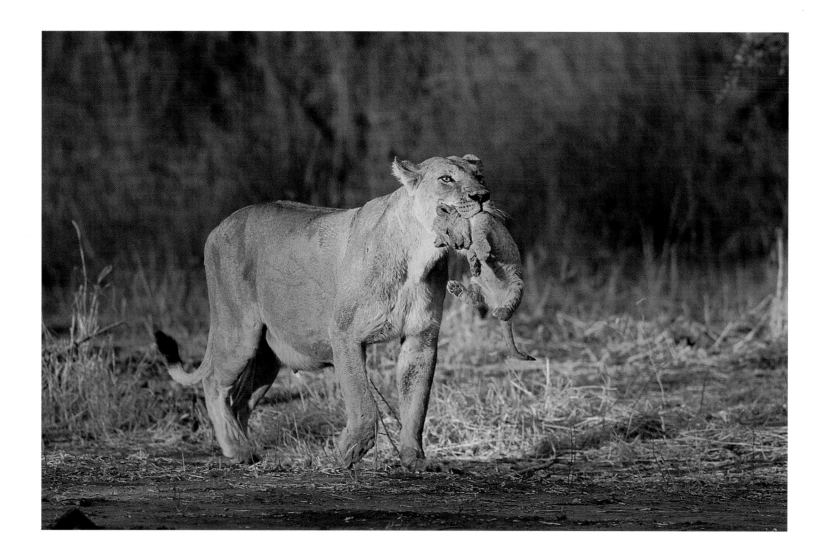

When we first arrived in Botswana, we came across a resident pride of ten lions, comprising six adult lionesses and four huge males, probably all closely related. The lionesses form the core of the pride, and this strong coalition of males provided the stability necessary for the lionesses to raise their young. Adult females are generally either pregnant or busy raising dependent young. Hence the absence of any cubs was promising for the near future. On our return two months later, it was with great excitement that we discovered two lactating lionesses, which were regularly entering an impenetrable thicket in a stand of leadwood trees. Gerald sat patiently by on several mornings until finally he was rewarded with a clear view as a lioness emerged with a tiny cub in her jaws. Even at just two months old these vulnerable cubs were enthusiastically demanding towards their mothers and ever playful with each other. We would watch this pride grow to two dozen individuals. One day these tiny bundles of fur would become elephant-killers.

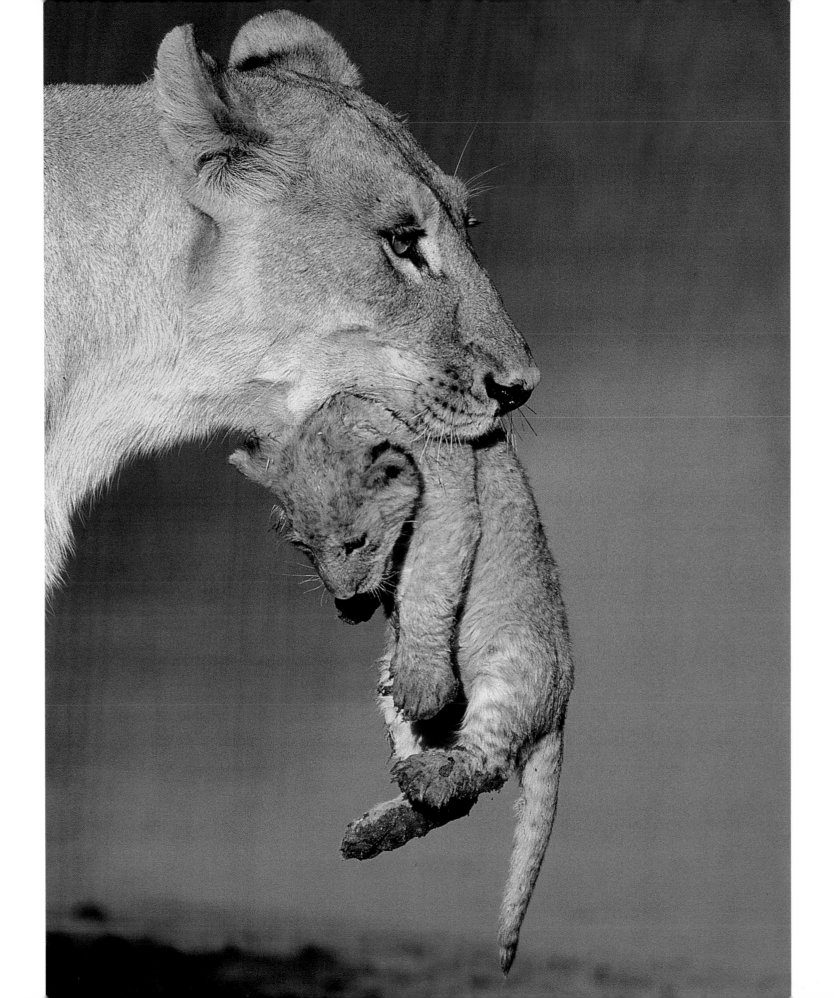

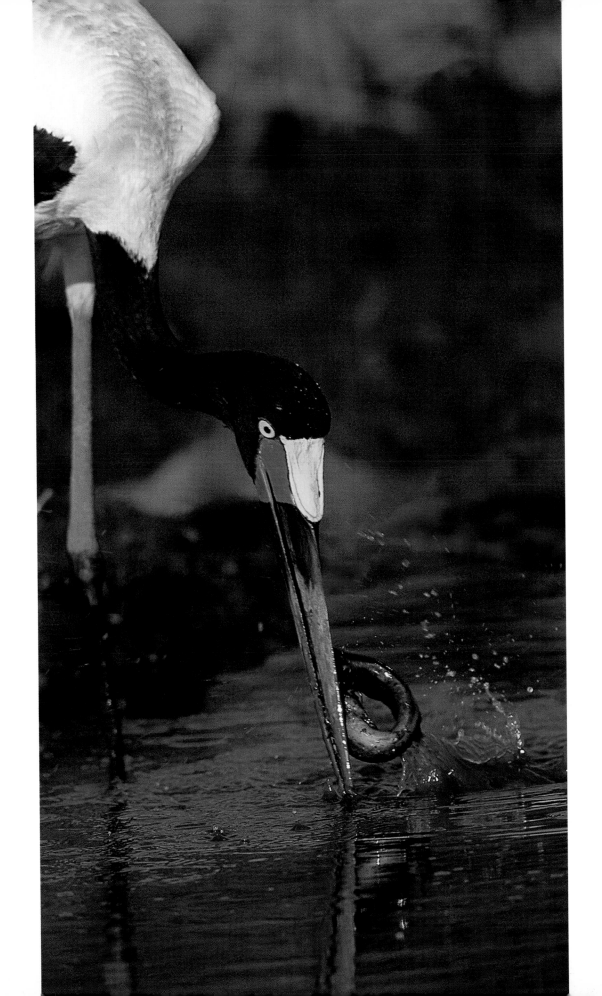

Opposite   Saddlebill storks are among the most impressive birds of the African wetlands and, happily, are quite common. This pair of storks was very territorial and would jealously defend their stretch of river against certain other waterbirds, although hamerkops were surprisingly exempt from this, despite the fact that they eat the same food. Curiously, the female stork plainly disliked sacred ibises and grey herons, both occasional visitors. If either of these flew in and settled she would charge in from her resting-place nearby and chase the intruders off. Despite their huge size the storks are capable of remarkable aerial manoeuvrability.

Below   Fish eagles often resort to piracy to obtain food from other fish-catching birds. However, these storks appeared to take pleasure in chasing off the lord of the waterways.

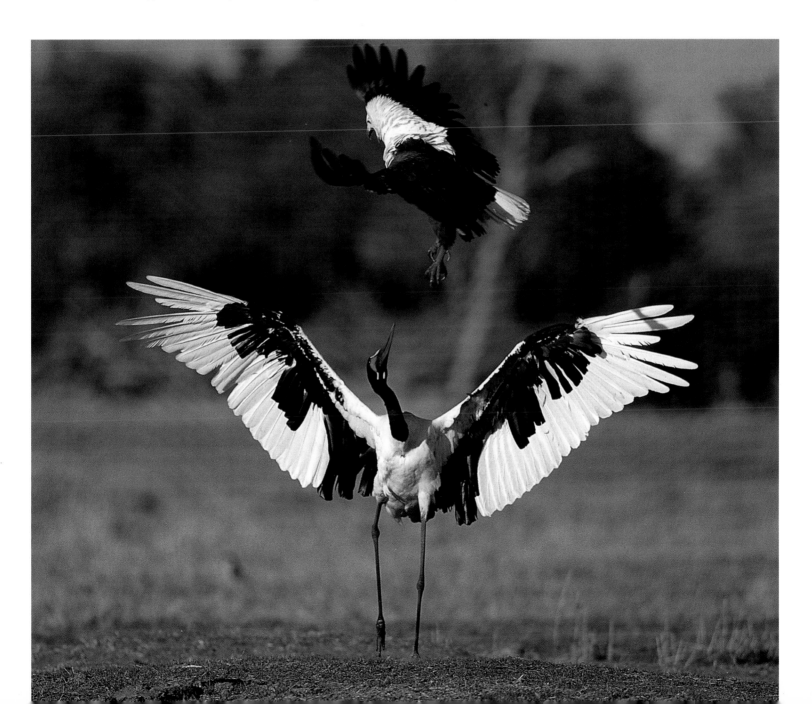

Timeless Wilderness

The period before dawn is my favourite time of day. Long before first light the diurnal birds start to add their songs to the sounds of the night singers. The first robins join nightjar, fruitbat and hyaena in the dawn chorus. Ostriches (*opposite top*) gather in the early light, males booming impressively. Guinea fowl (*opposite middle*) and baboons (*opposite bottom*) begin to come down, reluctantly, from their safe roosting places.

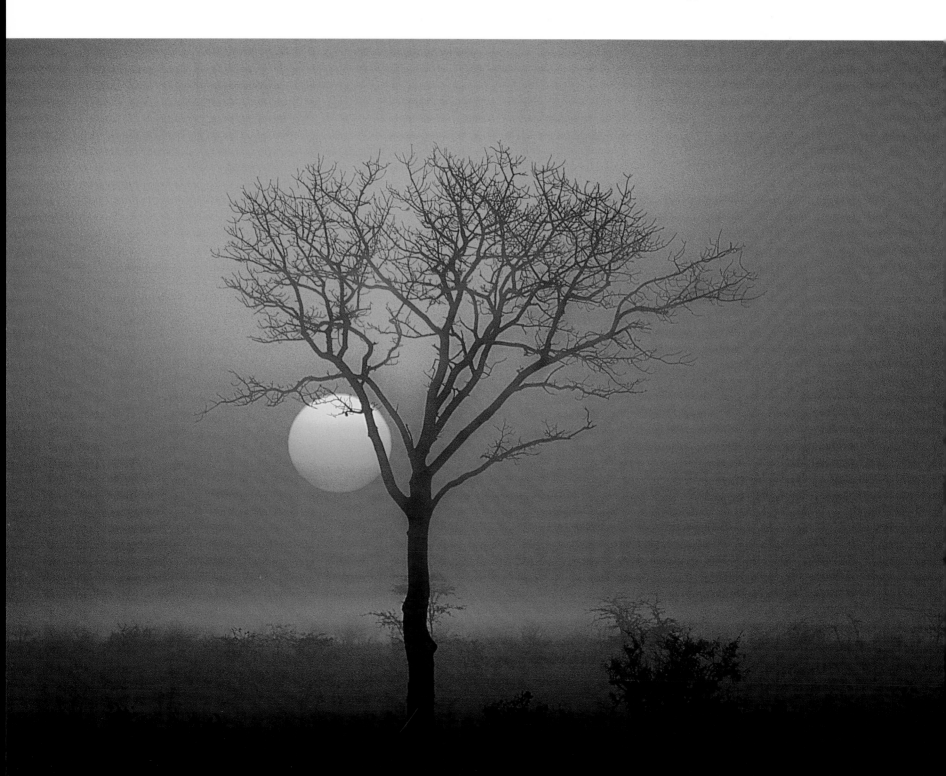

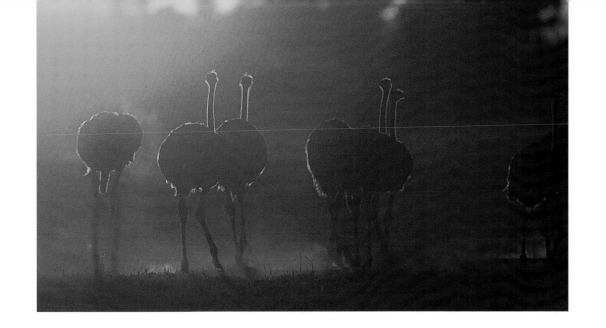

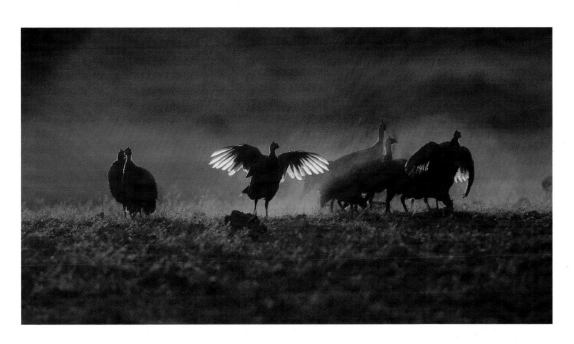

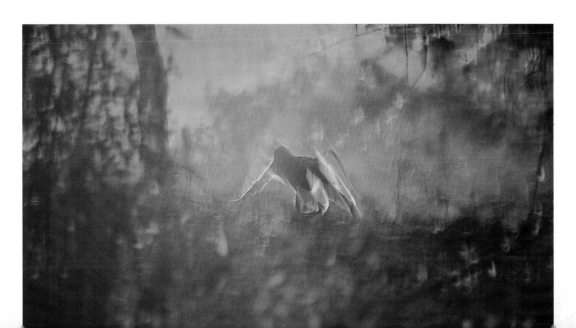

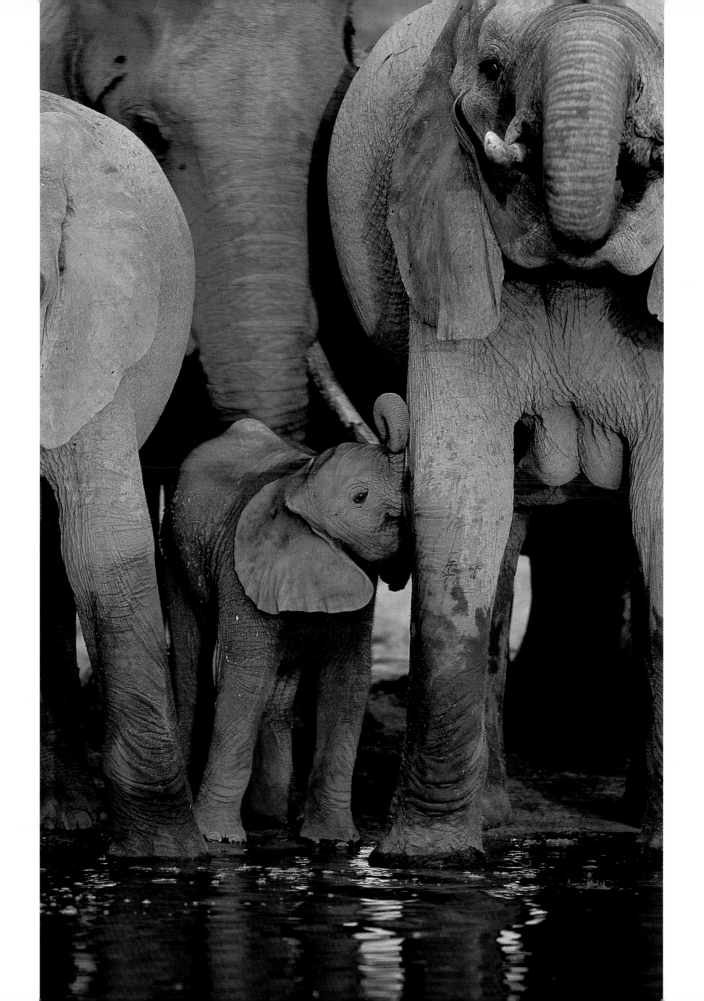

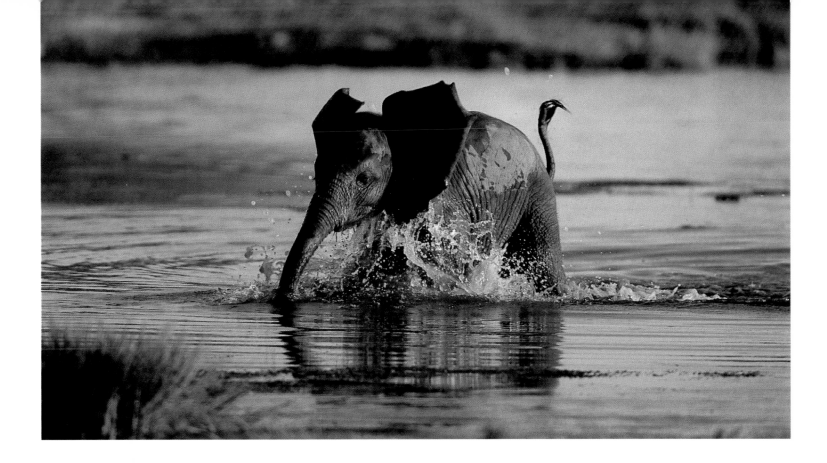

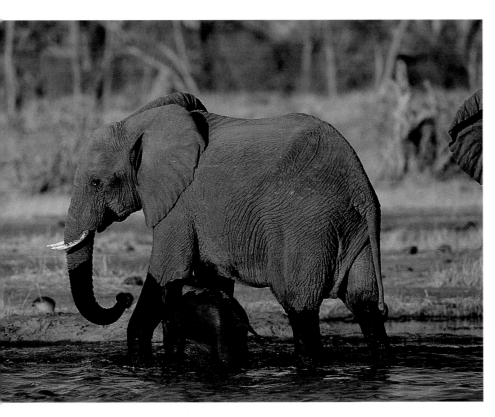

During the late afternoon the thirsty breeding herds arrive at the river, hurrying their way out of the dry and dusty mopane forests. The bulls have visited throughout the day, and after drinking, splash and mudbathe. The water has become a brown soup but the herds seem mostly indifferent. I couldn't work out any pattern with regard to where and when the elephants would drink. Some days many herds would come down, but normally to different sections of the river. Once the serious business of thirst-quenching has been taken care of, the waterhole becomes a social gathering place where the elephants celebrate and play. Palls of dust hang in the air, and the tranquil scene is continuously interrupted by squeals and stomach rumbles.

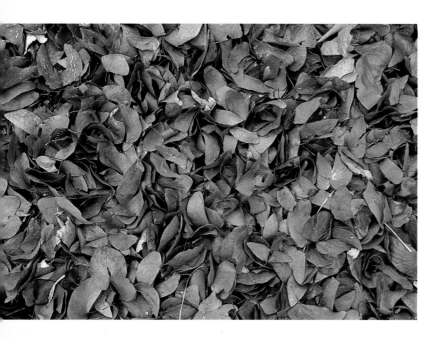

The shades of colour that dominate the summer woodlands
are the greens of the dense mopane trees and the lush grasses.
In the dry winter this is replaced by earthy colours of brown,
grey and red, providing a stark and intriguingly beautiful
contrast. The prevailing easterly winds have blown the mopane
trees bare, and their naked, stunted shapes and broken limbs
are a mute testimony to the brutal pruning wreaked by
the elephants. The deep piles of autumnal mopane leaves
lie bunched against fallen logs and form russet carpets in
the shallow depressions.

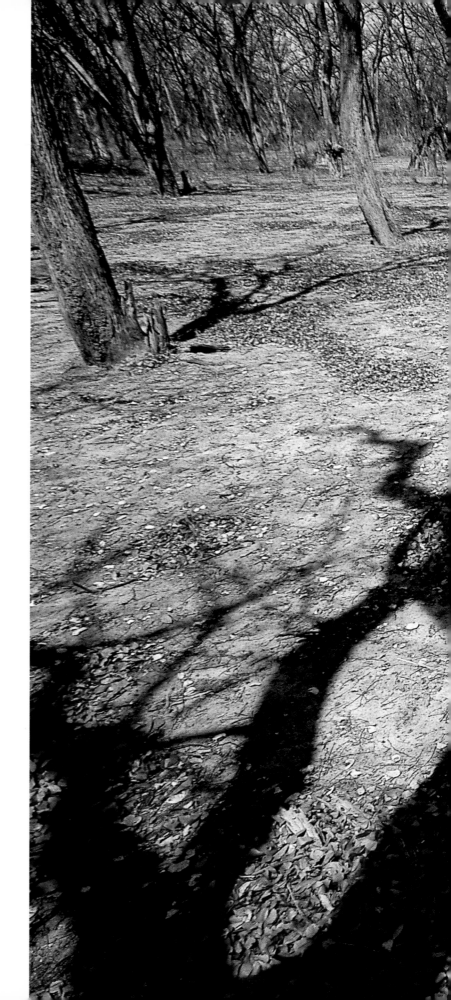

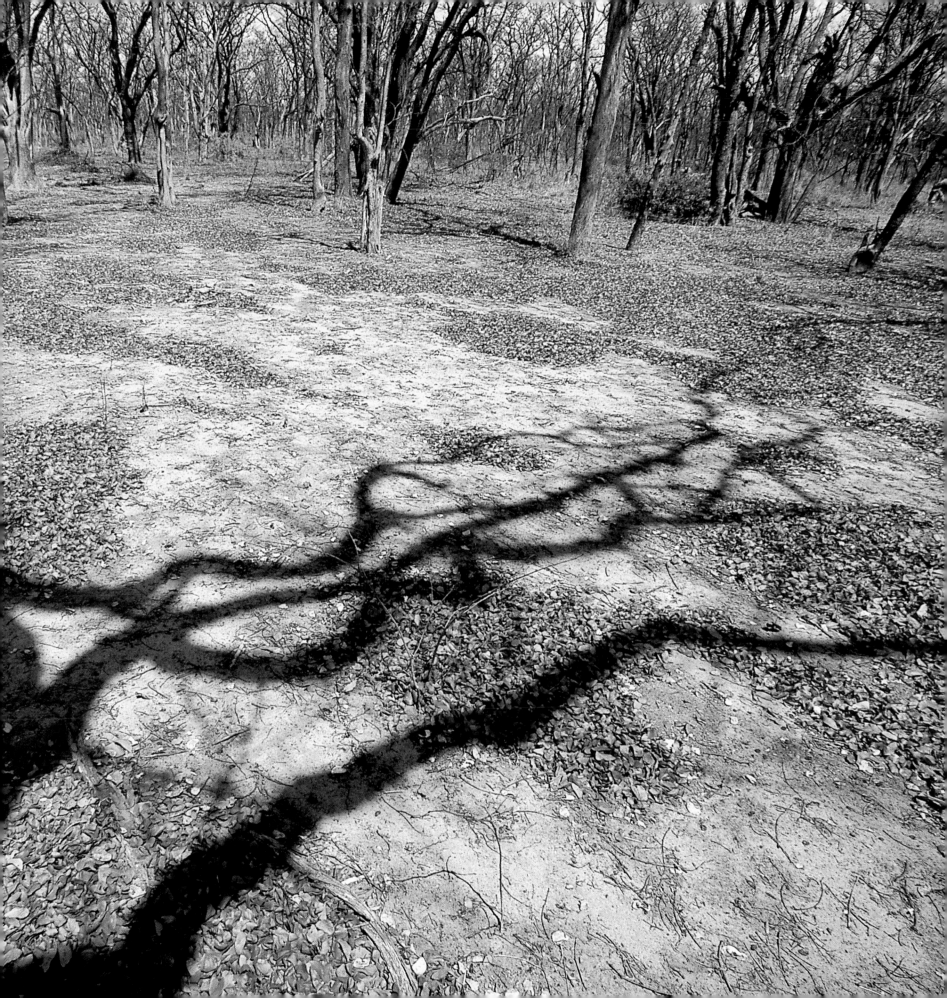

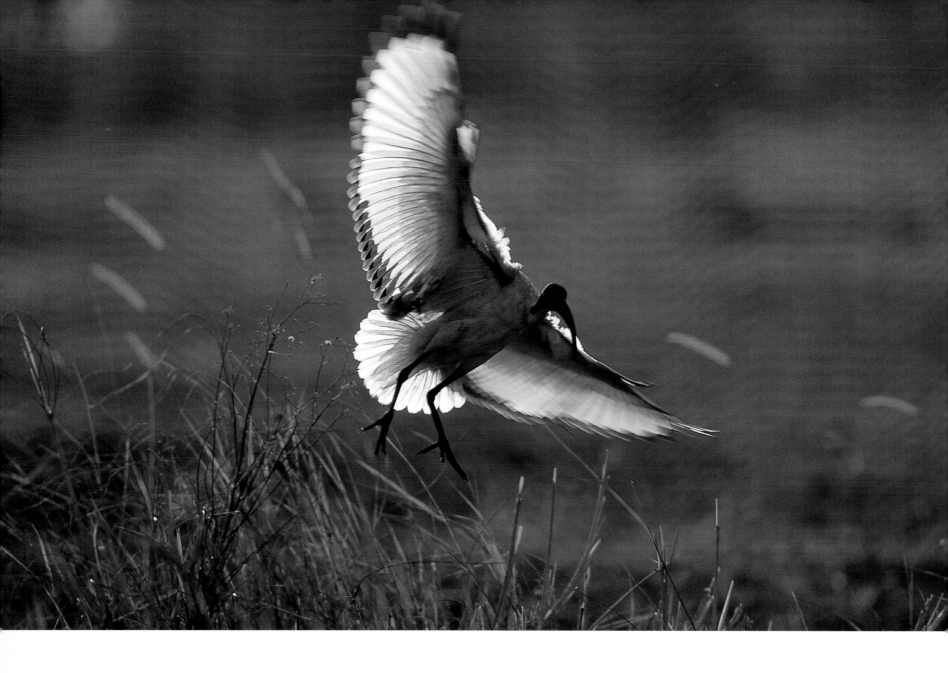

Deep water is the home of crocodile and tigerfish, and few birds venture here. The extensive shallows, in contrast, are rich feeding grounds and attract water birds in abundance. The exploitation of different habitats and food sources requires certain adaptations, and as a result the variety of sizes and shapes of water birds' beaks is quite bewildering. One needs to imagine a bird's bill as the 'hand' which its owner uses for grooming, nest building and protection. However, the design of this essential feeding tool is dictated primarily by diet and foraging style. The waders have long legs and long beaks. The floaters have specialist bills but can make do with short legs and webbed feet. The long, curved bill of the sacred ibis is used for probing in mud, whereas the pink-backed pelican has a large bill with an expandable throat pouch for scooping up numerous small fish at once. The bill of the marabou is unspecialized but huge, and serves as an imposing weapon.

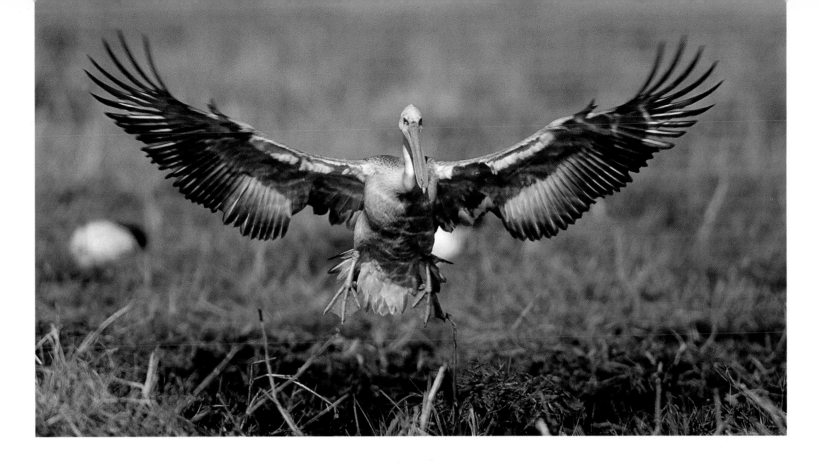

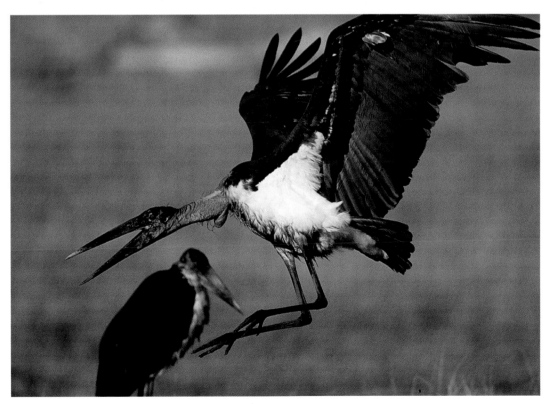

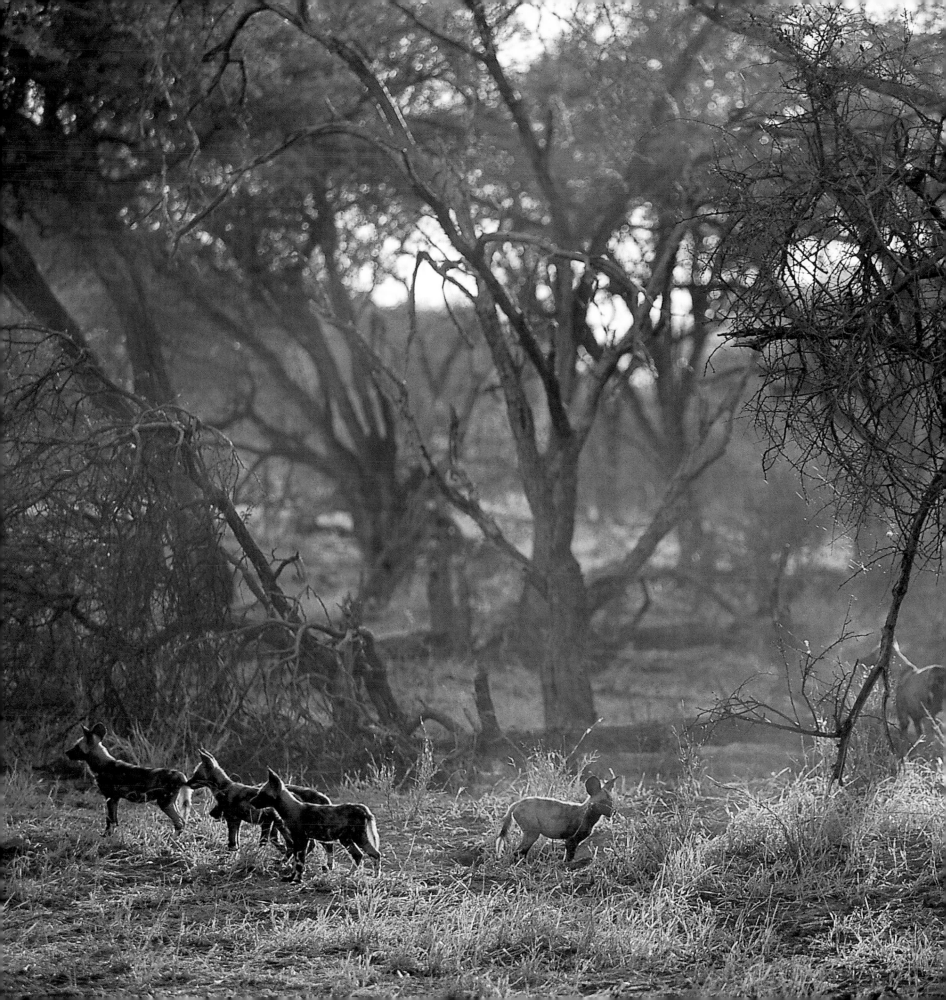

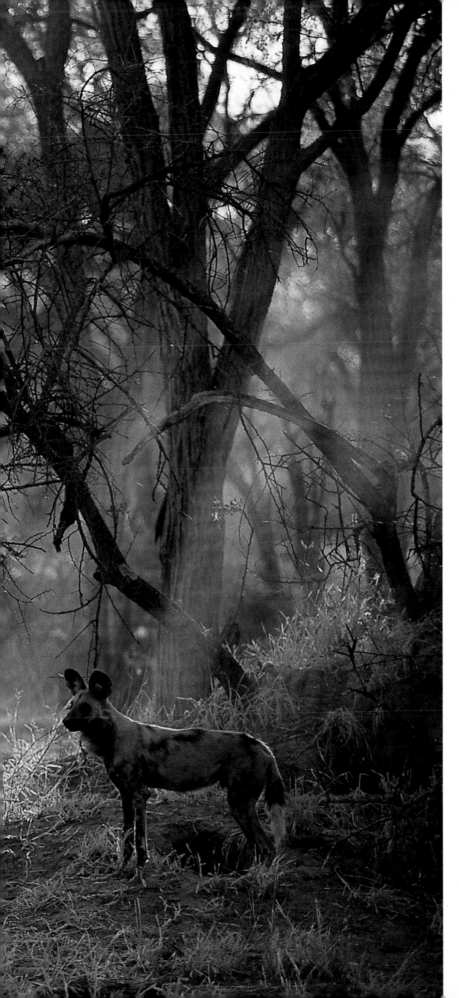

The Gathering

Wild dogs are seasonal breeders and in mid-winter the alpha female will give birth to her puppies in an underground den. The tiny pups emerge after a few weeks and litters can be as large as 18, the largest of any carnivore. The protective mother remains behind as the adults hunt daily – leaving the den site from well before dawn and occasionally on moonlit nights. The pups will follow the adults on hunts after a few months, resting for protection at well-known burrows at night. It is extraordinary how intimately familiar the dogs are with their territory. I once followed a pack that raced through the woodlands for hours and many kilometres before successfully making a kill. After feeding they all ran directly back to the den, through a maze of featureless mopane woodland, to regurgitate for the hungry pups.

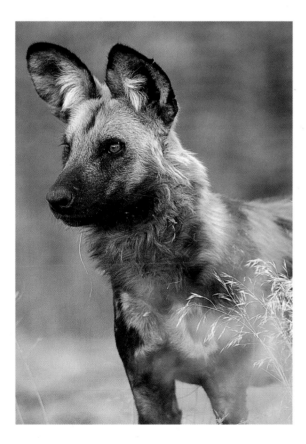

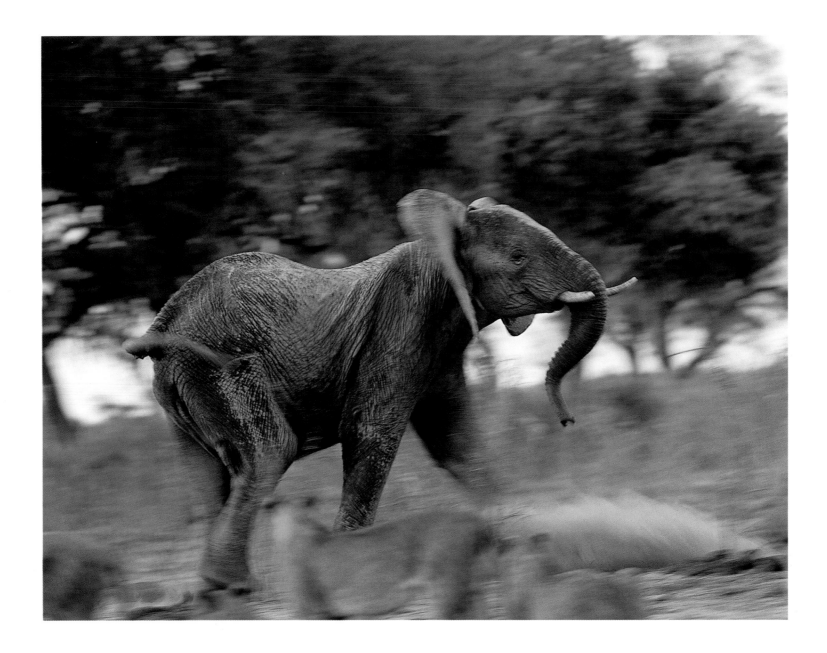

Lions are the most successful predators in this region, dominating all others. Lions gang up in prides, and the huge resident pride near our camp, of 24 individuals, represented some 3 000 kilograms of collective muscle. By hunting together, such prides are capable of killing large animals, including adult giraffe, hippo and buffalo – and even elephant. And remarkably that is what they do (*above and opposite*) at this time of year.

The lions target mostly young elephants up to ten years old. Tiny baby elephants do not appear to fall victim, possibly since their mothers are so protective. Older calves are more confident and thus more vulnerable.

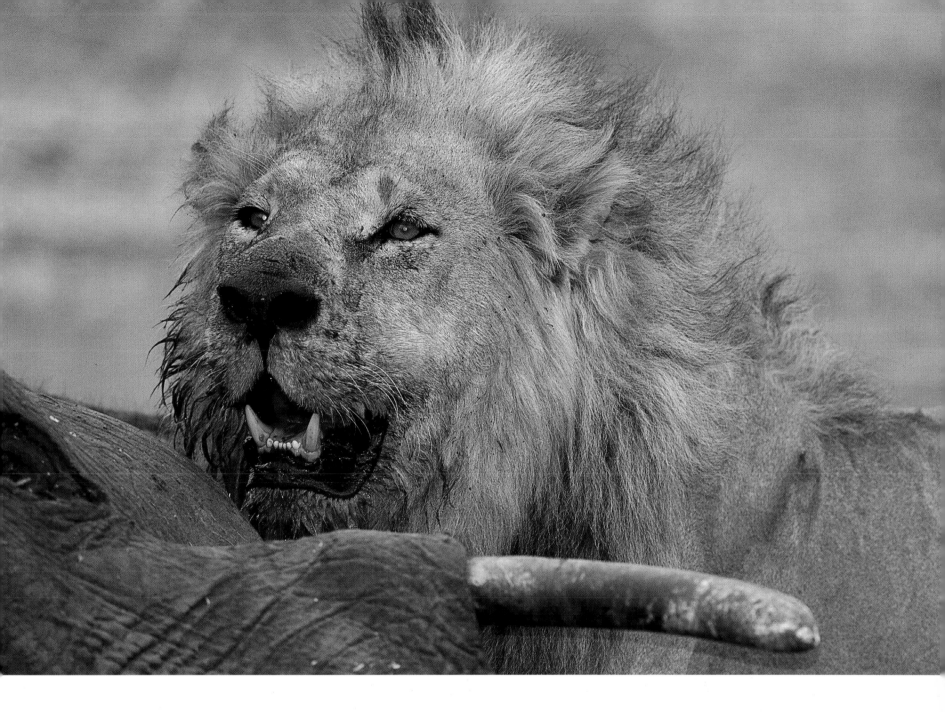

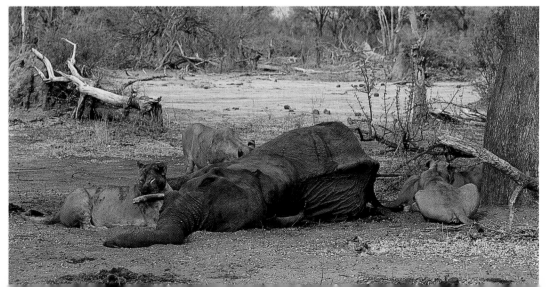

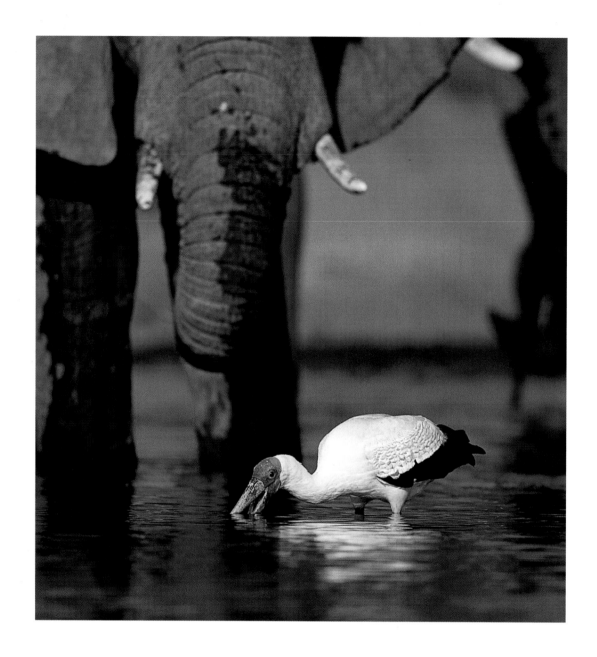

Yellow-billed storks are tactile feeders, their bill snapping shut as a reflex action when prey stimulates the sensitive bill tip. The nostrils are situated high up on the beak so they can breathe as they engage in slow-motion bill-swinging and foot-stirring to dislodge hidden morsels. This stork was totally engrossed in his fishing, and had forgotten that elephants seem to enjoy chasing any creature that ventures too close to them. Here (*above and opposite top*) a bull elephant frightens off a startled stork with a well-directed trunk splash. After a long day in the sun a stork will engage in a vigorous bathing and grooming session (*opposite bottom*).

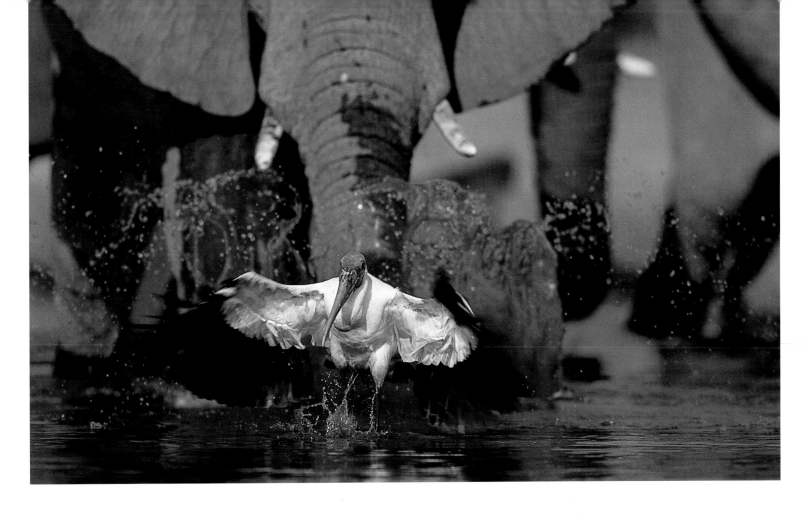

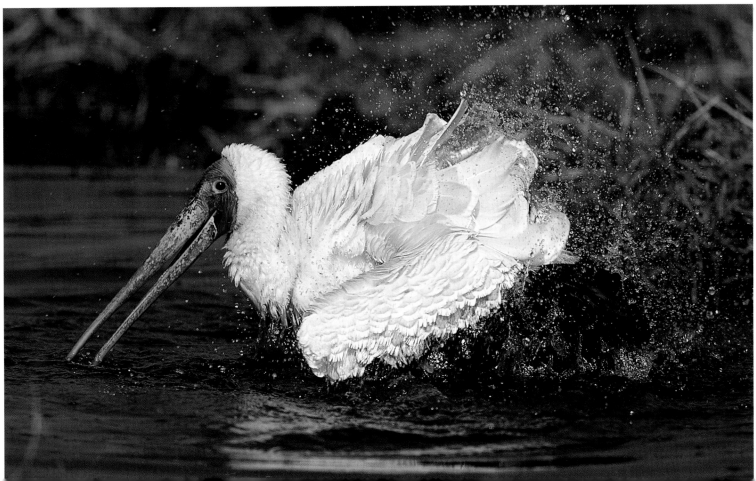

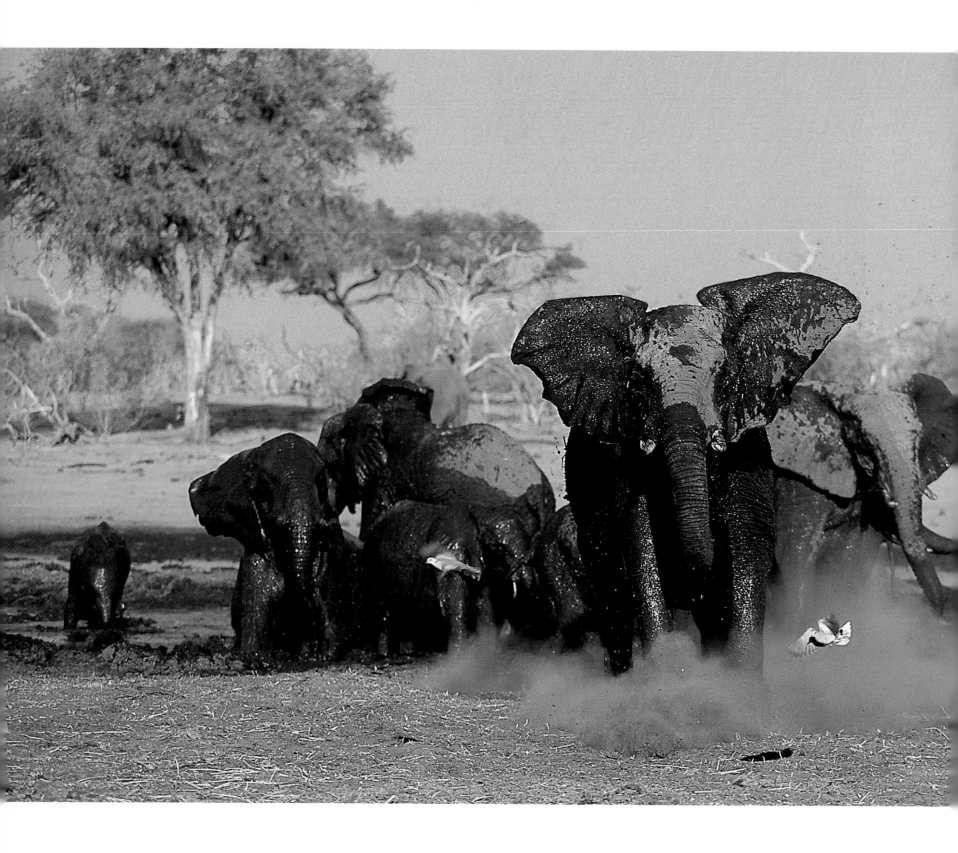

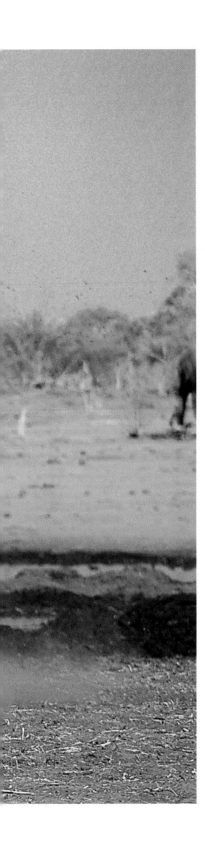

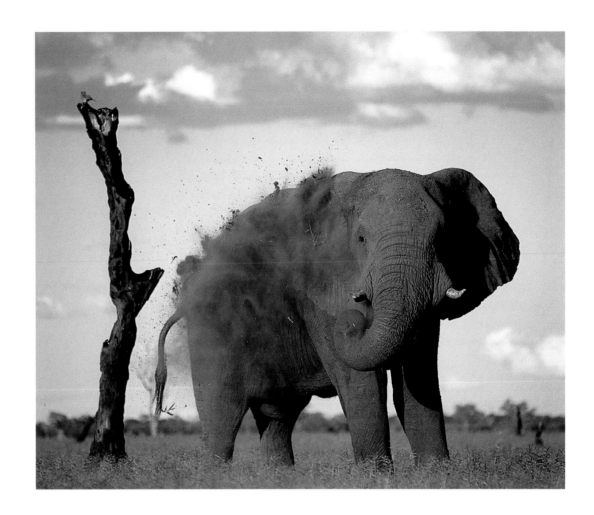

Opposite An elephant's mock charge is one of the most terrifying demonstrations of anger in Nature. It gets the message across – get out of here! Young elephants are fond of charging all creatures within range, whereas the old bulls seldom do more than flap their giant ears. The charge of a cow protective of a youngster should always be taken very seriously.

Above Old elephant bulls are particularly common along the Khwai at this time of year. The river provides a clue to the origin of the well-known myths of elephant graveyards, as the old elephants generally spend their final days close to water. Here their great bones accumulate along the waterways, where they can lie for decades before finally rotting away.

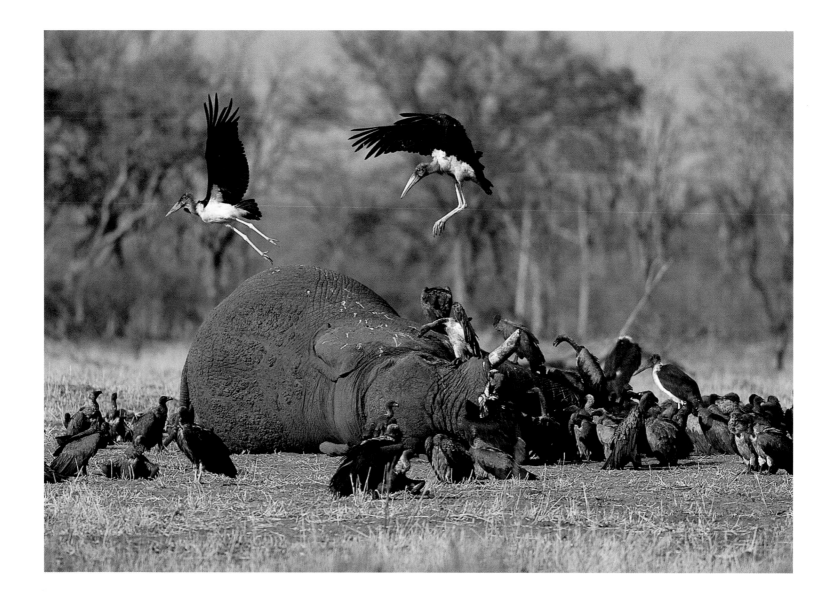

Alone, this giant bull elephant walked slowly out of the forest and down towards the river. His huge head, sunken temples and thick tusks showed his great age. But something in his gait revealed that all was not well. He paused, and then moved on a few more metres. Standing still with his trunk on the ground and his head bowed, the great beast swayed and then staggered, crashing over onto his side. He made one last, brief shudder and was dead before the dust settled. The old bull died late on a winter afternoon – a time of year when many elephants perish. Over the next ten days a multitude of scavengers visited the carcass. As always the vultures were first to arrive, and at times I counted nearly 300 vultures standing around. Marabou storks followed close on the vultures' heels.

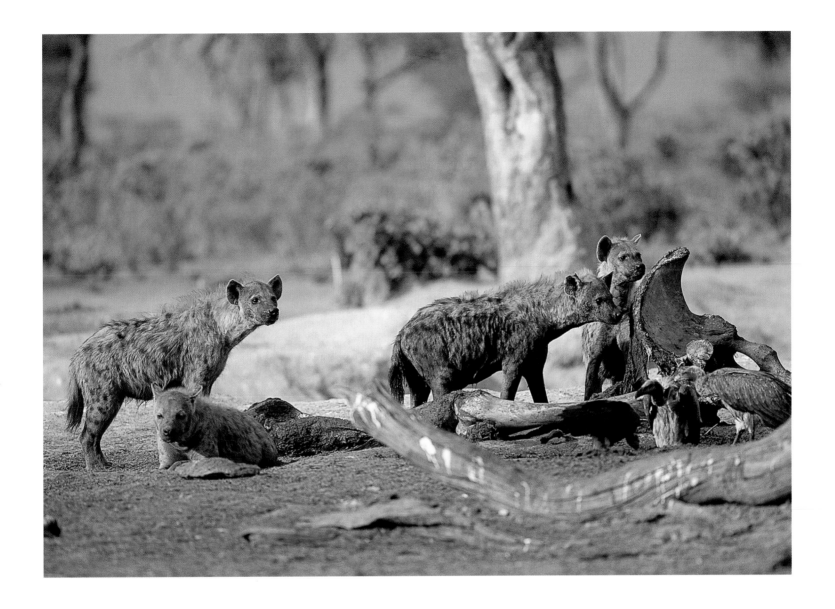

At night up to six hyaenas could be seen gathered around the dead elephant bull's carcass — the clans are small in this area. Other visitors included a pair of young nomadic lions, which squabbled with the hyaenas over the rotting flesh. One evening I was surprised to see three huge crocodiles crawl out of the nearby river to join the feast. The dust stirred by the sudden thrash of a crocodile's tail, the clap of vulture wings in the trees, the dull stench on a gentle wind, with heavy grey clouds rendering the scene colourless — all lent a primal atmosphere to a scene that could have taken place a million years ago.

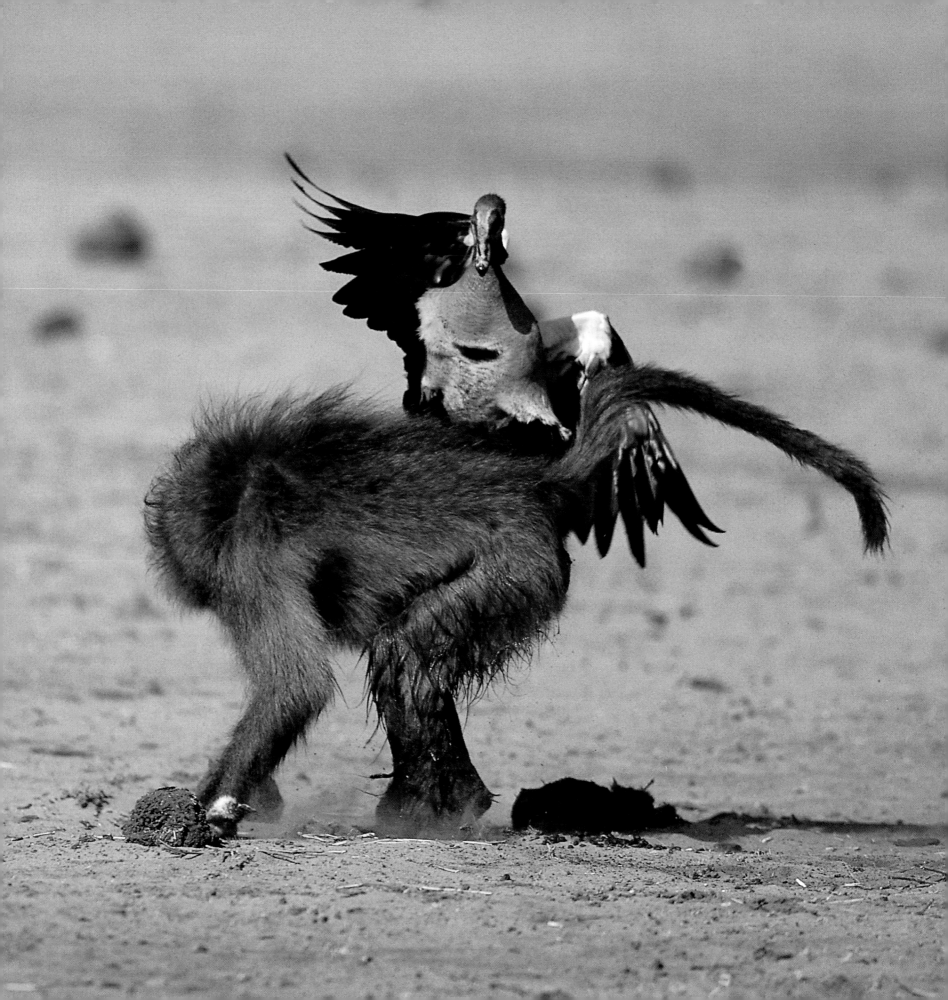

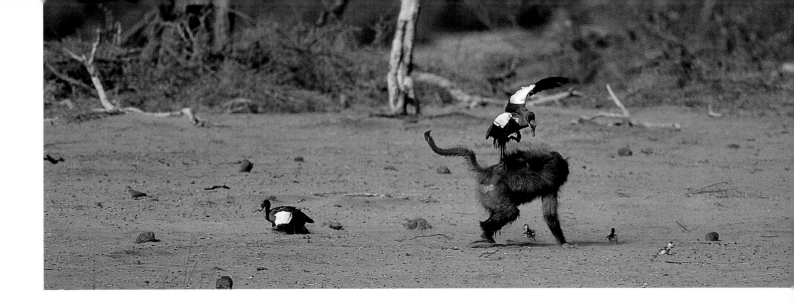

One morning I encountered two Egyptian geese and their brand new family of eight goslings at the tip of the river – just a small puddle of slowly trickling water. For the past months the female would have sat on her clutch of eggs, probably high up in the hollow trunk of a centuries-old leadwood tree. She would have called the goslings, once hatched, from the ground below, and they would have leapt down fearlessly. On this morning the river was a mere 100 metres away, but a month ago, it had been over four kilometres distant. Somehow, as they began nest building and incubation, they knew the water would arrive. It was exceptionally good timing, except for one thing; a troop of baboons was foraging at the water's edge. Spring is a difficult time, for food is scarce, and for a large male baboon a batch of tiny goslings makes a tempting opportunity. As I sat watching a large male baboon raced at them – with intent. What followed was an extraordinary few minutes. Splashing through the narrow channel the baboon raced in, catching the goslings one by one, stuffing them into his mouth pouches. A furious and desperate male goose smashed his wings against the ape, who sat down calmly and quickly devoured the youngsters alive. The attack was over in a few minutes, and after-wards I sat in a state of bewilderment. It was so savage, so fast and shocking – the pathetic desperation of the babies and the great courage of the parents left me amazed. As calm returned, an observant kite swooped down and grabbed a scrap of a tiny leg.

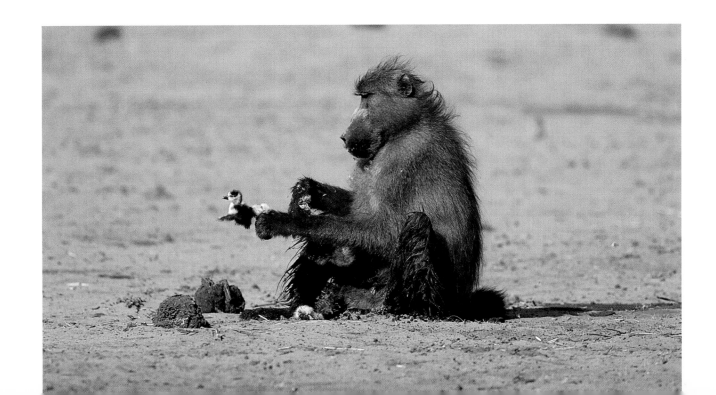

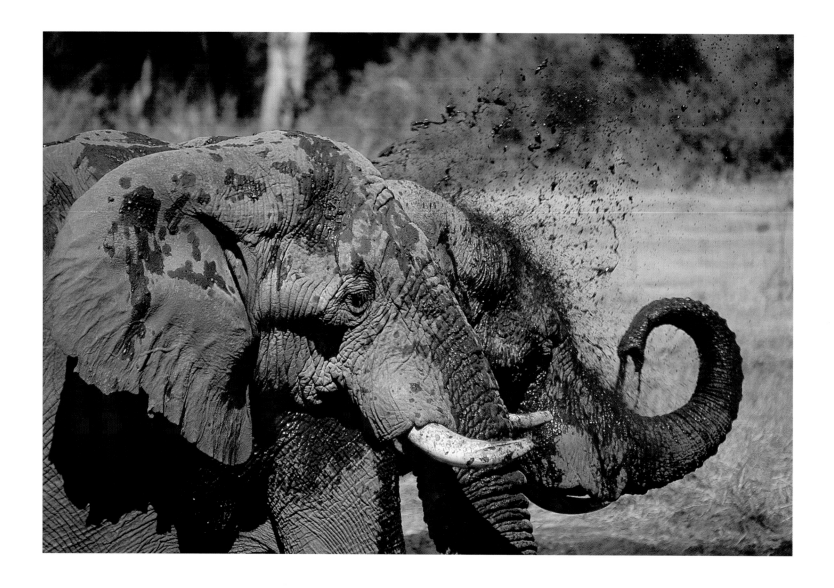

Above and Opposite The edges of the dry riverbed are pockmarked with an irregular pattern of shallow pits that refill as muddy pools when the trickling river arrives. It is the work of those great architects of the wilderness, the elephants. After a drink on a warm afternoon they visit these wallows, slurrying up the mud with their feet and trunks. They suck up copious litres of mud in their trunks which they squirt all over their giant forms, methodically covering their whole bodies. This amounts to kilograms of mud being carried from the river in a process that opens up wallows and eventually may create mainstream river pools.

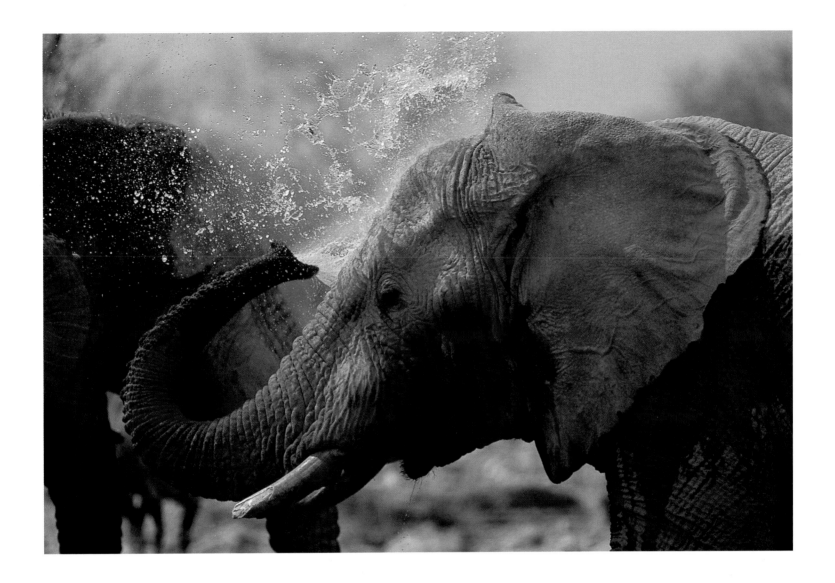

Overleaf For many visitors a safari without lions can be a great disappointment. Happily they are common and maintain a high profile in this region, and the chances of finding them are always good. Animals adapt to their particular environmental circumstances and their behaviour patterns can vary accordingly. A case in point is lions — these successful predators are great opportunists and are masters of exploiting particular situations. So, while lions are typically nocturnal, some prides or individuals take to daytime hunting because it is well worth the effort. Gerald often spent time with a small pride of lionesses that would become active from mid-morning. They would walk slowly along the edge of the water searching for antelope or warthog that they could ambush. They were particularly interested in the warthogs and Gerald was fortunate enough to witness several kills in the middle of the day.

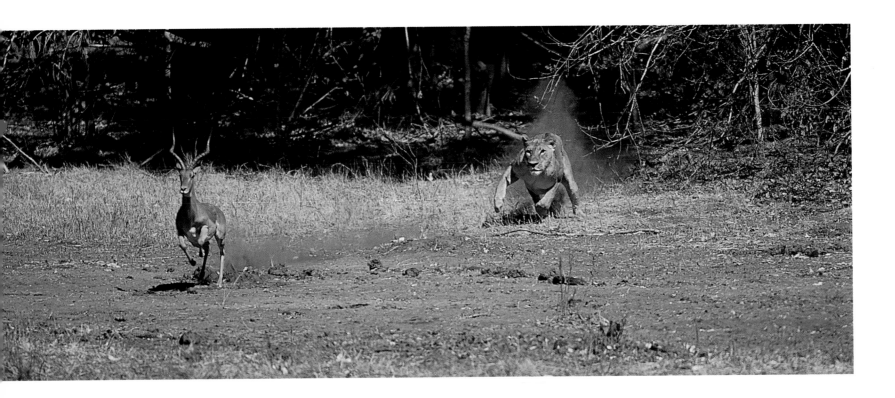

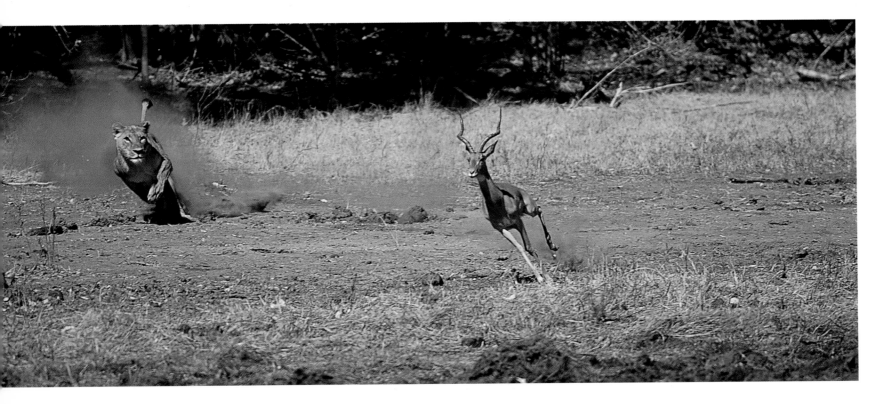

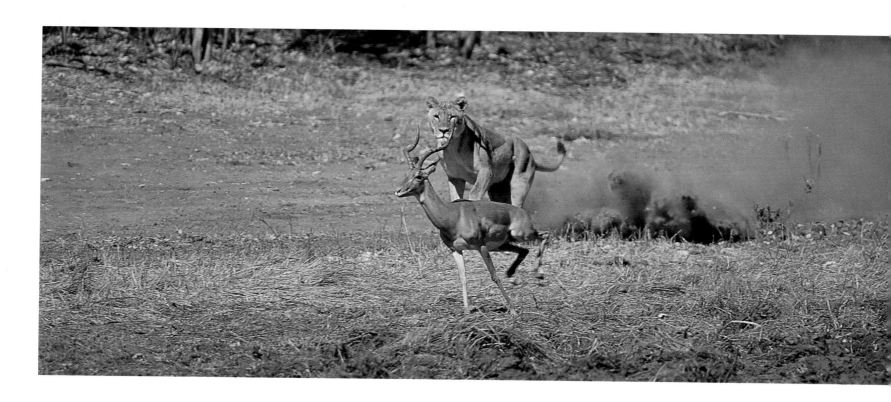

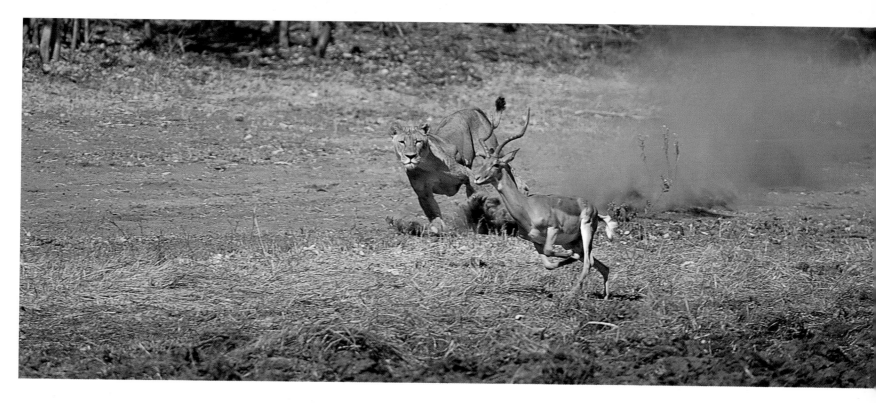

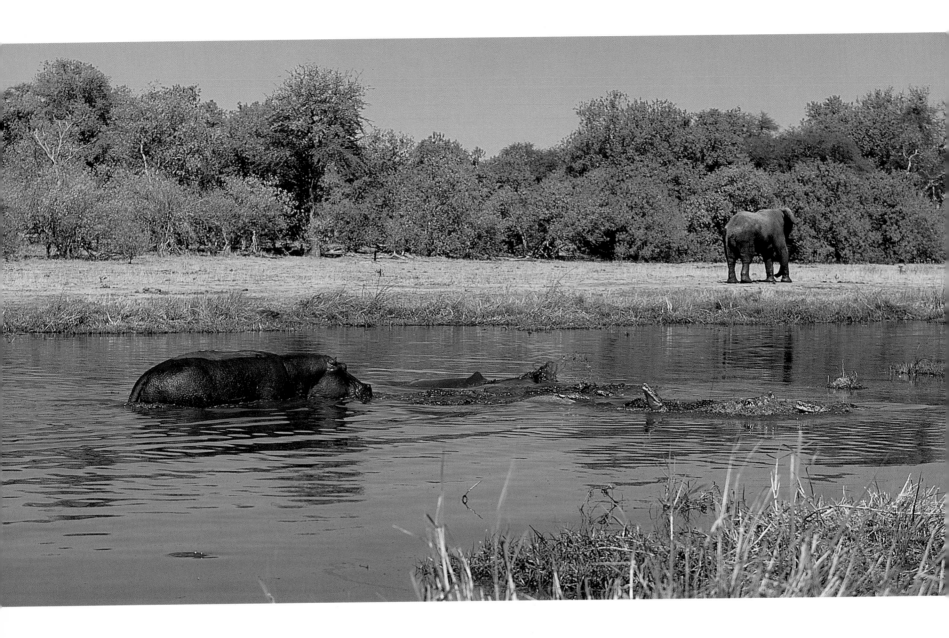

Above, Opposite and Overleaf   There are some well-documented cases of hippos showing interest in dead animals. A commotion had developed in one of the large hippo pools; the carcass of a baby hippo was being fed on by a group of a dozen large crocodiles. A hippo came wading over, threat-yawning to chase away the crocodiles, and proceeded to mouth and lick the carcass. Over a period of several hours at least two of the hippos would repeat this. The tolerance the hippos show for the crocodiles is surprising – at times the hippo would shove the reptiles away with their mouths. Eventually they moved off to sleep the day away and the crocodiles quickly returned to feast, spinning and splashing until there was nothing left.

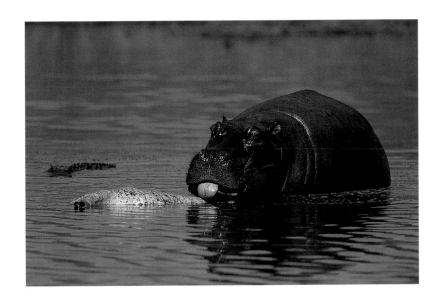

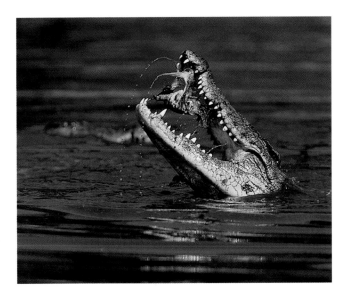

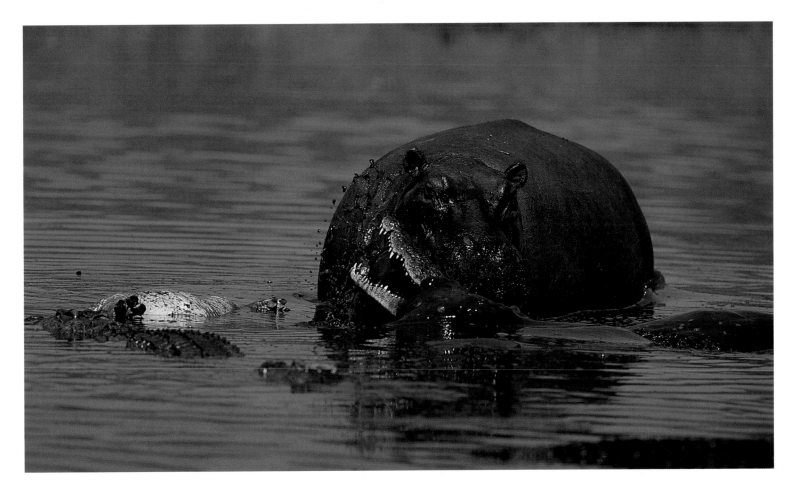

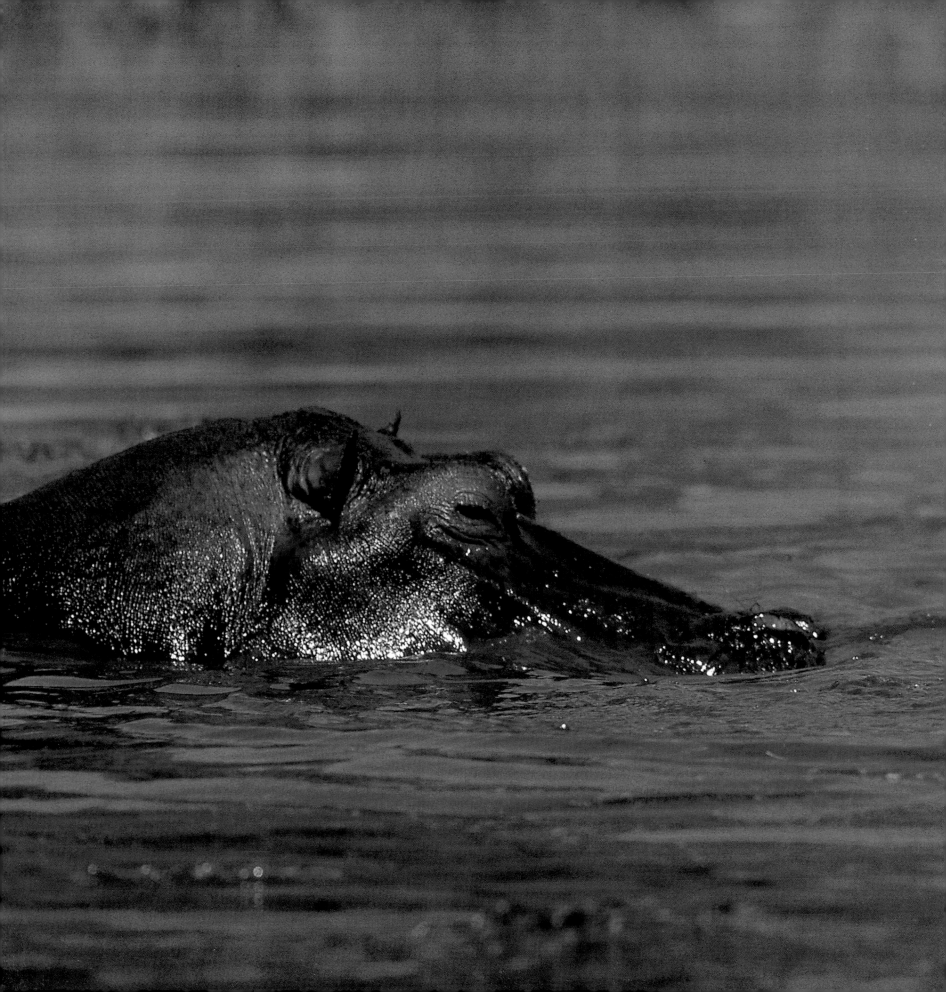

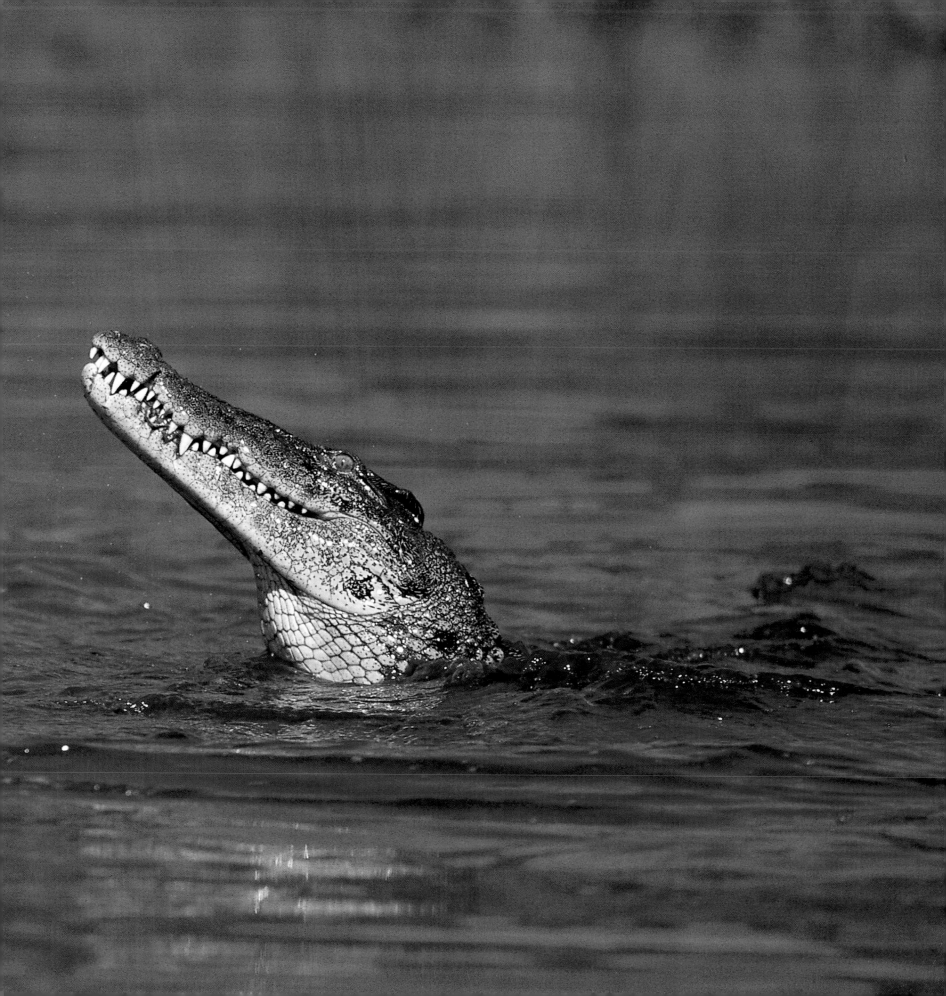

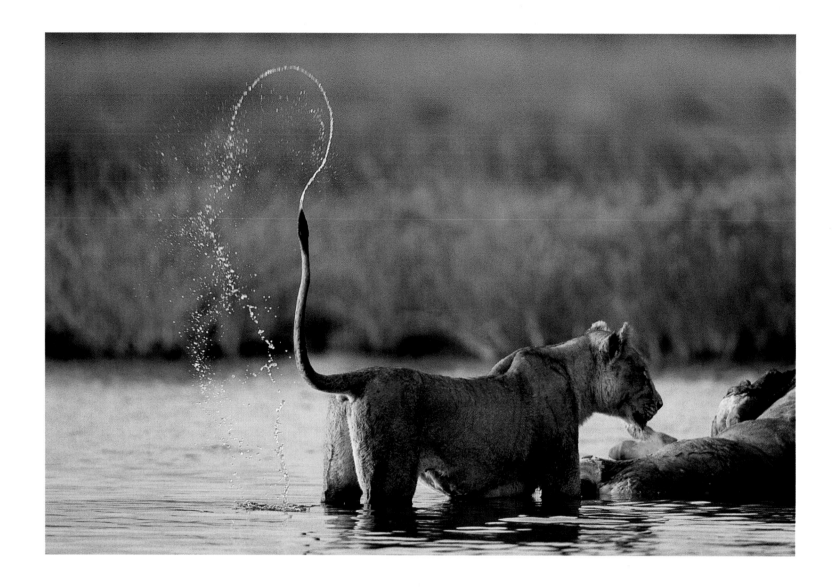

Above In Nature serious fighting is rare and seldom lasts long, especially when large and dangerous animals are involved, as the chances of injury or death are high. However, a battle between two equally dominant bull hippos was an exception to this and raged for many hours under the cover of darkness. Several days later a bull died in the shallow water, providing a feast for crocodiles and vultures. Attracted by the stench, a lioness feeds on the rotting carcass, wary of the crocodiles that are lurking nearby.

Opposite Giraffe drink every several days when water is available. It is a difficult procedure for such a tall creature, and it involves straddling or bending the front legs. After drinking the giraffe jumps back, and this action is accompanied by a characteristic and simultaneous flick of the head.

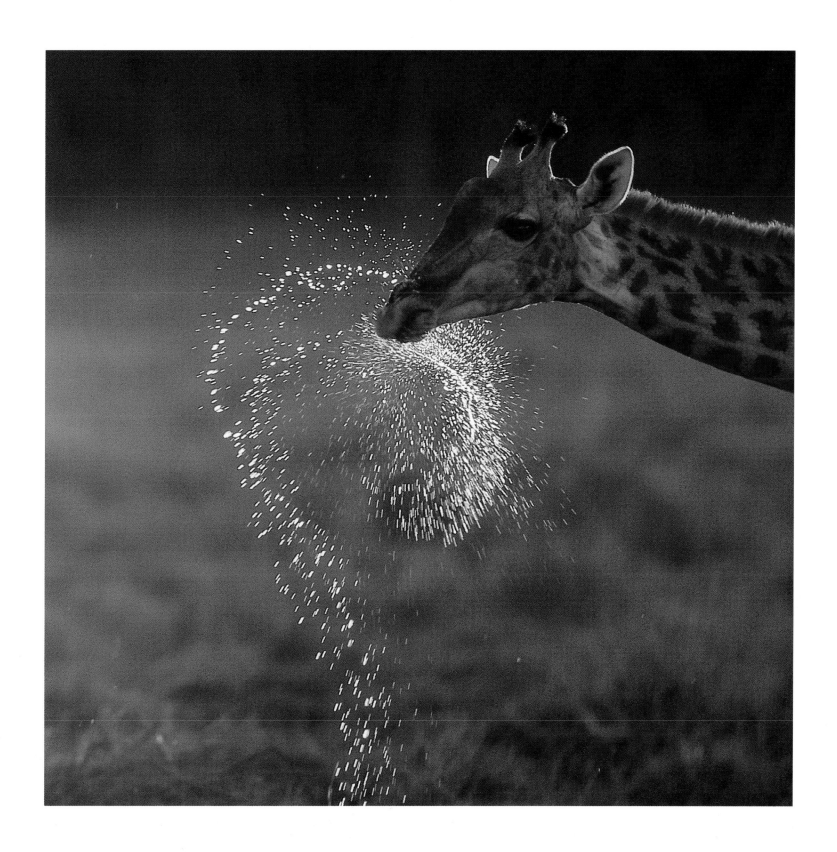

For most of the day wild dogs lie sprawled in the shade, their tortoiseshell camouflage rendering them invisible amongst mopane leaves. Periodically the pups will awake and hungrily beg a parent to regurgitate. Twittering and squeaking, they solicit meat, that is willingly spewed out. The little pups wolf it down, and after a while calm returns. We loved being around the wild dogs – they have such a great exuberance for life, seemingly carefree and fun-loving. Finding these rare and threatened predators hunting along a river's edge or simply crossing an anonymous floodplain is always thrilling, and the great wilderness of Botswana is one of their last strongholds. After the Ethiopian wolf, the wild dog is Africa's most endangered carnivore, with only about 5 000 of them surviving in the wild.

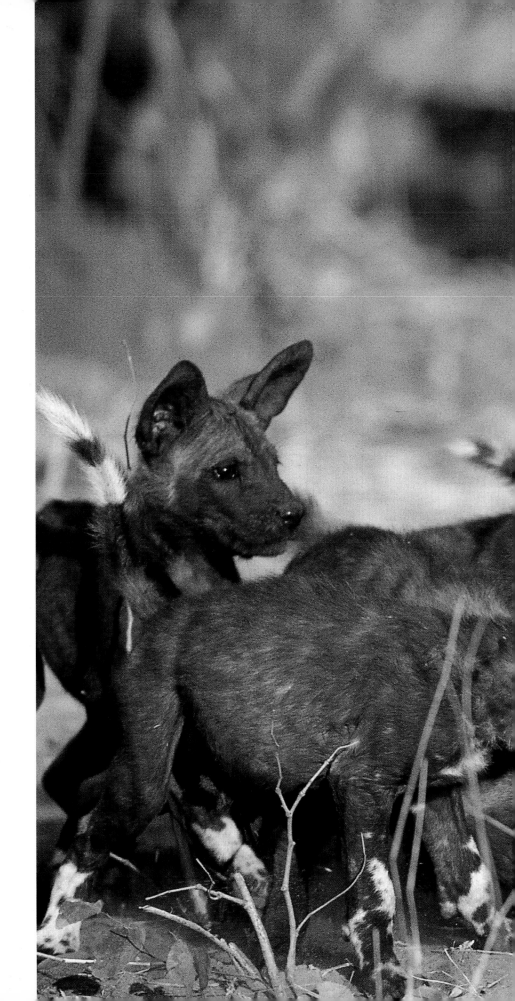

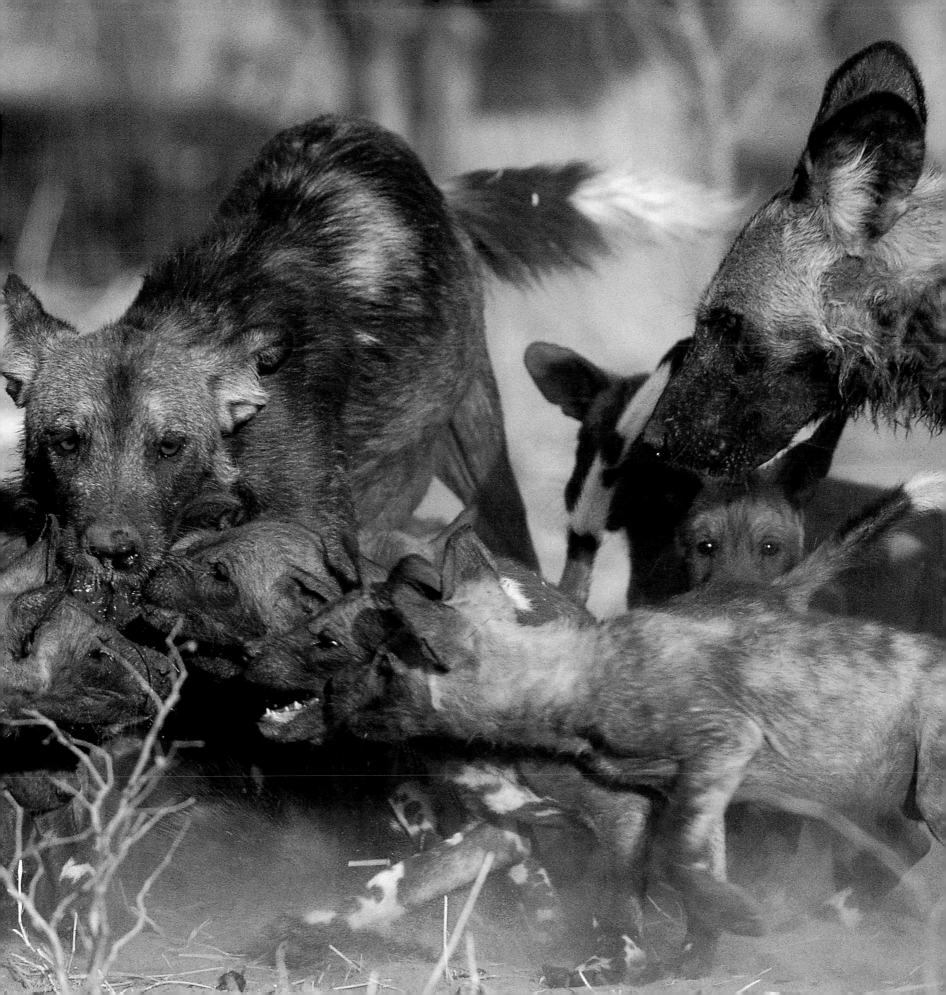

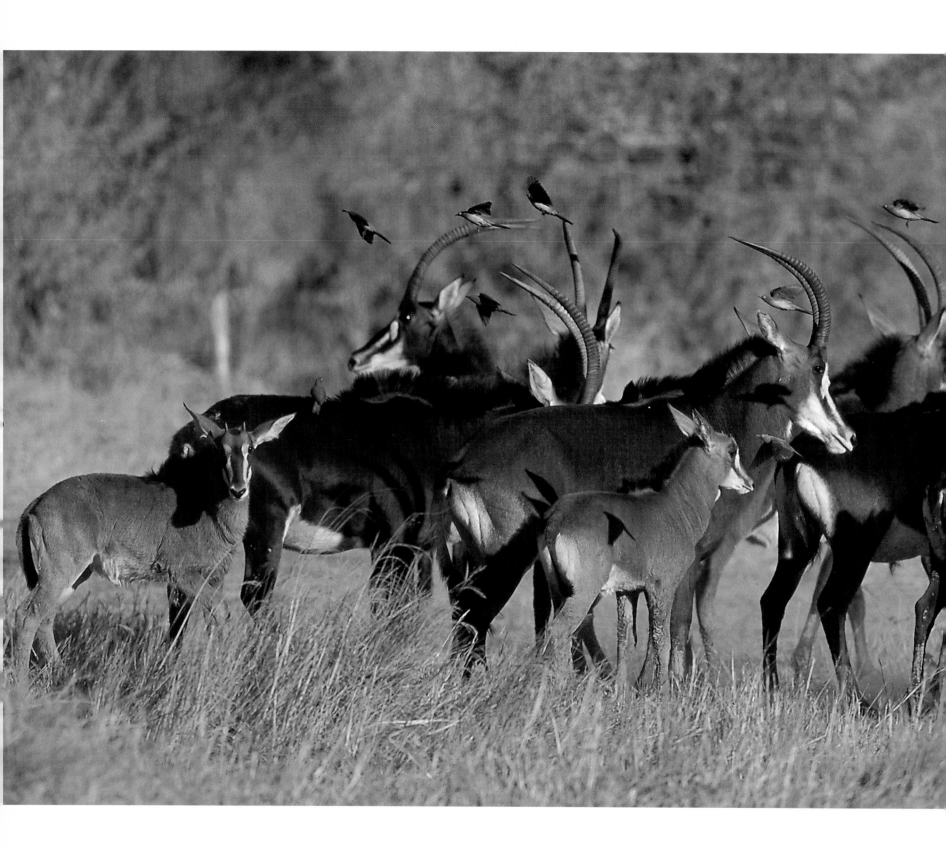

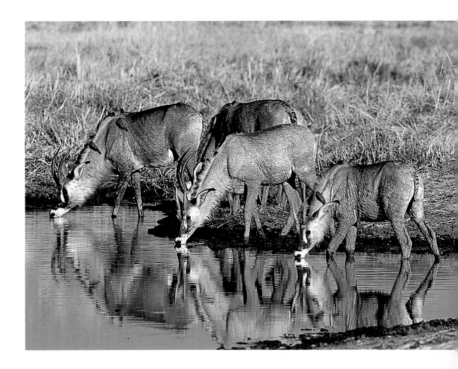

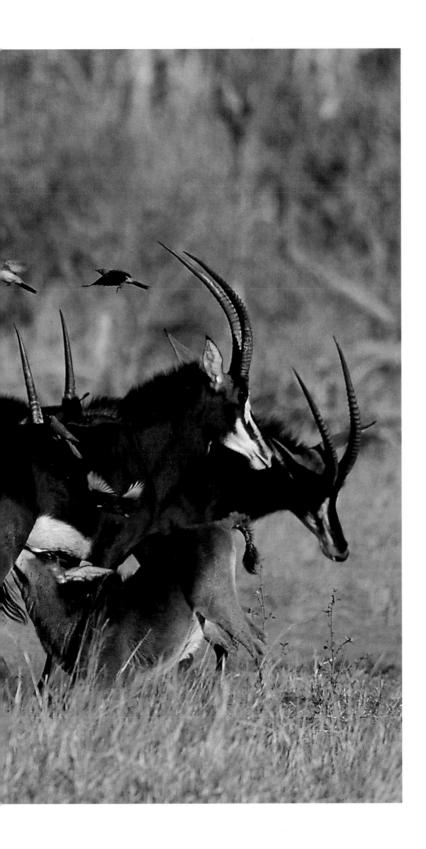

The genus *Hippotragus* is represented by two species in southern Africa, sable (***left***) and roan (***above***) antelope. The blue buck, which occurred in the southern part of the Cape, was also a member of this elegant group, but sadly became extinct almost 200 years ago. Both sable and roan are uncommon antelope, and were only occasional visitors to the river. They are normally fairly nervous, as they live in the distant forests and woodlands. Although smaller than the roan, the sable is surely the most magnificent of our antelope, and both sexes are horned. The males are jet black and the females more brown, and as in most related species, the young are born a pale colour.

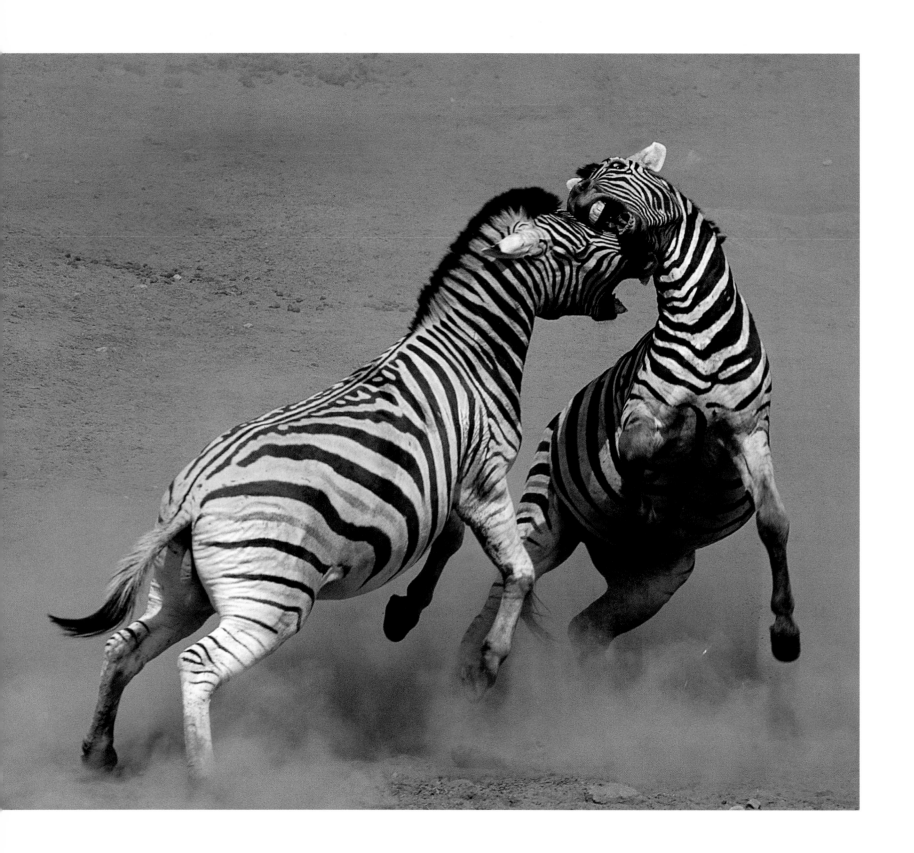

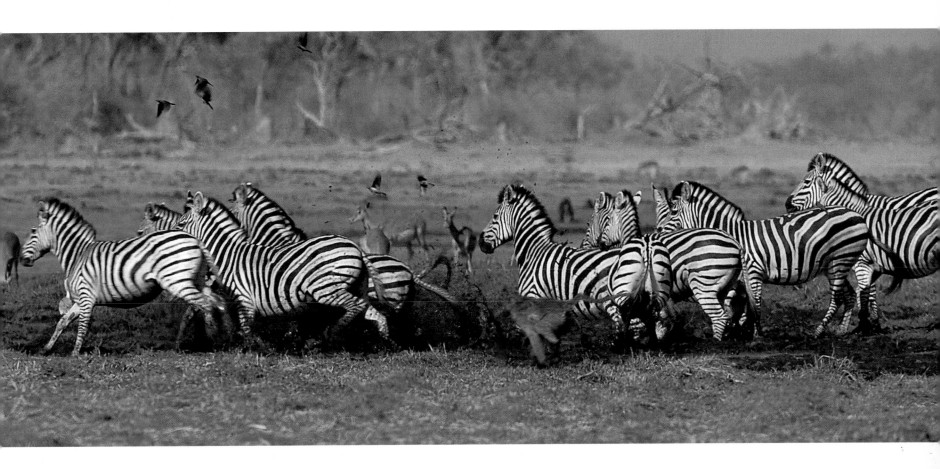

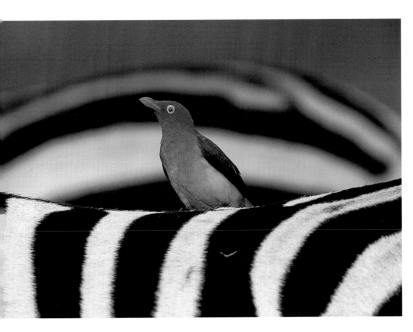

Colour combinations of black and white are common in Nature, with many birds and mammals sporting impressive pied coats. Since such colour patterns are so striking it must serve a purpose. In a land where brown and grey predominate the most spectacular and confusing of all is that of the zebra. Many explanations have been put forward but no single theory is accepted. If you observe zebras at a distance or in poor light, the effectiveness of this coat pattern as camouflage is most noticeable. Some suggest the stripes enable individuals to recognize one another, or present a dazzling and confusing sight to an attacking lion. We should remember, however, that other animals see very differently to humans. Our eyes are colour sensitive and best for diurnal vision; who knows quite what a lion's visual perception is on a dark African night?

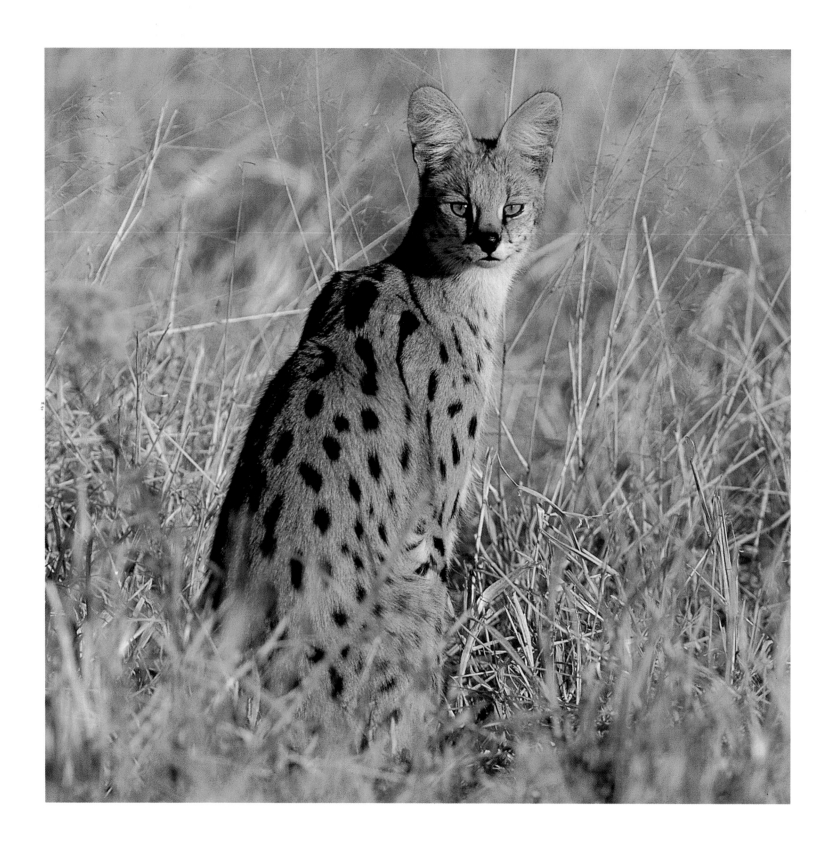

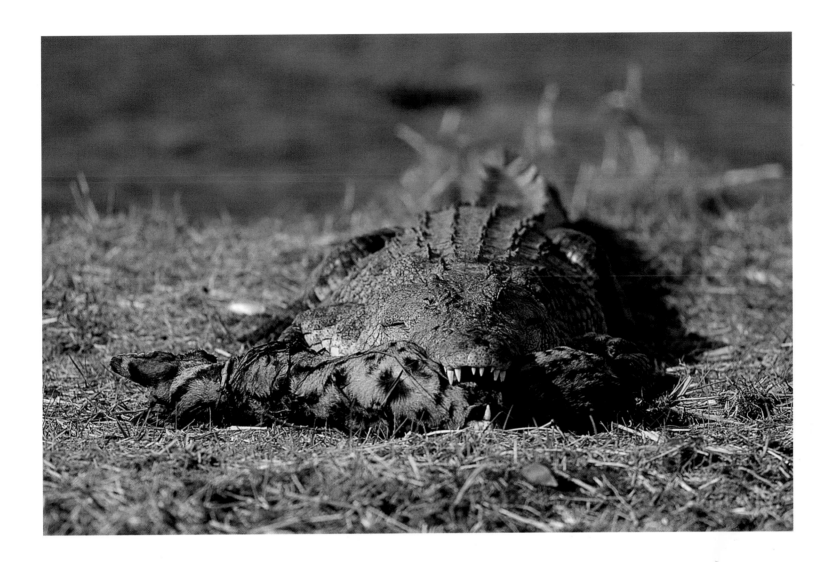

Opposite   Gerald found this relaxed serval out mousing one afternoon. This seldom-seen cat is primarily solitary and nocturnal, living in grassy areas close to water where it can hunt for small vlei creatures. For its size, the elegant serval has the longest legs of any member of the cat family, but it is not a particularly fast runner. It uses its large ears to help locate prey before pouncing on its victims with a spectacular leap. Large paws swat the life out of its favourite rats and mice, but small birds and frogs also get devoured.

Above   Early one morning I chanced upon a huge crocodile lying out on the riverbank. On approaching, I noticed something clamped firmly in its jaws, and to my amazement I recognized the typical stripes and spots of a large serval. How could such an athletic cat have been caught? I still wonder how he met his end. The croc stared at me beady-eyed before lifting the carcass and sliding quietly into the still, dark waters of the Khwai.

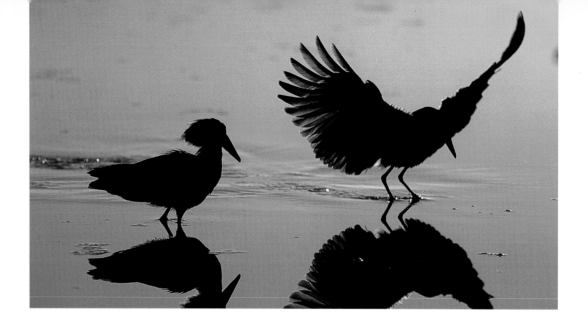

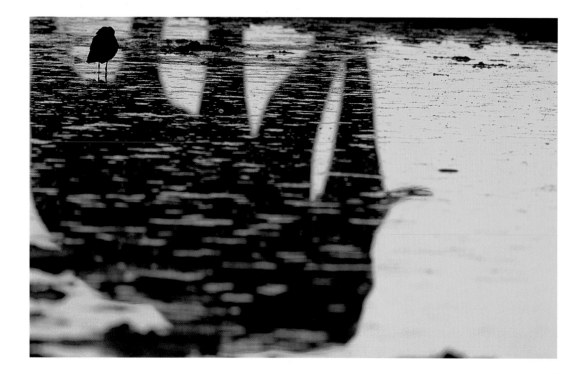

With its flow at a mere trickle, the river has finally reached the end of its journey. The relentless sun, and the continuous visitations of thirsty elephants and other beasts, have halted the river's progress altogether.

At the tip of the river the muddy flow releases frogs from their dry cocoon of mud where they have hibernated for months. It is here that the hamerkops (*top*) wait to grab and swallow the hapless amphibians. The river's terminus is always busy. While elephants seldom visit the river in the early morning, on this chilly morning I saw a herd march down to drink (*above and opposite*).

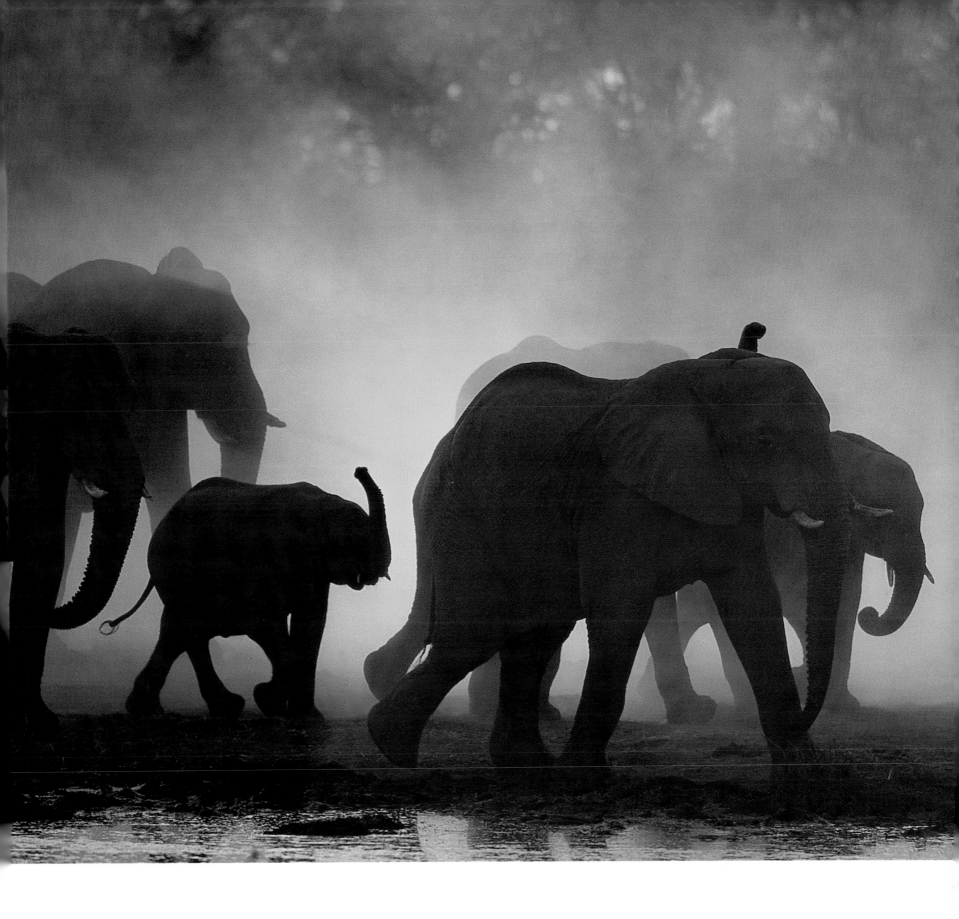

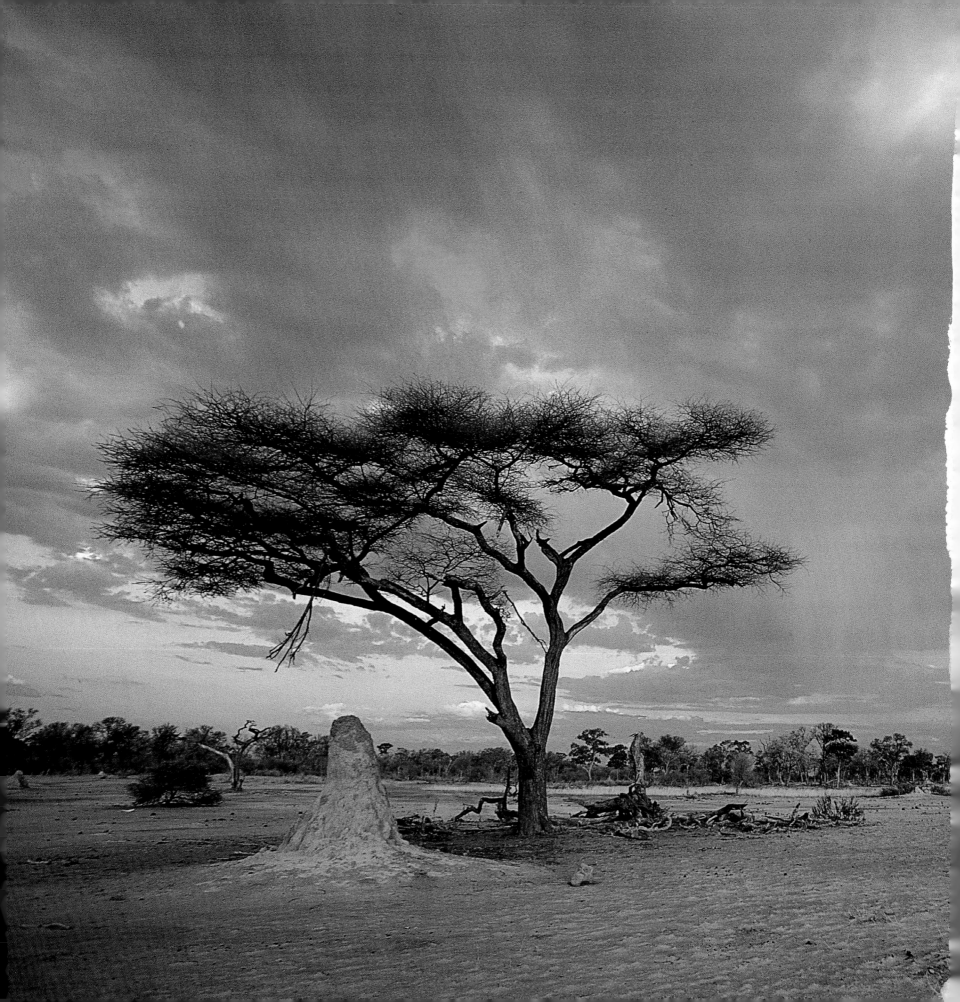

The Waiting

for the first stirrings of summer

*I*T IS EARLY SUMMER AND nearly half a year since the last rains fell. The land and its inhabitants wait patiently, and within the earth plants lie dormant and small creatures hibernate. The river has stopped flowing and the big pools are beginning to dry up. In some years the rains do not materialise at all, and devastating droughts can prevail.

October is the hottest month in Botswana, with endless days of debilitating heat. Hot winds prevail from the east, blowing relentlessly day in and day out. Dust clouds are whipped up, causing the most beautiful sunsets of red, orange and gold. The dust is everywhere, and there is no more moisture for the sun to steal from the soil.

Then comes a feeling of change in the air. For several weeks storm clouds gather each day. By late afternoon fluffy white cloud puffs have grown into huge grey and white thunderheads rich with the promise of rain. In the evenings thunder grumbles in the distance and lightning flickers late into night. Despite the promise, however, no rain falls. By morning the clouds will have dissipated, and once more the sky will be as blue as a roller's wing. This cycle will repeat itself for weeks, slowly building momentum towards eventual respite for the thirsty land.

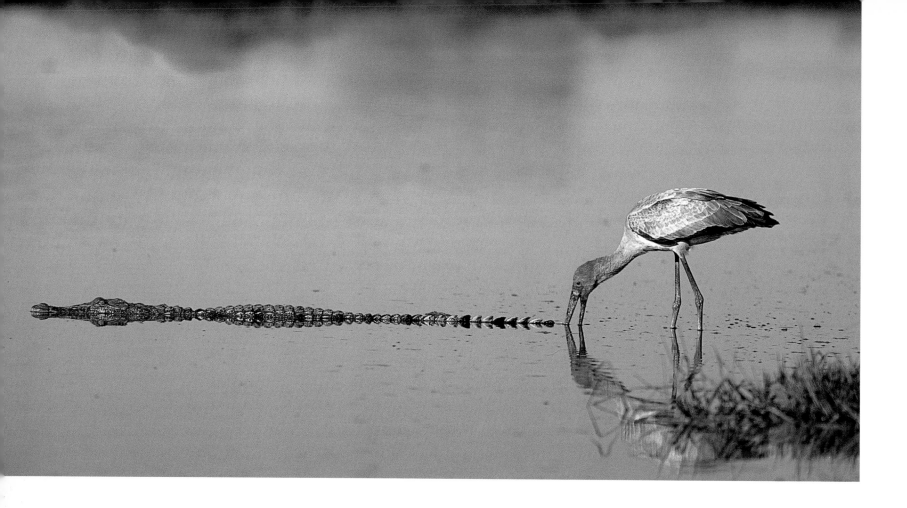

One morning a close examination of a scruffy acacia tree reveals green buds on the thin branch tips – the trees have exploited waters deep beneath the sandy surface. This is good news for the browsers, who will quickly find these new shoots. Impalas both graze and browse, and have an edge over the grazers who must still survive on dusty hay.

Once more the earth has travelled its full orbit around the sun and another cycle of the seasons has been completed. The only constant in Nature is change itself; all things change. Along the banks of the River Khwai there unfolds the life and death of individuals, fluctuations in populations, and floods and droughts come and go. The long wait for the rains goes on, but relief will come.

Previous pages A spring rainbow confirms rain falling from a distant thundercloud. Some kilometres from the river this lone camelthorn tree stands gauntly on a floodplain totally devoid of the rich grasses that flourished there just half a year ago.

Above An immature yellow-bellied stork probes carefully for food against a crocodile's tail. Most waterbirds seem to wade and swim oblivious to the presence of crocs and I often wonder if they ever end up in the jaws of these fearsome reptiles. Although this crocodile (***opposite***) later answered my question, I am still not sure who the unfortunate victim was. Gulping it down headfirst and whole, the few visible feathers sticking out of the crocodile's mouth suggested a spur-winged goose.

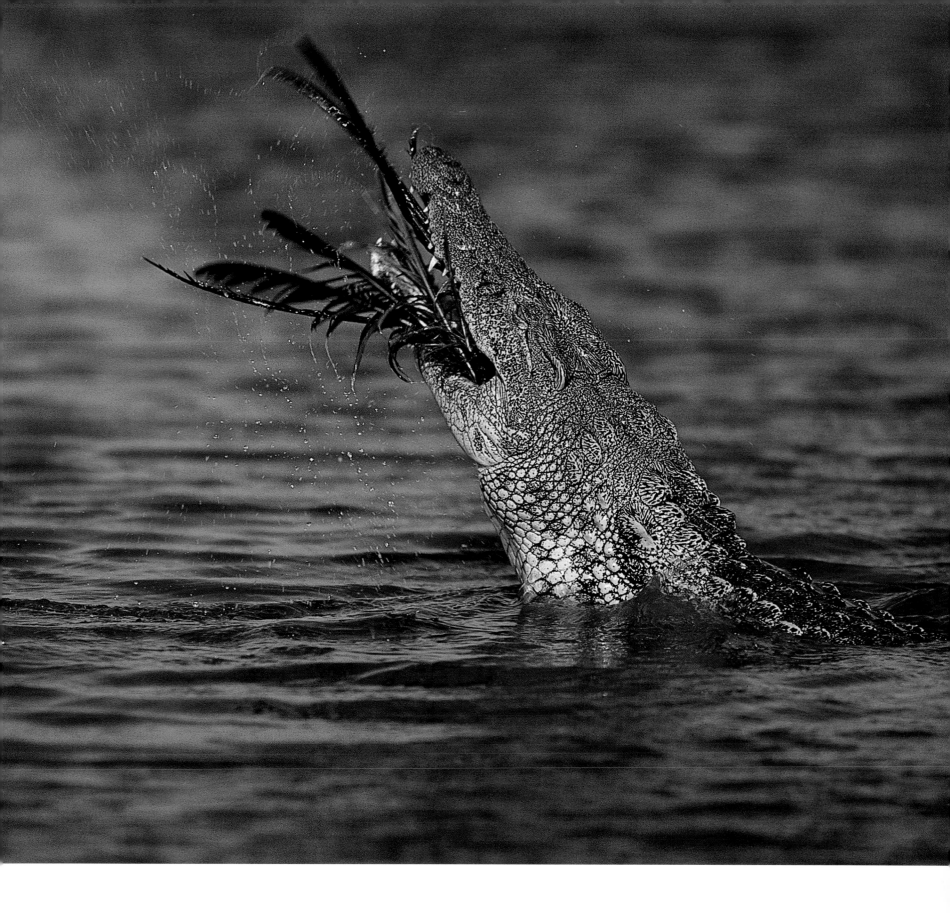

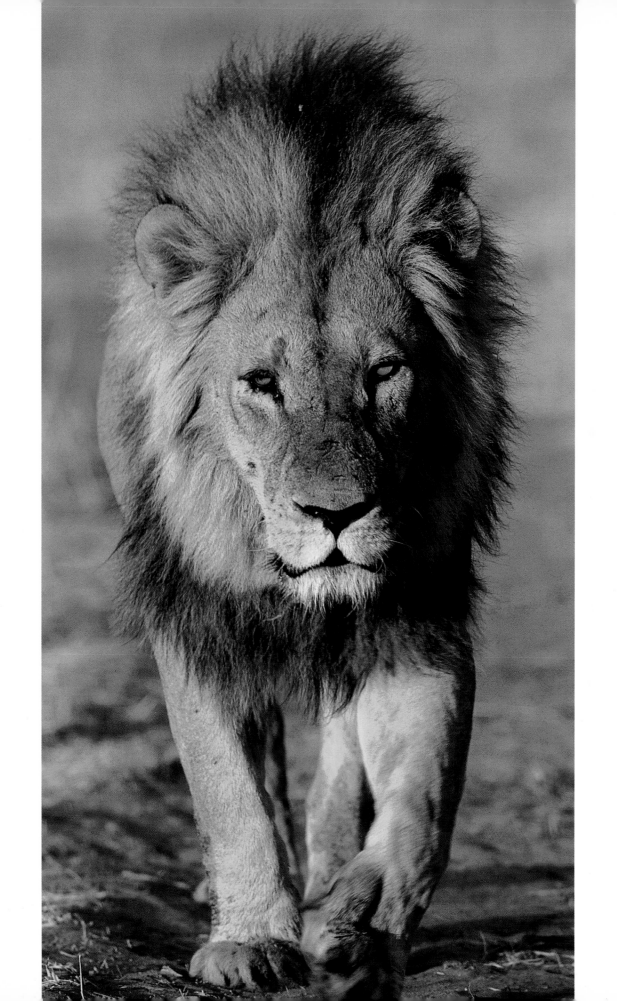

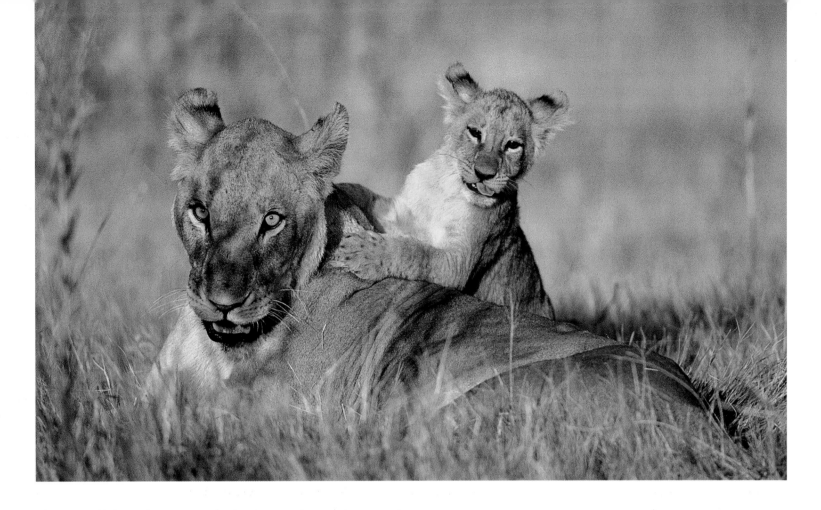

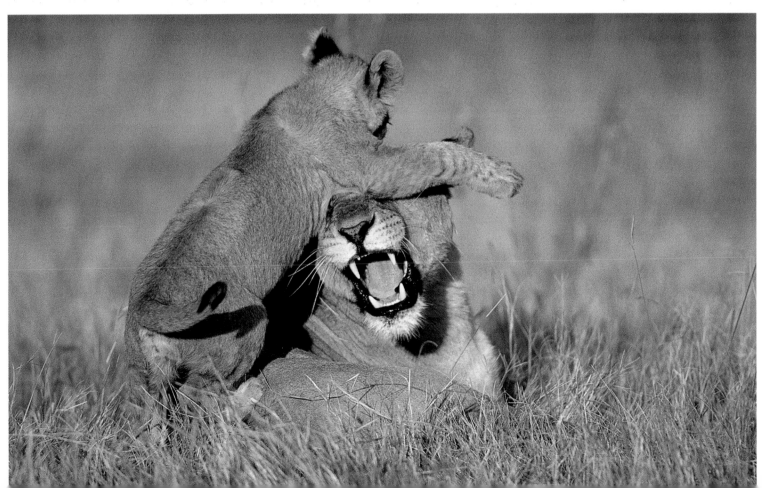

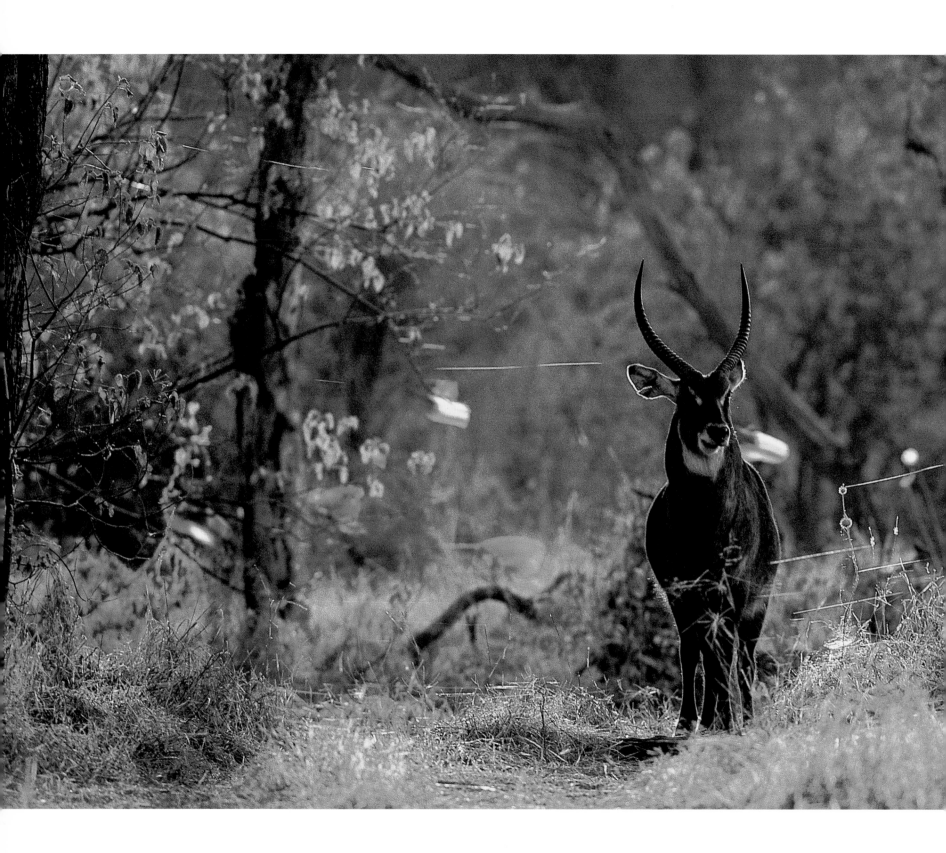

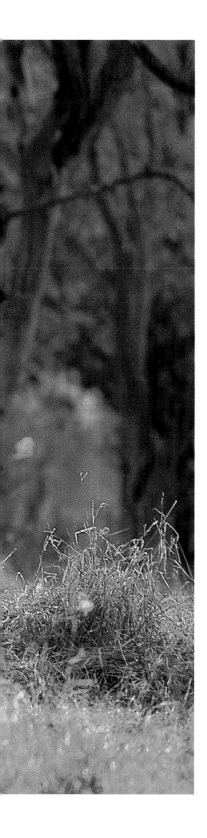

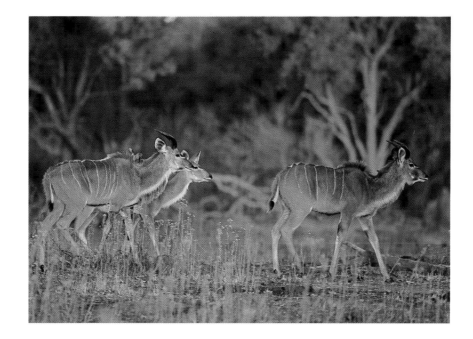

Previous pages   Lions are famous for killing anything they can, whether they eat it or not. Pride wars result in the death of many lion cubs as dominant males annex a new territory. They move quickly to kill the offspring of the previous dominant male, and waste no time trying to mate with the lionesses to create offspring of their own and so ensure the continuation of their genetic line.

Left and Above   The antelope family is one of the most successful of all mammal groups, with more than 30 species occurring in southern Africa. All the males have permanent horns that last a lifetime, although fierce clashes between competing rams often result in these being broken off. It is tough to survive in an environment where every year resources become so limited. Come the end of winter, all aspects of competition are intensified, of which the highly visible predators are but one concern; there are the limitations of food and water, and ectoparasites in the form of biting flies and ticks tax the animals. Endoparasites are also common, taking a huge toll on even a healthy host. The climate can also be extreme – with spells of hot and cold weather and even hailstorms and fires. The period before the first rains is always the hardest time of year for many creatures; particularly for pregnant ewes whose extra weight compromises their speed and taxes their resources to the limit. Simply being alive is ample testimony to an extraordinary ability to survive.

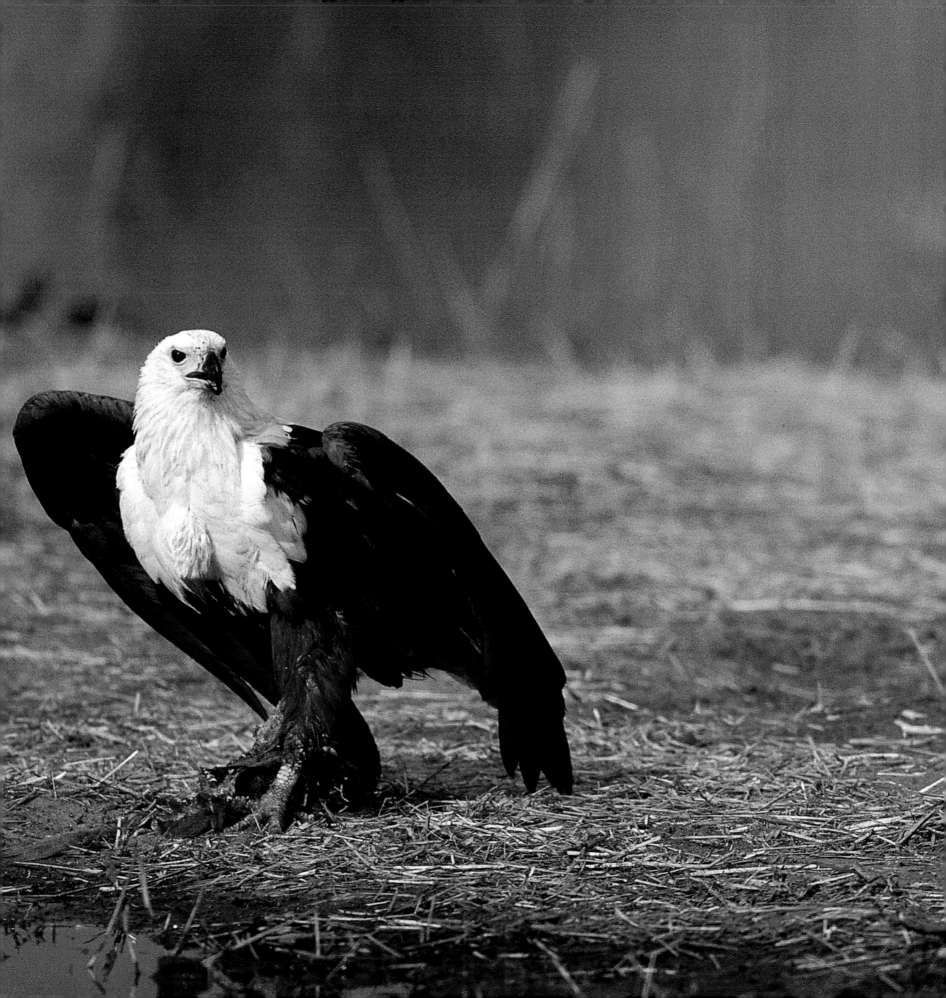

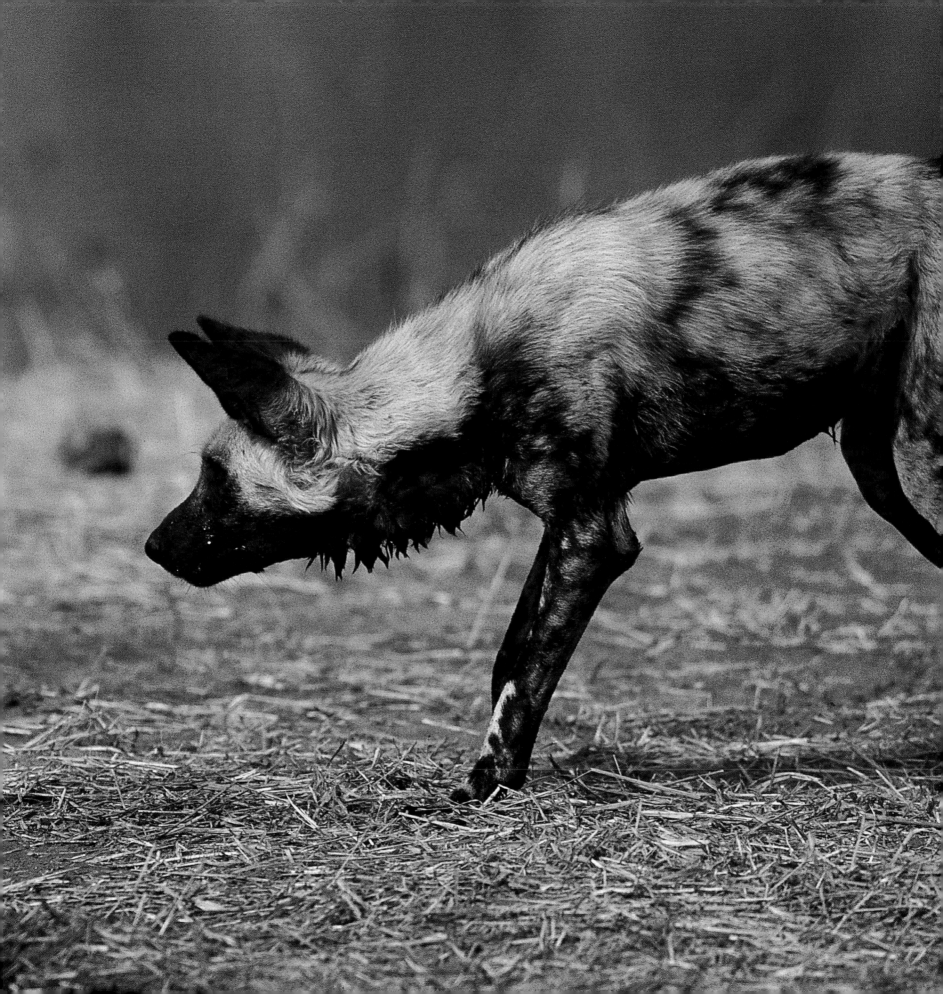

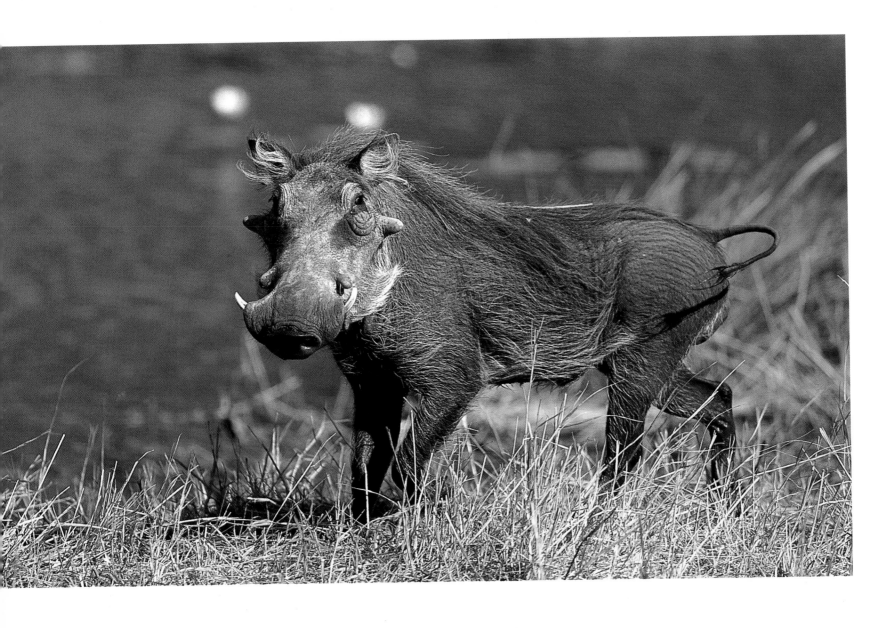

Previous pages This fish eagle would not have permitted such a close approach by a member of the cat species. Wild dogs are naturally inquisitive, and sometimes to their regret. But not this time. After sniffing the worried eagle the dog jumped back and ran off to join the rest of the pack.

Above and Opposite Large male warthogs are a formidable match for most predators, with the exception of lions, and I have seen many leopards and cheetahs come off second best in tangles with them. Their thick necks make them difficult to strangle, and their tusks are effective weapons, especially the razor-sharp lower pair. The males are recognisable by their two sets of large warts; females have only one pair.

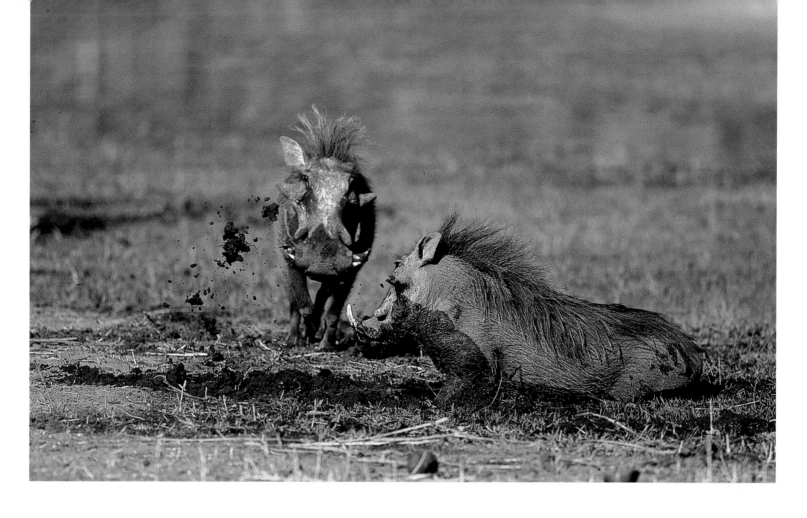

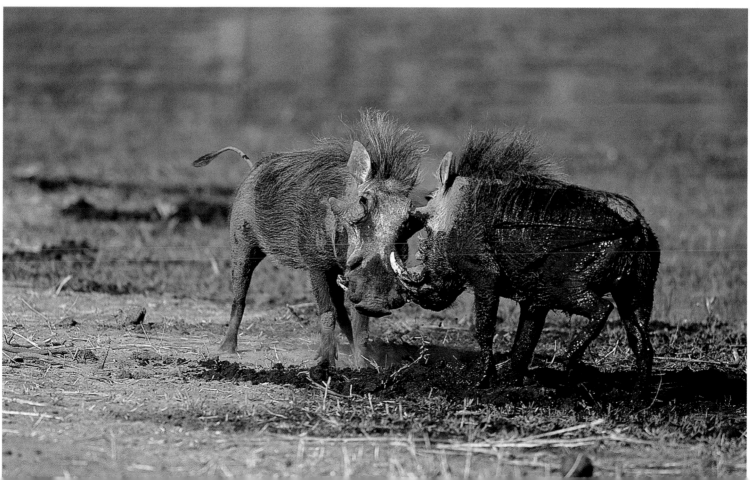

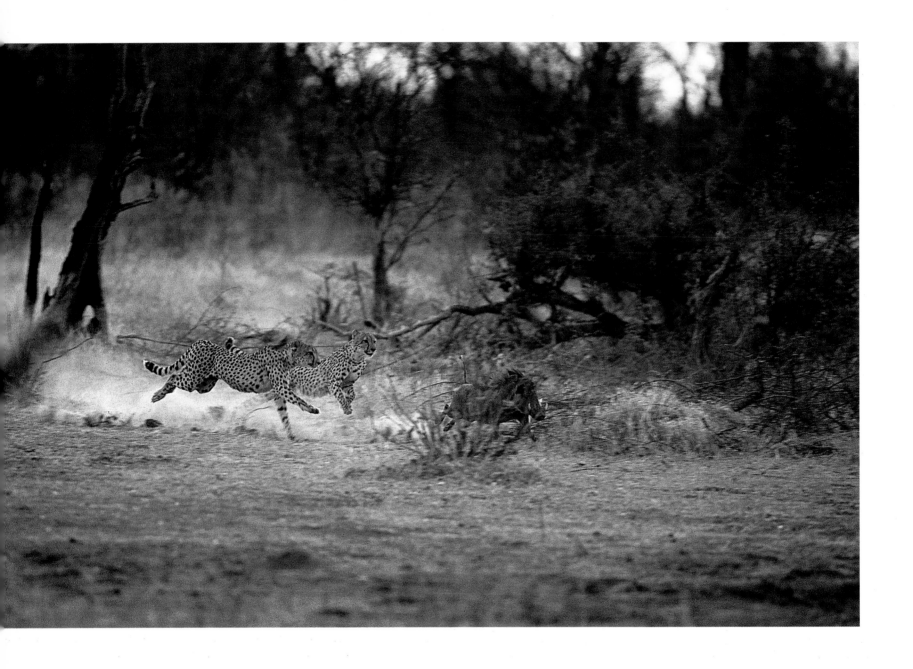

Cheetahs are scarce here, but Gerald found these two males hunting one morning. Most male cheetahs live together in coalitions of two and sometimes three individuals. They are capable of hunting prey larger than the smaller solitary females can manage. After identifying this warthog as a smaller subadult, the two male cheetahs gave chase across a dusty woodland.

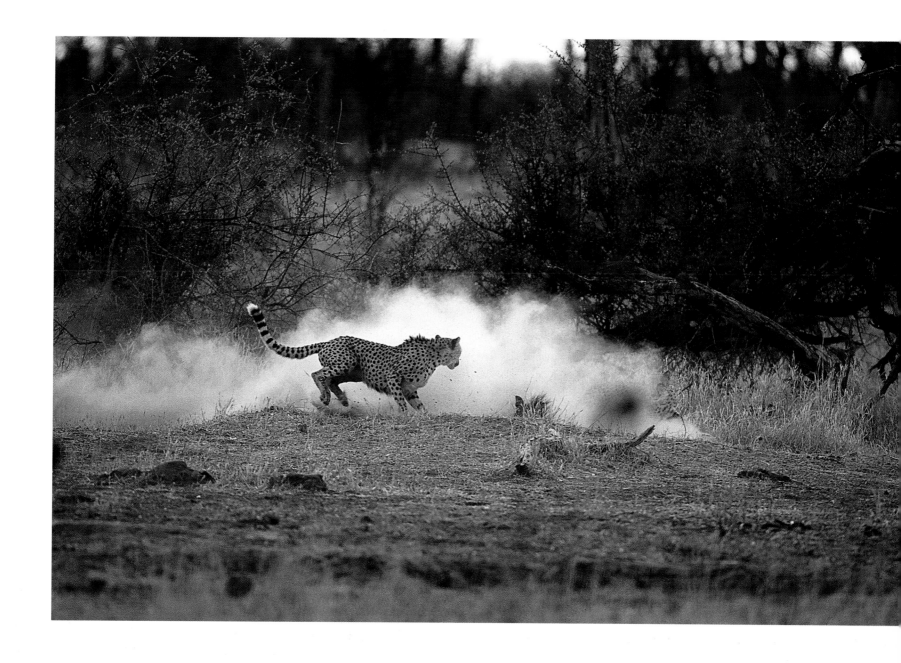

Racing to take refuge in a nearby burrow the hog spins and enters backwards, presenting his threatening tusks and protecting his vulnerable rump. This hunt was unsuccessful; these experienced cheetahs did not want to risk injury. A deep gash would be a handicap, and a blinded eye or broken limb would prove fatal.

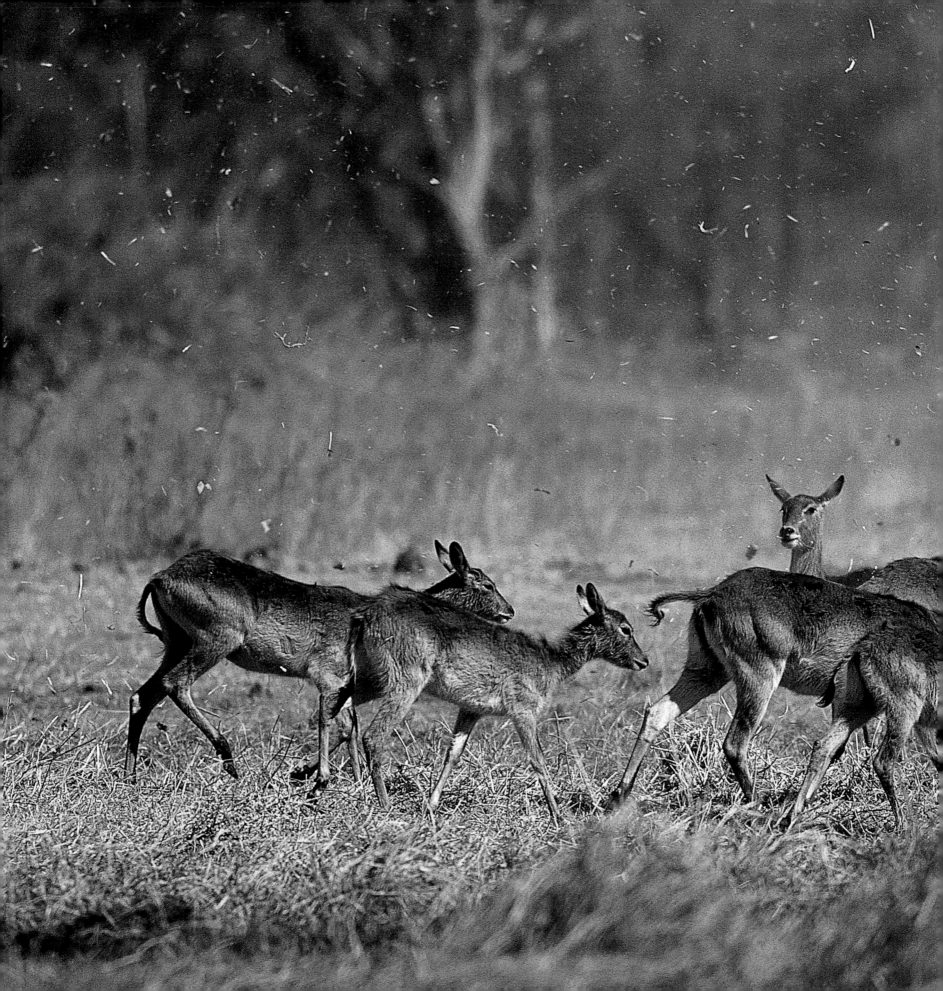

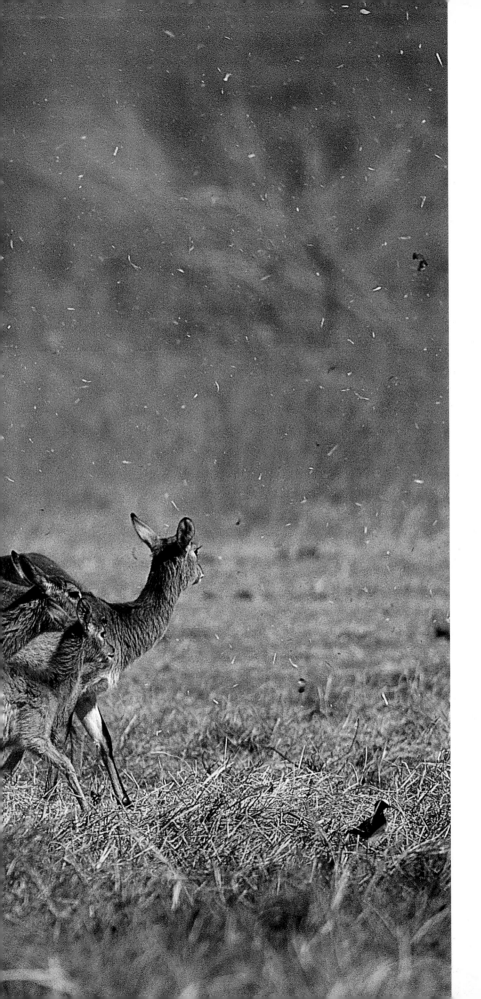

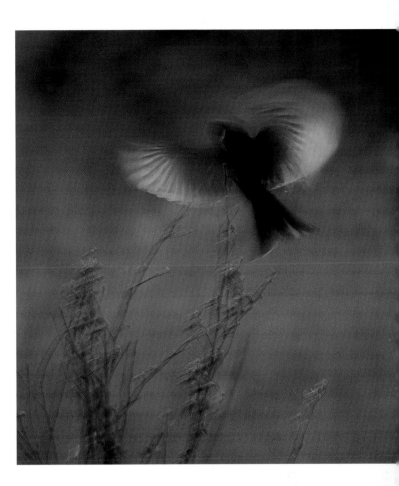

Above The fork-tailed drongo is a colourful character; these pugnacious little birds boldly chase away dangerous birds of prey, and loudly warn other birds of the threat.

Left Lechwe ewes are engulfed by a passing whirlwind. As the furious swirls of air tumble up dry leaves and grass, the dusty air stings their eyes shut. But their nostrils are flared, for on the wind comes a promising message of change, the faint scent of distant rain. The transition to the long-awaited wet season could be imminent. However, until that moment arrives they must stoically wait, preoccupied with the daily challenges of finding food and avoiding danger.

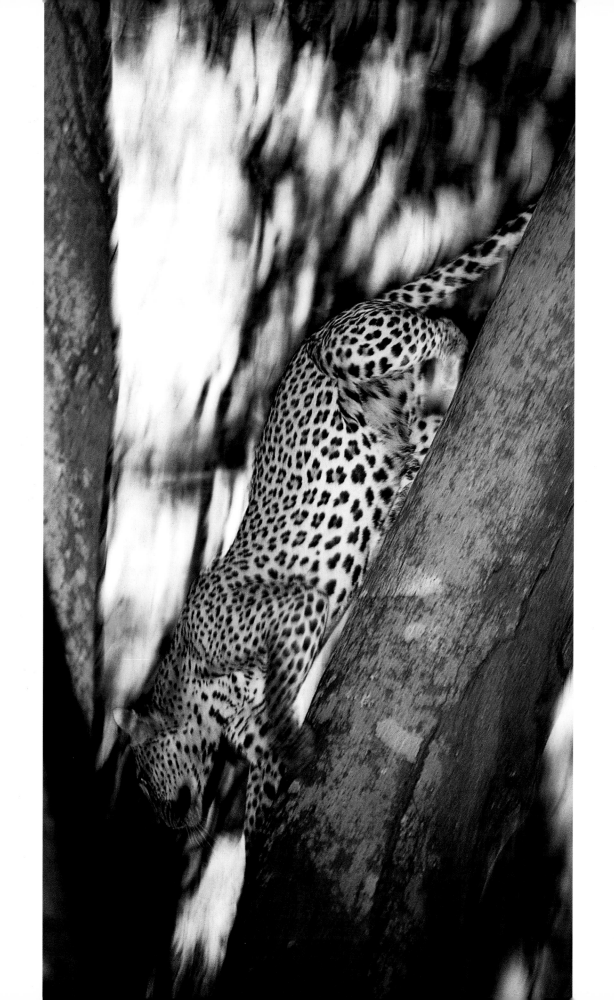

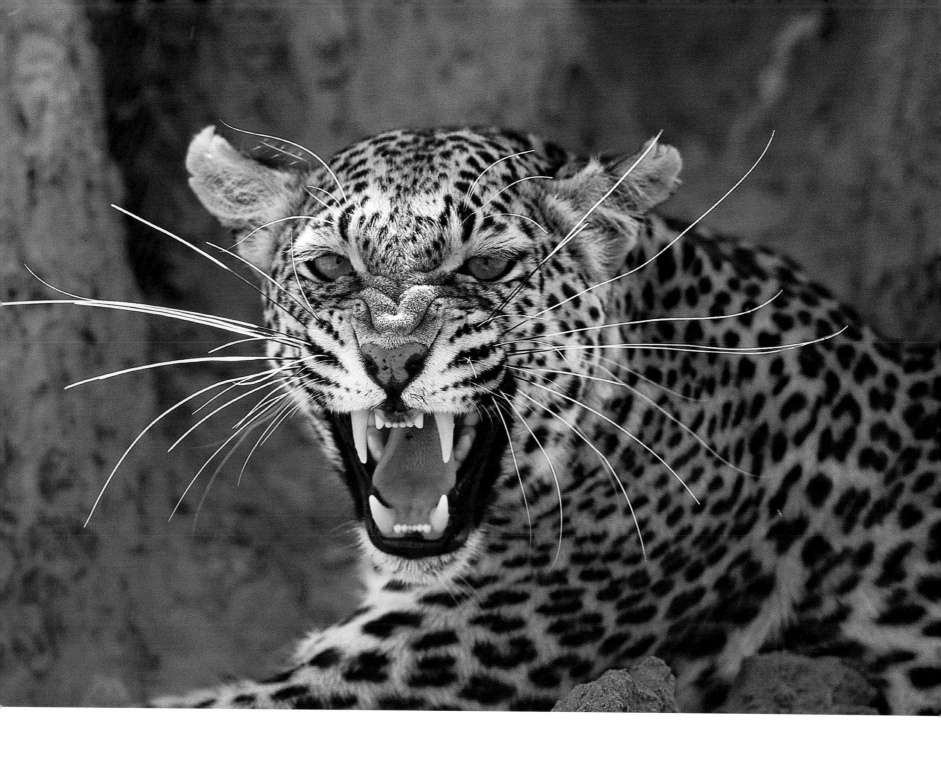

Leopards are common in Botswana but, true to their legendary secretiveness, they are seldom seen. Early one morning the chatter of monkeys alerted us to this female leopard on the ground near some tall knobthorn trees. She had caught an adult impala during the night, but it was too large for her to hoist to safety. She spent the day in a bad mood, fending off jackals and vultures. When the hyaenas arrived at dusk she quickly melted away into the shadows. The carcass was not worth fighting over.

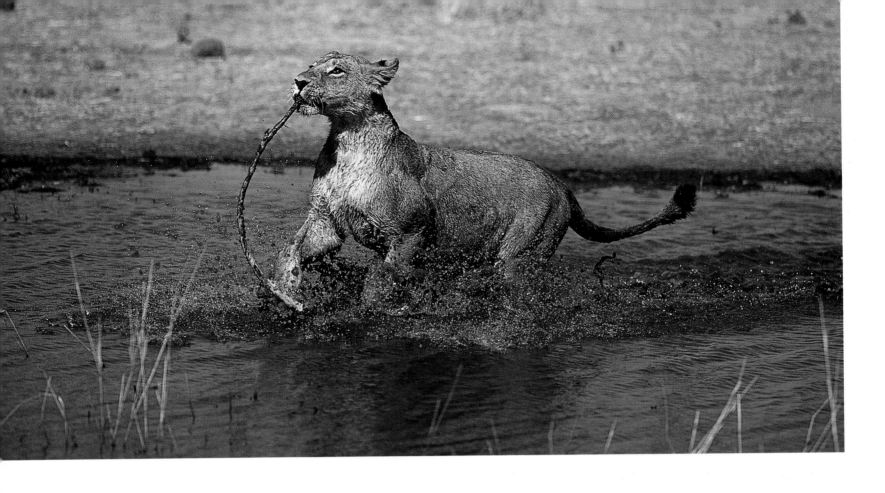

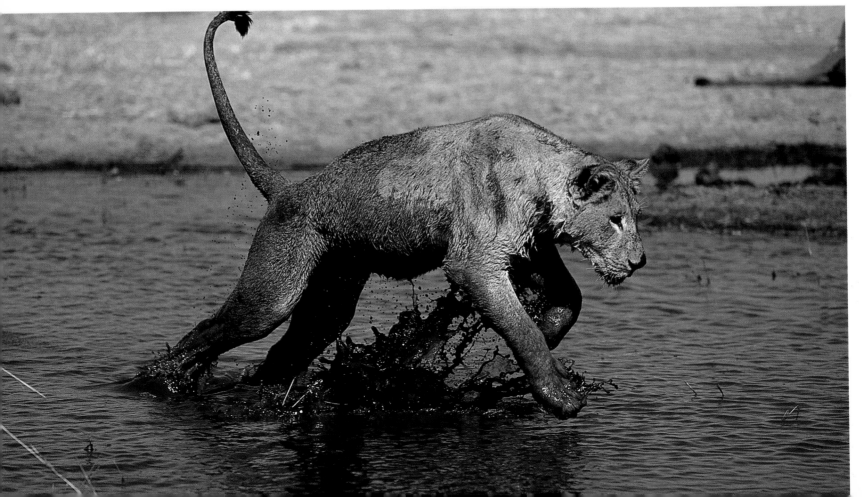

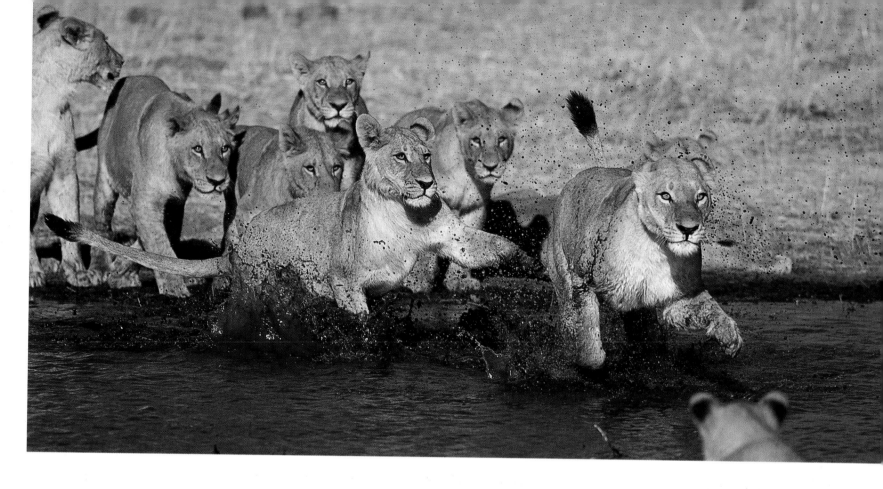

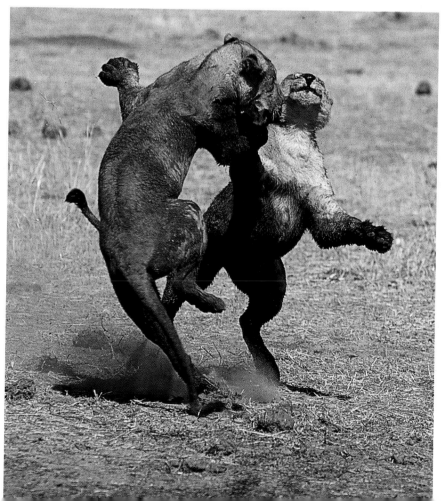

This pride of 24 lions was sprawled at the water's edge one morning, lying in full-bellied slumber as only lions can. They had caught an eight-year-old elephant, and eaten him over a period of two days. As the day warmed up they came to life, the young subadults in particular becoming energetic and playful. One young male tried his luck at chasing catfish in the shallows (*opposite below*), but with no success. These river lions are quite happy crossing the shallow water, but were reluctant to swim the deeper stretches. The whole pride would stand undecided at the water's edge before swimming, showing their concern by snarling and hissing at invisible crocodiles!

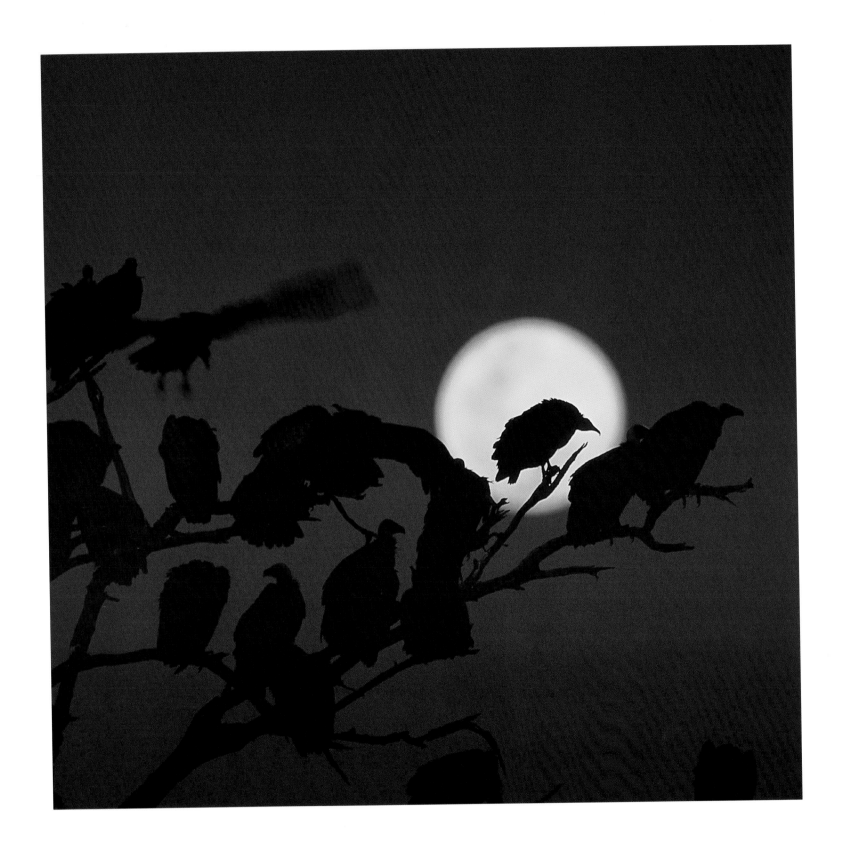

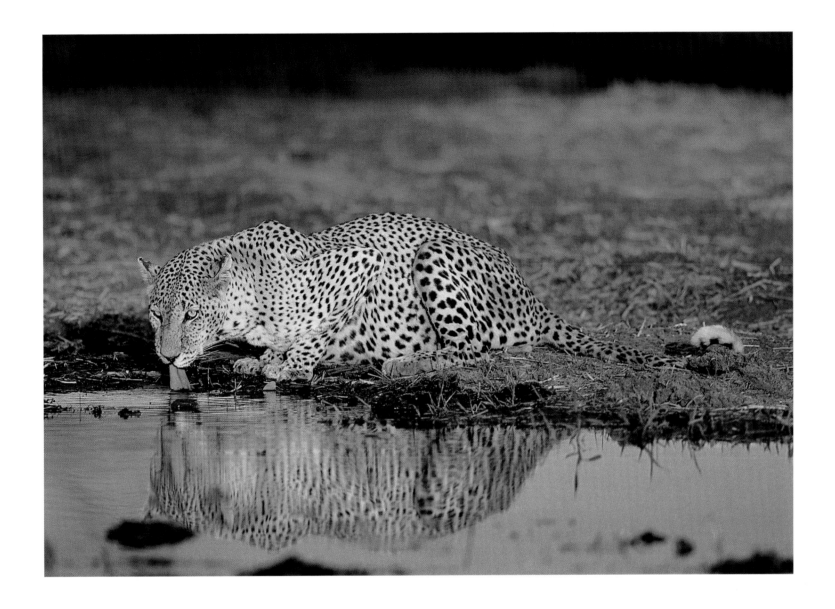

Opposite   White-backed and hooded vultures jostle on a night perch as the full moon rises. Under the cover
of darkness the predators reign. The darker the night, the more successful the lions' hunt.

Above   A shaft of late evening light warmed the coat of this grizzled old male leopard as he slaked his thirst,
still beautiful in his twilight years. His spotted coat blended him in so well I almost missed him as he lay close
to the water's edge. This relaxed individual is a legend in the area and the local guides have many stories to
tell. Some years back he caught and killed a litter of three lion cubs, which he stashed and ate high up in the
boughs of a raintree. Lions don't have it all their own way.

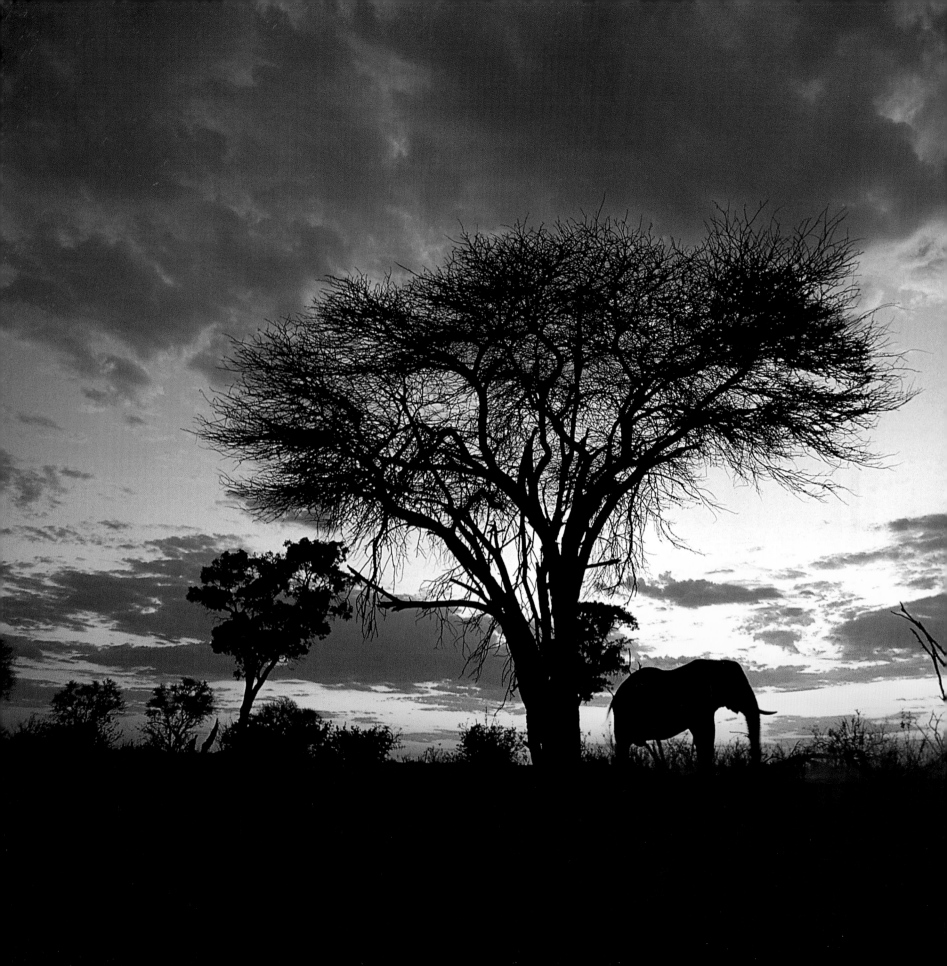

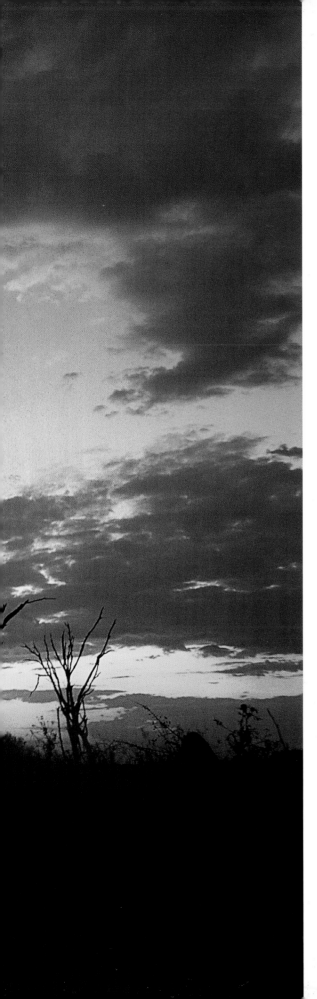

There is no good or bad in Nature, and animals are neither brave nor cowardly. They simply do that which is most expedient to ensure their personal survival, and hence that of their species. We witnessed many extraordinary events in the course of our year on the Khwai, and being so close to Nature helps one gain a greater understanding of Life. Mankind is also part of Nature, even though we so often distance ourselves from her. Surely the inner peace we feel in wild places is testimony to this.

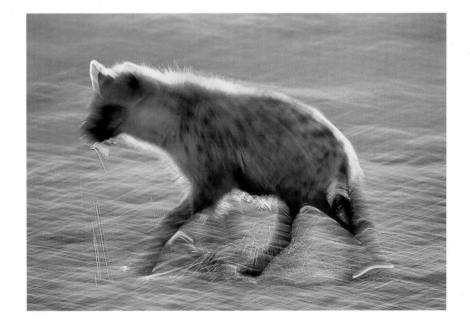

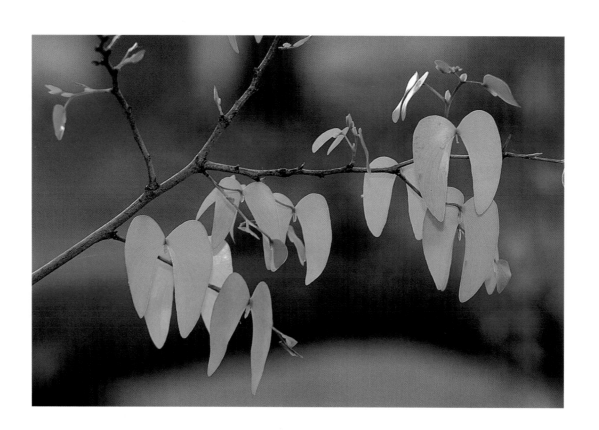

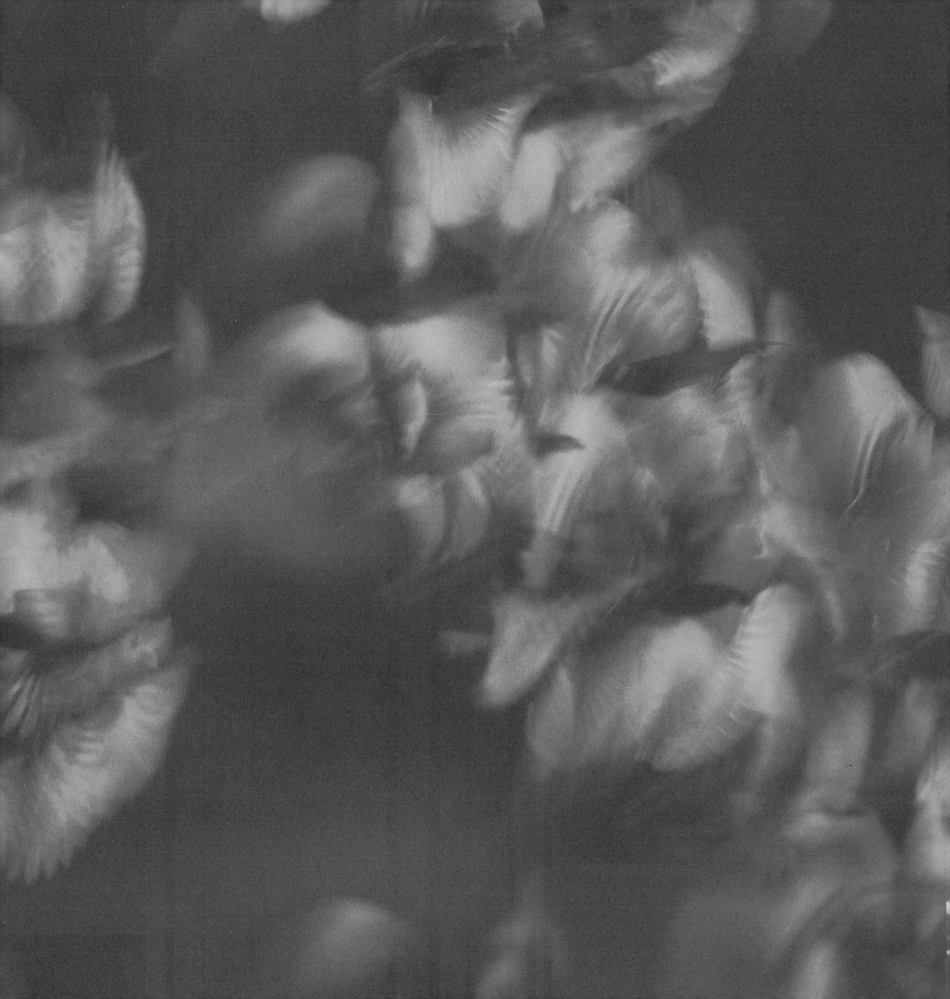